Alice in Wonderland

This Book
Belongs To:

....

....

Lewis Carroll's

Alice in Wonderland

With original and unabridged text

p

Illustrated by June Goulding

First published in 1865

This is a Parragon book
This edition published in 2003

Parragon
Queen Street House
4 Queen Street
Bath, BA1 1HE, UK

ISBN 1-40541-954-7

♥ Contents ♥

Alice's Adventures in Wonderland

Through the Looking-Glass
And what Alice found there

List of Full-Page Illustrations

FROM THE AUTHOR'S PREFACE
TO THE EIGHTY-SIXTH THOUSAND
OF THE 6/- EDITION, 1897

Enquiries have so often been addressed to me, as to whether any answer to the Hatter's Riddle (see p. 70) can be imagined, that I may as well put on record here what seems to me to be a fairly appropriate answer; viz. "Because it can produce a few notes, though they are very flat; and it is never put with the wrong end in front!" This, however, is merely an after-thought: the Riddle, as originally invented, had no answer at all.

Christmas, 1896

All in the golden afternoon
  Full leisurely we glide;
For both our oars, with little skill,
  By little arms are plied,
While little hands make vain pretence
  Our wanderings to guide.

Ah, cruel Three! In such an hour,
  Beneath such dreamy weather,
To beg a tale of breath too weak
  To stir the tiniest feather!
Yet what can one poor voice avail
  Against three tongues together?

Imperious Prima flashes forth
  Her edict "to begin it":
In gentler tone Secunda hopes
  "There will be nonsense in it!"
While Tertia interrupts the tale
  Not more than once a minute.

Anon, to sudden silence won,
  In fancy they pursue
The dream-child moving through a land
  Of wonders wild and new,
In friendly chat with bird or beast –
  And half believe it true.

And ever, as the story drained
   The wells of fancy dry,
And faintly strove that weary one
   To put the subject by,
"The rest next time –" "It is next time!"
   The happy voices cry.

Thus grew the tale of Wonderland:
   Thus slowly, one by one,
Its quaint events were hammered out –
   And now the tale is done,
And home we steer, a merry crew,
   Beneath the setting sun.

Alice! A childish story take,
   And, with a gentle hand
Lay it where Childhood's dreams are twined
   In Memory's mystic band,
Like pilgrim's wither'd wreath of flowers
   Pluck'd in a far-off land.

♥ ♥ ♥

Alice's Adventures in Wonderland

CHAPTER ONE
♥ Down the Rabbit-Hole ♥

Alice was beginning to get very tired of sitting by her sister on the bank, and of having nothing to do: once or twice she had peeped into the book her sister was reading, but it had no pictures or conversations in it, "and what is the use of a book," thought Alice, "without pictures or conversations?"

So she was considering in her own mind (as well as she could, for the hot day made her feel very sleepy and stupid) whether the pleasure of making a daisy-chain would be worth the trouble of getting up and picking the daisies, when suddenly a White Rabbit with pink eyes ran close by her.

There was nothing so *very* remarkable in that; nor did Alice think it so *very* much out of the way to hear the Rabbit say to itself, "Oh dear! Oh dear! I shall be too late!" (when she thought it over afterwards, it occurred to her that she ought to have wondered at this, but at the time it all seemed quite natural); but when the Rabbit actually *took a watch out of its waistcoat-pocket*, and looked at it, and then hurried on, Alice started to her feet, for it flashed across her mind that she had never before seen a rabbit with either a waistcoat-pocket or a watch to take out of it, and, burning with curiosity, she ran across the field after it, and was just in time to see it pop down a large rabbit-hole under the hedge.

In another moment down went Alice after it, never once considering how in the world she was to get out again.

The rabbit-hole went straight on like a tunnel for some way, and then dipped suddenly down, so suddenly that Alice had not a moment to think about stopping herself before she found herself falling down a very deep well.

Either the well was very deep, or she fell very slowly, for she had plenty of time as she went down to look about her, and to wonder what was going to happen next. First, she tried to look down and make out what she was coming to, but it was too dark to see anything: then she looked at the sides of the well, and noticed that they were filled with cupboards and book-shelves: here and there she saw maps and pictures hung upon pegs. She took down a jar from one of the shelves as she passed: it was labelled "ORANGE MARMALADE", but to her great disappointment it was empty: she did not like to drop the jar, for fear of killing somebody underneath, so managed to put it into one of the cupboards as she fell past it.

"Well!" thought Alice to herself. "After such a fall as this, I shall think nothing of tumbling down-stairs! How brave they'll all think me at home! Why, I wouldn't say anything about it, even if I fell off the top of the house!" (Which was very likely true.)

Down, down, down. Would the fall *never* come to an end?

"I wonder how many miles I've fallen by this time?" she said aloud. "I must be getting somewhere near the centre of the earth. Let me see: that would be four thousand miles down, I think –" (for, you see, Alice had learnt several things of this sort in her lessons in the schoolroom, and though this was not a *very* good opportunity for showing off her knowledge, as there was no one to listen to her, still it was good practice to say it over) "– yes, that's about the right distance – but then I wonder what Latitude or Longitude I've got to?" (Alice had no idea what Latitude was, or Longitude either, but she thought they were nice grand words to say.)

Presently she began again. "I wonder if I shall fall right *through* the earth! How funny it'll seem to come out among the people that walk with their heads downwards! The Antipathies, I think –" (she was rather glad there *was* no one listening, this time, as it didn't sound at all the right word) "– but I shall have to ask them what the name of this country is, you know. Please, Ma'am, is this New Zealand? Or Australia?" (and she tried to curtsey as she spoke – fancy *curtseying* as you're falling through the air! Do you think you could manage it?) "And what an ignorant little girl she'll think me for asking! No, it'll never do to ask: perhaps I shall see it written up somewhere."

Down, down, down. There was nothing else to do, so Alice soon began talking again. "Dinah'll miss me very much to-night, I should think!" (Dinah was the cat.) "I hope they'll remember her saucer of milk at tea-time. Dinah, my dear! I wish you were down here with me! There are no mice in the air, I'm afraid, but you might catch a bat, and that's very like a mouse, you know. But do cats eat bats, I wonder?" And here

Alice began to get rather sleepy, and went on saying to herself, in a dreamy sort of way, "Do cats eats bats? Do cats eat bats?" and sometimes, "Do bats eat cats?" for, you see, as she couldn't answer either question, it didn't much matter which way she put it. She felt that she was dozing off, and had just begun to dream that she was walking hand in hand with Dinah, and was saying to her very earnestly, "Now, Dinah, tell me the truth: did you ever eat a bat?" when suddenly, thump! thump! down she came upon a heap of dry leaves, and the fall was over.

Alice was not a bit hurt, and she jumped up on to her feet in a moment: she looked up, but it was all dark overhead; before her was another long passage, and the White Rabbit was still in sight, hurrying down it. There was not a moment to be lost: away went Alice like the wind, and was just in time to hear it say, as it turned a corner, "Oh my ears and whiskers, how late it's getting!" She was close behind it when she turned the corner, but the Rabbit was no longer to be seen: she found herself in a long, low hall, which was lit up by a row of lamps hanging from the roof.

There were doors all round the hall, but they were all locked; and when Alice had been all the way down one side and up the other, trying every door, she walked sadly down the middle, wondering how she was ever going to get out again.

Suddenly she came upon a little three-legged table, all made of solid glass: there was nothing on it but a tiny golden key, and Alice's first idea was that it might belong to one of the doors of the hall; but, alas! either the locks were too large, or the key was too small, but at any rate it would not open any of them. However, on the second time round, she came upon a

... she found herself in a long, low hall, which was lit up by a row of lamps hanging from the roof.

low curtain she had not noticed before, and behind it was a little door about fifteen inches high: she tried the little golden key in the lock, and to her great delight it fitted!

Alice opened the door and found that it led into a small passage, not much larger than a rat-hole: she knelt down and looked along the passage into the loveliest garden you ever saw. How she longed to get out of that dark hall, and wander about among those beds of bright flowers and those cool fountains, but she could not even get her head through the doorway; "and even if my head *would* go through," thought poor Alice, "it would be of very little use without my shoulders. Oh, how I wish I could shut up like a telescope! I think I could, if I only knew how to begin." For, you see, so many out-of-the-way things had happened lately, that Alice had begun to think that very few things were really impossible.

There seemed to be no use in waiting by the little door, so she went back to the table, half hoping she might find another key on it, or at any rate a book of rules for shutting people up like telescopes: this time she found a little bottle on it ("which certainly was not here before," said Alice), and tied round the neck of the bottle was a paper label, with the words "DRINK ME" beautifully printed on it in large letters.

It was all very well to say "Drink me", but the wise little Alice was not going to do *that* in a hurry. "No, I'll look first," she said, "and see whether it's marked '*poison*' or not"; for she had read several nice little stories about children who had got burnt, and eaten up by wild beasts, and other unpleasant things, all because they *would* not remember the simple rules their friends had taught them: such as, that a red-hot poker will burn you if you hold it too long; and that, if you cut your finger *very* deeply with a knife, it usually bleeds; and she had never forgotten that, if you drink much from a bottle marked "poison", it is almost certain to disagree with you, sooner or later.

However, this bottle was *not* marked "poison", so Alice ventured to taste it, and finding it very nice (it had, in fact, a sort of mixed flavour of cherry-tart, custard, pine-apple, roast turkey, toffy, and hot buttered toast), she very soon finished it off.

"What a curious feeling!" said Alice. "I must be shutting up like a telescope."

And so it was indeed: she was now only ten inches high, and her face brightened up at the thought that she was now the right size for going through the little door into that lovely garden. First, however, she waited for a few minutes to see if she was going to shrink any further: she felt a little nervous about this; "for it might end, you know," said Alice, "in my going out altogether, like a candle. I wonder what I should be like then?" And she tried to fancy what the flame of a candle is like after it is blown out, for she could not remember ever having seen such a thing.

After a while, finding that nothing more happened, she decided on going into the garden at once; but, alas for poor Alice! when she got to the door, she found she had forgotten the little golden key, and when she went back to the table for it, she found she could not possibly reach it: she could see it quite plainly through the glass, and she tried her best to climb up one of the table-legs, but it was too slippery; and when she had tired herself out with trying, the poor little thing sat down and cried.

"Come, there's no use in crying like that!" said Alice to herself, rather sharply. "I advise you to leave off this minute!" She generally gave herself very good advice (though she very seldom followed it), and sometimes she scolded herself so severely as to bring tears in to her eyes; and once she remembered trying to box her own ears for having cheated herself in a game of croquet she was playing against herself, for this curious child was very fond of pretending to be two people. "But it's no use now," thought poor Alice, "to pretend to be two people! Why, there's hardly enough of me left to make *one* respectable person!"

Soon her eye fell on a little glass box that was lying under the table: she opened it, and found in it a very small cake, on which the words "EAT ME" were beautifully marked in currants. "Well, I'll eat it," said Alice, "and if it makes me grow larger, I can reach the key; and if it makes me grow smaller, I can creep under the door: so either way I'll get into the garden, and I don't care which happens!"

She ate a little bit, and said anxiously to herself, "Which way? Which way?", holding her hand on the top of her head to feel which way it was growing; and she was quite surprised to find that she remained the same size. To be sure, this is what generally happens when one eats cake; but Alice had got so much into the way of expecting nothing but out-of-the-way things to happen, that it seemed quite dull and stupid for life to go on in the common way.

So she set to work, and very soon finished off the cake.

CHAPTER TWO
♥ The Pool of Tears ♥

"Curiouser and curiouser!" cried Alice (she was so much surprised, that for the moment she quite forgot how to speak good English). "Now I'm opening out like the largest telescope that ever was! Good-bye, feet!" (for when she looked down at her feet, they seemed to be almost out of sight, they were getting so far off). "Oh my poor little feet, I wonder who will put on your shoes and stockings for you now, dears? I'm sure *I* shan't be able! I shall be a great deal too far off to trouble myself about you: you must manage the best way you can – but I must be kind to them," thought Alice, "or perhaps they won't walk the way I want to go! Let me see. I'll give them a new pair of boots every Christmas."

And she went on planning to herself how she would manage it. "They must go by the carrier," she thought; "and how funny it'll seem, sending presents to one's own feet! And how odd the directions will look!

Alice's Right Foot, Esq.,
Hearthrug,
near the Fender,
(with Alice's love)

Oh dear, what nonsense I'm talking!"

Just at this moment her head struck against the roof of the hall: in fact she was now rather more than nine feet high, and she at once took up the little golden key and hurried off to the garden door.

Poor Alice! It was as much as she could do, lying down on one side, to look through into the garden with one eye; but to get through was more hopeless than ever: she sat down and began to cry again.

"You ought to be ashamed of yourself," said Alice, "a great girl like you" (she might well say this), "to go on crying in this way! Stop this moment, I tell you!" But she went on all the same, shedding gallons of tears, until there was a large pool all round her, about four inches deep and reaching half down the hall.

After a time she heard a little pattering of feet in the distance, and she hastily dried her eyes to see what was coming. It was the White Rabbit returning, splendidly dressed, with a pair of white-kid gloves in one hand and a large fan in the other: he came trotting along in a great hurry, muttering to himself as he came, "Oh! the Duchess, the Duchess! Oh! *Won't* she be savage if I've kept her waiting!" Alice felt so desperate that she was ready to ask help of any one: so, when the Rabbit came near her, she began, in a low, timid voice, "If you please, Sir –" The Rabbit started violently, dropped the white-kid gloves and the fan, and skurried away into the darkness as hard as he could go.

Alice took up the fan and gloves, and, as the hall was very hot, she kept fanning herself all the time she went on talking. "Dear, dear! How queer everything is to-day! And yesterday things went on just as usual. I wonder if I've been changed in the night? Let me think: *was* I the same when I got up this morning? I almost think I can remember feeling a little different. But if I'm not the same, the next question is, 'Who in the world am I?' Ah, *that's* the great puzzle!" And she began thinking over all the children she knew that were of the same age as herself, to see if she could have been changed for any of them.

"I'm sure I'm not Ada," she said, "for her hair goes in such long ringlets, and mine doesn't go in ringlets at all; and I'm sure I can't be Mabel, for I know all sorts of things, and she, oh! she knows such a very little! Besides, *she's* she, and *I'm* I, and – oh dear, how puzzling it all is! I'll try if I know all the things I used to know. Let me see: four times five is twelve, and four times six is thirteen, and four times seven is – oh dear! I shall never get to twenty at that rate! However, the Multiplication Table doesn't signify: let's try Geography. London is the capital of Paris, and Paris is the capital of Rome, and Rome – no, *that's* all wrong, I'm certain! I must have changed for Mabel! I'll try and say '*How doth the little –*'," and she crossed her hands on her lap as if she were saying lessons, and began to repeat it, but her voice sounded hoarse and strange, and the words did not come the same as they used to do:

"How doth the little crocodile
Improve his shining tail,
And pour the waters of the Nile
On every golden scale!

How cheerfully he seems to grin,
How neatly spread his claws,
And welcomes little fishes in,
With gently smiling jaws!"

"I'm sure those are not the right words," said poor Alice, and her eyes filled with tears again as she went on, "I must be Mabel after all, and I shall have to go and live in that poky little house, and have next to no toys to play with, and oh, ever so many lessons to learn! No, I've made up my mind about it: if I'm Mabel, I'll stay down here! It'll be no use their putting their heads down and saying, 'Come up again, dear!' I shall only look up and say, 'Who am I, then? Tell me that first, and then, if I like being that person, I'll come up: if not I'll stay down here till I'm somebody else' – but, oh dear!" cried Alice with a sudden burst of tears, "I do wish they *would* put their heads down! I am so *very* tired of being all alone here!"

As she said this she looked down at her hands, and was surprised to see that she had put on one of the Rabbit's little white kid-gloves while she was talking. "How *can* I have done that?" she thought. "I must be growing small again." She got up and went to the table to measure herself by it, and found that, as nearly as she could guess, she was now about two feet high, and was going on shrinking rapidly: she soon found out that the cause of this was the fan she was holding, and she

"Dear, Dear! How queer everything is to-day! ...
I wonder if I've been changed in the night?"

dropped it hastily, just in time to save herself from shrinking away altogether.

"That *was* a narrow escape!" said Alice, a good deal frightened at the sudden change, but very glad to find herself still in existence. "And now for the garden!" And she ran with all speed back to the little door; but, alas! the little door was shut again, and the little golden key was lying on the glass table as before, "and things are worse than ever," thought the poor child, "for I never was so small as this before, never! And I declare it's too bad, that it is!"

As she said these words her foot slipped, and in another moment, splash! she was up to her chin in salt-water. Her first idea was that she had somehow fallen into the sea, "and in that case I can go back by railway," she said to herself. (Alice had been to the seaside once in her life, and had come to the general conclusion that wherever you go to on the English coast you find a number of bathing-machines in the sea, some children digging in the sand with wooden spades, then a row of lodging-houses, and behind them a railway station.) However, she soon made out that she was in the pool of tears which she had wept when she was nine feet high.

"I wish I hadn't cried so much!" said Alice, as she swam about, trying to find her way out. "I shall be punished for it now, I suppose, by being drowned in my own tears! That *will* be a queer thing, to be sure! However, everything is queer to-day."

Just then she heard something splashing about in the pool a little way off, and she swam nearer to make out what it was: at first she thought it must be a walrus or hippopotamus, but then she remembered how small she was now, and she soon made out that it was only a mouse that had slipped in like herself.

"Would it be of any use, now," thought Alice, "to speak to this mouse? Everything is so out-of-the-way down here, that I should think very likely it can talk: at any rate there's no harm in trying." So she began: "O Mouse, do you know the way out of this pool? I am very tired of swimming about here, O Mouse!" (Alice thought this must be the right way of speaking to a mouse: she had never done such a thing before, but she remembered having seen, in her brother's Latin Grammar, "A mouse – of a mouse – to a mouse – a mouse – O mouse!") The Mouse looked at her rather inquisitively, and seemed to her to wink with one of its little eyes, but it said nothing.

"Perhaps it doesn't understand English," thought Alice. "I dare say it's a French mouse, come over with William the Conqueror." (For, with all her knowledge of history, Alice had no very clear notion how long ago anything had happened.) So she began again: "*Où est ma chatte?*", which was the first sentence in her French lesson-book. The Mouse gave a sudden leap out of the water, and seemed to quiver all over with fright.

"Oh, I beg your pardon!" cried Alice hastily, afraid that she had hurt the poor animal's feelings. "I quite forgot you didn't like cats."

"Not like cats!" cried the Mouse in a shrill, passionate voice. "Would *you* like cats, if you were me?"

"Well, perhaps not," said Alice in a soothing tone: "don't be angry about it. And yet I wish I could show you our cat Dinah. I think you'd take a fancy to cats if you could only see her. She is such a dear quiet thing," Alice went on, half to herself, as she swam lazily about in the pool, "and she sits purring so nicely by the fire, licking her paws and washing her face – and she is such a nice soft thing to nurse – and she's such a capital one for catching mice – oh, I beg your pardon!" cried Alice again, for this time the Mouse was bristling all over, and she felt certain it must be really offended. "We won't talk about her any more, if you'd rather not."

"We, indeed!" cried the Mouse, who was trembling down to the end of his tail. "As if *I* would talk on such a subject! Our family always *hated* cats: nasty, low, vulgar things! Don't let me hear the name again!"

"I won't indeed!" said Alice, in a great hurry to change the subject of conversation. "Are you – are you fond – of – of dogs?" The Mouse did not answer, so Alice went on eagerly: "There is such a nice little dog near our house, I should like to show you! A little bright-eyed terrier, you know, with oh, such long curly brown hair! And it'll fetch things when you throw them, and it'll sit up and beg for its dinner, and all sorts of things – I can't remember half of them – and it belongs to a farmer, you know, and he says it's so useful, it's worth a hundred pounds! He says it kills all the rats and – oh dear!"

cried Alice in a sorrowful tone. "I'm afraid I've offended it again!" For the Mouse was swimming away from her as hard as it could go, and making quite a commotion in the pool as it went.

So she called softly after it, "Mouse dear! Do come back again, and we won't talk about cats, or dogs either, if you don't like them!" When the Mouse heard this, it turned round and swam slowly back to her: its face was quite pale (with passion, Alice thought), and it said in a low trembling voice, "Let us get to the shore, and then I'll tell you my history, and you'll understand why it is I hate cats and dogs."

It was high time to go, for the pool was getting quite crowded with the birds and animals that had fallen into it: there was a Duck and a Dodo, a Lory and an Eaglet, and several other curious creatures. Alice led the way, and the whole party swam to the shore.

Chapter Three

♥ A Caucus-Race and ♥ a Long Tale

They were indeed a queer-looking party that assembled on the bank – the birds with draggled feathers, the animals with their fur clinging close to them, and all dripping wet, cross, and uncomfortable.

The first question of course was, how to get dry again: they had a consultation about this, and after a few minutes it seemed quite natural to Alice to find herself talking familiarly with them, as if she had known them all her life. Indeed, she had quite a long argument with the Lory, who at last turned sulky, and would only say, "I am older than you, and must know better." And this Alice would not allow, without knowing how old it was, and, as the Lory positively refused to tell its age, there was no more to be said.

At last the Mouse, who seemed to be a person of some authority among them, called out, "Sit down, all of you, and listen to me! *I'll* soon make you dry enough!" They all sat down at once, in a large ring, with the Mouse in the middle. Alice kept her eyes anxiously fixed on it, for she felt sure she would catch a bad cold if she did not get dry very soon.

"Ahem!" said the Mouse with an important air. "Are you all ready? This is the driest thing I know. Silence all round, if you please! 'William the Conqueror, whose cause was favoured by the pope, was soon submitted to by the English, who wanted leaders, and had been of late much accustomed to usurpation and conquest. Edwin and Morcar, the earls of Mercia and Northumbria –'"

"Ugh!" said the Lory, with a shiver.

"I beg your pardon!" said the Mouse, frowning, but very politely. "Did you speak?"

"Not I!" said the Lory, hastily.

"I thought you did," said the Mouse. "I proceed. 'Edwin and Morcar, the earls of Mercia and Northumbria, declared for him; and even Stigand, the patriotic Archbishop of Canterbury, found it advisable –'"

"Found *what*?" said the Duck.

"Found *it*," the Mouse replied rather crossly: "of course you know what 'it' means."

"I know what 'it' means well enough, when *I* find a thing," said the Duck: "it's generally a frog, or a worm. The question is, what did the Archbishop find?"

The Mouse did not notice this question, but hurriedly went on, "'– found it advisable to go with Edgar Atheling to meet William and offer him the crown. William's conduct at first was moderate. But the insolence of his Normans –' How are you getting on now, my dear?" it continued, turning to Alice as it spoke.

"As wet as ever," said Alice in a melancholy tone: "it doesn't seem to dry me at all."

"In that case," said the Dodo solemnly, rising to its feet, "I move that the meeting adjourn, for the immediate adoption of more energetic remedies –"

"Speak English!" said the Eaglet. "I don't know the meaning of half those long words, and, what's more, I don't believe you do either!" And the Eaglet bent down its head to hide a smile: some of the other birds tittered audibly.

"What I was going to say," said the Dodo in an offended tone, "was, that the best thing to get us dry would be a Caucus-race."

"What *is* a Caucus-race?" said Alice; not that she much wanted to know, but the Dodo had paused as if it thought that *somebody* ought to speak, and no one else seemed inclined to say anything.

"Why," said the Dodo, "the best way to explain it is to do it." (And, as you might like to try the thing yourself, some winter day, I will tell you how the Dodo managed it.)

First it marked out a race-course, in a sort of circle ("the exact shape doesn't matter," it said), and then all the party were placed along the course, here and there. There was no "One, two, three, and away!" but they began running when they liked, and left off when they liked, so that it was not easy to know when the race was over. However, when they had been running half an hour or so, and were quite dry again, the Dodo suddenly called out, "The race is over!" and they all crowded round it, panting, and asking, "But who has won?"

This question the Dodo could not answer without a great deal of thought, and it stood for a long time with one finger

"The race is over!" and they all crowded round it, panting, and asking, "But who has won?"

pressed upon its forehead (the position in which you usually see Shakespeare, in the pictures of him), while the rest waited in silence. At last the Dodo said, "*Everybody* has won, and all must have prizes."

"But who is to give the prizes?" quite a chorus of voices asked.

"Why, *she*, of course," said the Dodo, pointing to Alice with one finger; and the whole party at once crowded round her, calling out, in a confused way, "Prizes! Prizes!"

Alice had no idea what to do, and in despair she put her hand in to her pocket, and pulled out a box of comfits (luckily the salt-water had not got into it), and handed them round as prizes. There was exactly one a-piece, all round.

"But she must have a prize herself, you know," said the Mouse.

"Of course," the Dodo replied very gravely. "What else have you got in your pocket?" he went on, turning to Alice.

"Only a thimble," said Alice sadly.

"Hand it over here," said the Dodo.

Then they all crowded round her once more, while the Dodo solemnly presented the thimble, saying, "We beg your acceptance of this elegant thimble"; and, when it had finished this short speech, they all cheered.

Alice thought the whole thing very absurd, but they all looked so grave that she did not dare to laugh; and, as she could not think of anything to say, she simply bowed, and took the thimble, looking as solemn as she could.

The next thing was to eat the comfits: this caused some noise and confusion, as the large birds complained that they could not taste theirs, and the small ones choked and had to be patted on the back. However, it was over at last, and they sat down again in a ring, and begged the Mouse to tell them something more.

"You promised to tell me your history, you know," said Alice, "and why it is you hate – C and D," she added in a whisper, half afraid that it would be offended again.

"Mine is a long and sad tale!" said the Mouse, turning to Alice and sighing.

"It *is* a long tail, certainly," said Alice, looking down with wonder at the Mouse's tail; "but why do you call it sad?" And she kept puzzling about it while the Mouse was speaking, so that her idea of the tale was something like this:

> "Fury said to a mouse, That he
> met in the house, 'Let us
> both go to the law: *I* will
> prosecute *you*. –
> Come, I'll take
> no denial: We
> must have the
> trial; For really
> this morning I've
> nothing to do.' Said
> the mouse to the cur,
> 'Such a trial, dear sir,
> With no jury or
> judge, would be
> wasting our breath.'
> 'I'll be judge, I'll be
> jury,' said cunning
> old Fury: 'I'll try the
> whole cause and
> condemn you to
> death.'"

"You are not attending!" said the Mouse to Alice, severely. "What are you thinking of?"

"I beg your pardon," said Alice very humbly: "you had got to the fifth bend, I think?"

"I had *not*!" cried the Mouse, sharply and very angrily.

"A knot!" said Alice, always ready to make herself useful, and looking anxiously about her. "Oh, do let me help to undo it!"

"I shall do nothing of the sort," said the Mouse, getting up and walking away. "You insult me by talking such nonsense!"

"I didn't mean it!" pleaded poor Alice. "But you're so easily offended, you know!"

The Mouse only growled in reply.

"Please come back, and finish your story!" Alice called after it. And the others all joined in chorus, "Yes, please do!" But the Mouse only shook its head impatiently, and walked a little quicker.

"What a pity it wouldn't stay!" sighed the Lory, as soon as it was quite out of sight. And an old Crab took the opportunity of saying to her daughter, "Ah, my dear! Let this be a lesson to you never to lose *your* temper!" "Hold your tongue, Ma!" said the young Crab, a little snappishly. "You're enough to try the patience of an oyster!"

"I wish I had our Dinah here, I know I do!" said Alice aloud, addressing nobody in particular. "She'd soon fetch it back!"

"And who is Dinah, if I might venture to ask the question?" said the Lory.

Alice replied eagerly, for she was always ready to talk about her pet: "Dinah's our cat. And she's such a capital one for catching mice, you can't think! And oh, I wish you could see her after the birds! Why, she'll eat a little bird as soon as look at it!"

This speech caused a remarkable sensation among the party. Some of the birds hurried off at once: one old Magpie began wrapping itself up very carefully, remarking, "I really must be getting home: the night-air doesn't suit my throat!" And a Canary called out in a trembling voice, to its children, "Come away, my dears! It's high time you were all in bed!" On various pretexts they all moved off, and Alice was soon left alone.

"I wish I hadn't mentioned Dinah!" she said to herself in a melancholy tone. "Nobody seems to like her, down here, and I'm sure she's the best cat in the world! Oh, my dear Dinah! I wonder if I shall ever see you any more!" And here poor Alice began to cry again, for she felt very lonely and low-spirited. In a little while, however, she again heard a little pattering of footsteps in the distance, and she looked up eagerly, half hoping that the Mouse had changed his mind, and was coming back to finish his story.

CHAPTER FOUR

♥ The Rabbit Sends in ♥ a Little Bill

It was the White Rabbit, trotting slowly back again, and looking anxiously about as it went, as if it had lost something; and she heard it muttering to itself, "The Duchess! The Duchess! Oh, my dear paws! Oh, my fur and whiskers! She'll get me executed, as sure as ferrets are ferrets! Where *can* I have dropped them, I wonder?" Alice guessed in a moment that it was looking for the fan and the pair of white kid-gloves, and she very goodnaturedly began hunting about for them, but they were nowhere to be seen – everything seemed to have changed since her swim in the pool; and the great hall, with the glass table and the little door, had vanished completely.

Very soon the Rabbit noticed Alice, as she went hunting about, and called out to her, in an angry tone, "Why Mary Ann, what *are* you doing out here? Run home this moment, and fetch me a pair of gloves and a fan! Quick, now!" And Alice was so much frightened that she ran off at once in the direction it pointed to, without trying to explain the mistake it had made.

"He took me for his housemaid," she said to herself as she ran. "How surprised he'll be when he finds out who I am! But I'd better take him his fan and gloves – that is, if I can find them." As she said this, she came upon a neat little house, on the door of which was a bright brass plate with the name "W. RABBIT" engraved upon it. She went in without knocking, and hurried upstairs, in great fear lest she should meet the real Mary Ann, and be turned out of the house before she had found the fan and gloves.

"How queer it seems," Alice said to herself, "to be going messages for a rabbit! I suppose Dinah'll be sending me on messages next!" And she began fancying the sort of thing that would happen: "'Miss Alice! Come here directly, and get ready for your walk!' 'Coming in a minute, nurse! But I've got to watch this mousehole till Dinah comes back, and see that the mouse doesn't get out.' Only I don't think," Alice went on, "that they'd let Dinah stop in the house if she began ordering people about like that!"

By this time she had found her way into a tidy little room with a table in the window, and on it (as she had hoped) a fan and two or three pairs of tiny white kid-gloves: she took up the fan and a pair of the gloves, and was just going to leave the room, when her eye fell upon a little bottle that stood near the looking-glass. There was no label this time with the words "DRINK ME", but nevertheless she uncorked it and put it to her lips. "I know *something* interesting is sure to happen," she said to herself, "whenever I eat or drink anything: so I'll just see what this bottle does. I do hope it'll make me grow large again, for really I'm quite tired of being such a tiny little thing!"

It did so indeed, and much sooner than she had expected: before she had drunk half the bottle, she found her head pressing against the ceiling, and had to stoop to save her neck from being broken. She hastily put down the bottle, saying to herself, "That's quite enough – I hope I shan't grow any more – As it is, I can't get out at the door – I do wish I hadn't drunk quite so much!"

Alas! It was too late to wish that! She went on growing and growing, and very soon had to kneel down on the floor: in another minute there was not even room for this, and she tried the effect of lying down with one elbow against the door, and the other arm curled round her head. Still she went on growing, and, as a last resource, she put one arm out of the window, and one foot up the chimney, and said to herself, "Now I can do no more, whatever happens. What *will* become of me?"

Luckily for Alice, the little magic bottle had now had its full effect, and she grew no larger: still it was very uncomfortable, and, as there seemed to be no sort of chance of her ever getting out of the room again, no wonder she felt unhappy.

"It was much pleasanter at home," thought poor Alice, "when one wasn't always growing larger and smaller, and being ordered about by mice and rabbits. I almost wish I hadn't gone down that rabbit-hole – and yet – and yet – it's rather curious, you know, this sort of life! I do wonder what *can* have happened to me! When I used to read fairy tales, I fancied that kind of thing never happened, and now here I am in the middle of one! There ought to be a book written about me, that there ought! And when I grow up, I'll write one – but I'm grown up now," she added in a sorrowful tone: "at least there's no room to grow up any more *here*."

"But then," thought Alice, "shall I *never* get any older than I am now? That'll be a comfort, one way – *never* to be an old woman – but then – always to have lessons to learn! Oh, I shouldn't like *that*!"

"Oh, you foolish Alice!" she answered herself. "How can you learn lessons in here? Why, there's hardly room for *you*, and no room at all for any lesson-books!"

And so she went on, taking first one side and then the other, and making quite a conversation of it altogether; but after a few minutes she heard a voice outside, and stopped to listen.

"Mary Ann! Mary Ann!" said the voice. "Fetch me my gloves this moment!" Then came a little pattering of feet on the stairs. Alice knew it was the Rabbit coming to look for her, and she trembled till she shook the house, quite forgetting that she was now about a thousand times as large as the Rabbit, and had no reason to be afraid of it.

Presently the Rabbit came up to the door, and tried to open it; but, as the door opened inwards, and Alice's elbow was pressed hard against it, that attempt proved a failure. Alice heard it say to itself, "Then I'll go round and get in at the window."

"*That* you won't!" thought Alice, and, after waiting till she fancied she heard the Rabbit just under the window, she suddenly spread out her hand, and made a snatch in the air. She did not get hold of anything, but she heard a little shriek and a fall, and a crash of broken glass, from which she concluded that it was just possible it had fallen into a cucumber-frame, or something of the sort.

Next came an angry voice – the Rabbit's – "Pat! Pat!
Where are you?" And then a voice she had never heard before,
"Sure then I'm here! Digging for apples, yer honour!"

"Digging for apples, indeed!" said the Rabbit angrily.
"Here! Come and help me out of *this*!" (Sounds of more broken
glass.)

"Now tell me, Pat, what's that in the window?"

"Sure, it's an arm, yer honour!" (He pronounced it
"arrum".)

"An arm, you goose! Who ever saw one that size? Why, it
fills the whole window!"

"Sure, it does, yer honour: but it's an arm for all that."

"Well, it's got no business there, at any rate: go and take
it away!"

There was a long silence after this, and Alice could only
hear whispers now and then; such as, "Sure, I don't like it, yer
honour, at all, at all!" "Do as I tell you, you coward!", and at
last she spread out her hand again, and made another snatch
in the air. This time there were *two* little shrieks, and more
sounds of broken glass. "What a number of cucumber-frames
there must be!" thought Alice. "I wonder what they'll do next!
As for pulling me out of the window, I only wish they *could*! I'm
sure *I* don't want to stay in here any longer!"

She waited for some time without hearing anything more:
at last came a rumbling of little cart-wheels, and the sound of
a good many voices all talking together: she made out the
words: "Where's the other ladder? – Why, I hadn't to bring but
one. Bill's got the other – Bill! Fetch it here, lad! – Here, put
'em up at this corner – No, tie 'em together first – they don't
reach half high enough yet – Oh! they'll do well enough. Don't

She did not get hold of anything, but she heard a little shriek and a fall, and a crash of broken glass ...

be particular – Here, Bill! Catch hold of this rope – Will the roof bear? – Mind that loose slate – Oh, it's coming down! Heads below!" (a loud crash) – "Now, who did that? – It was Bill, I fancy – Who's to go down the chimney? – Nay, *I* shan't! – *You* do it! *That* I won't, then! – Bill's got to go down – Here, Bill! The master says you've got to go down the chimney!"

"Oh! So Bill's got to come down the chimney, has he?" said Alice to herself. "Why, they seem to put everything upon Bill! I wouldn't be in Bill's place for a good deal: this fireplace is narrow to be sure; but I *think* I can kick a little!"

She drew her foot as far down the chimney as she could, and waited till she heard a little animal (she couldn't guess of what sort it was) scratching and scrambling about in the chimney close above her: then, saying to herself, "This is Bill," she gave one sharp kick, and waited to see what would happen next.

The first thing she heard was a general chorus of "There goes Bill!" then the Rabbit's voice alone – "Catch him, you by the hedge!" then silence, and then another confusion of voices – "Hold up his head – Brandy now – Don't choke him – How was it, old fellow? What happened to you? Tell us all about it!"

Last came a feeble, squeaking voice ("That's Bill," thought Alice), "Well, I hardly know – No more, thank ye; I'm better now – but I'm a deal too flustered to tell you – all I know is, something comes at me like a Jack-in-the-box, and up I goes like a sky-rocket!"

"So you did, old fellow!" said the others.

"We must burn the house down!" said the Rabbit's voice. And Alice called out as loud as she could, "If you do, I'll set Dinah at you!"

There was a dead silence instantly, and Alice thought to herself, "I wonder what they *will* do next! If they had any sense, they'd take the roof off." After a minute or two, they began moving about again, and Alice heard the Rabbit say, "A barrowful will do, to begin with."

"A barrowful of *what*?" thought Alice. But she had not long to doubt, for the next moment a shower of little pebbles came rattling in at the window, and some of them hit her in the face. "I'll put a stop to this," she said to herself, and shouted out, "You'd better not do that again!", which produced another dead silence.

Alice noticed, with some surprise, that the pebbles were all turning into little cakes as they lay on the floor, and a bright idea came into her head. "If I eat one of these cakes," she thought, "it's sure to make *some* change in my size; and, as it can't possibly make me larger, it must make me smaller, I suppose."

So she swallowed one of the cakes, and was delighted to find that she began shrinking directly. As soon as she was small enough to get through the door, she ran out of the house, and found quite a crowd of little animals and birds waiting outside. The poor little Lizard, Bill, was in the middle, being held up by two guinea-pigs, who were giving it something out of a bottle. They all made a rush at Alice the moment she appeared; but she ran off as hard as she could, and soon found herself safe in a thick wood.

"The first thing I've got to do," said Alice to herself, as she wandered about in the wood, "is to grow to my right size again; and the second thing is to find my way into that lovely garden. I think that will be the best plan."

It sounded an excellent plan, no doubt, and very neatly and simply arranged: the only difficulty was that she had not the smallest idea how to set about it; and, while she was peering about anxiously among the trees, a little sharp bark just over her head made her look up in a great hurry.

An enormous puppy was looking down at her with large round eyes, and feebly stretching out one paw, trying to touch her. "Poor little thing!" said Alice, in a coaxing tone, and she tried hard to whistle to it; but she was terribly frightened all the time at the thought that it might be hungry, in which case it would be very likely to eat her up in spite of all her coaxing.

Hardly knowing what she did, she picked up a little bit of stick, and held it out to the puppy: whereupon the puppy jumped into the air off all its feet at once, with a yelp of delight, and rushed at the stick, and made believe to worry it: then Alice dodged behind a great thistle, to keep herself from being run over; and, the moment she appeared on the other side, the puppy made another rush at the stick, and tumbled head over heels in its hurry to get hold of it: then Alice, thinking it was very like having a game of play with a cart-horse, and expecting every moment to be trampled under its feet, ran round the thistle again: then the puppy began a series of short charges at the stick, running a very little way forwards each time and a long way back, and barking hoarsely all the while, till at last it sat down a good way off, panting, with its tongue hanging out of its mouth, and its great eyes half shut.

This seemed to Alice a good opportunity for making her escape: so she set off at once, and ran till she was quite tired and out of breath, and till the puppy's bark sounded quite faint in the distance.

"And yet what a dear little puppy it was!" said Alice, as she leant against a buttercup to rest herself, and fanned herself with one of the leaves. "I should have liked teaching it tricks very much, if – if I'd only been the right size to do it! Oh dear! I'd nearly forgotten that I've got to grow up again! Let me see – how *is* it to be managed? I suppose I ought to eat or drink something or other; but the great question is, what?"

The great question certainly was, "What?" Alice looked all round her at the flowers and the blades of grass, but she could not see anything that looked like the right thing to eat or drink under the circumstances. There was a large mushroom growing near her, about the same height as herself, and when she had looked under it, and on both sides of it, and behind it, it occurred to her that she might as well look and see what was on the top of it.

She stretched herself up on tiptoe, and peeped over the edge of the mushroom, and her eyes immediately met those of a large blue caterpillar, that was sitting on the top, with its arms folded, quietly smoking a long hookah, and taking not the smallest notice of her or of anything else.

Chapter Five
♥ Advice from a Caterpillar ♥

The Caterpillar and Alice looked at each other for some time in silence: at last the Caterpillar took the hookah out of its mouth, and addressed her in a languid, sleepy voice.

"Who are *you*?" said the Caterpillar.

This was not an encouraging opening for a conversation. Alice replied, rather shyly, "I – I hardly know, sir, just at present – at least I know who I *was* when I got up this morning, but I think I must have been changed several times since then."

"What do you mean by that?" said the Caterpillar sternly. "Explain yourself!"

"I can't explain *myself*, I'm afraid, Sir," said Alice, "because I'm not myself, you see."

"I don't see," said the Caterpillar.

"I'm afraid I can't put it more clearly," Alice replied, very politely, "for I can't understand it myself to begin with; and being so many different sizes in a day is confusing."

"It isn't," said the Caterpillar.

"Well, perhaps you haven't found it so yet," said Alice; "but when you have turned into a chrysalis – you will some day, you know – and then after that into a butterfly, I should think you'll feel it a little queer, won't you?"

"Not a bit," said the Caterpillar.

"Well, perhaps *your* feelings may be different," said Alice; "all I know is, it would feel very queer to *me*."

"You!" said the Caterpillar contemptuously. "Who are *you*?"

Which brought them back again to the beginning of the conversation. Alice felt a little irritated at the Caterpillar's making such *very* short remarks, and she drew herself up and said, very gravely, "I think you ought to tell me who *you* are, first."

"Why?" said the Caterpillar.

Here was another puzzling question; and, as Alice could not think of any good reason, and as the Caterpillar seemed to be in a *very* unpleasant state of mind, she turned away.

"Come back!" the Caterpillar called after her. "I've something important to say!"

This sounded promising, certainly. Alice turned and came back again.

"Keep your temper," said the Caterpillar.

"Is that all?" said Alice, swallowing down her anger as well as she could.

"No," said the Caterpillar.

Alice thought she might as well wait, as she had nothing else to do, and perhaps after all it might tell her something worth hearing. For some minutes it puffed away without speaking; but at last it unfolded its arms, took the hookah out of its mouth again, and said, "So you think you're changed, do you?"

"I'm afraid I am, sir," said Alice. "I can't remember things as I used – and I don't keep the same size for ten minutes together!"

"Can't remember *what* things?" said the Caterpillar.

"Well, I've tried to say 'How doth the little busy bee,' but it all came different!" Alice replied in a very melancholy voice.

"Repeat 'You are old, Father William,'" said the Caterpillar.

Alice folded her hands, and began:

"You are old, Father William," the young man said,
 "And your hair has become very white;
And yet you incessantly stand on your head –
 Do you think, at your age, it is right?"

"In my youth," Father William replied to his son,
 "I feared it might injure the brain;
But, now that I'm perfectly sure I have none,
 Why, I do it again and again."

"You are old," said the youth, "as I mentioned before,
 And have grown most uncommonly fat;
Yet you turned a back-somersault in at the door –
 Pray, what is the reason of that?"

"In my youth," said the sage, as he shook his grey locks,
 "I kept all my limbs very supple
By the use of this ointment – one shilling the box –
 Allow me to sell you a couple?"

"You are old," said the youth, "and your jaws are too weak
   For anything tougher than suet;
Yet you finished the goose, with the bones and the beak –
   Pray, how did you manage to do it?"

"In my youth," said his father, "I took to the law,
   And argued each case with my wife;
And the muscular strength, which it gave to my jaw,
   Has lasted the rest of my life."

"You are old," said the youth; "one would hardly suppose
   That your eye was as steady as ever;
Yet you balanced an eel on the end of your nose –
   What made you so awfully clever?"

"I have answered three questions, and that is enough,"
   Said his father. "Don't give yourself airs!
Do you think I can listen all day to such stuff?
   Be off, or I'll kick you down-stairs!"

"That is not said right," said the Caterpillar.

"Not *quite* right, I'm afraid," said Alice, timidly; "some of the words have got altered."

"It is wrong from beginning to end," said the Caterpillar decidedly; and there was silence for some minutes.

The Caterpillar was the first to speak.

"What size do you want to be?" it asked.

"Oh, I'm not particular as to size," Alice hastily replied; "only one doesn't like changing so often, you know."

"I *don't* know," said the Caterpillar.

Alice said nothing: she had never been so much contradicted in all her life before, and she felt that she was losing her temper.

"Are you content now?" said the Caterpillar.

"Well, I should like to be a *little* larger, Sir, if you wouldn't mind," said Alice: "three inches is such a wretched height to be."

"It is a very good height indeed!" said the Caterpillar angrily, rearing itself upright as it spoke (it was exactly three inches high).

"But I'm not used to it!" pleaded poor Alice in a piteous tone. And she thought to herself, "I wish the creatures wouldn't be so easily offended!"

"You'll get used to it in time," said the Caterpillar; and it put the hookah into its mouth and began smoking again.

This time Alice waited patiently until it chose to speak again. In a minute or two the Caterpillar took the hookah out of its mouth, and yawned once or twice, and shook itself. Then it got down off the mushroom, and crawled away into the grass, merely remarking as it went, "One side will make you grow taller, and the other side will make you grow shorter."

... the Caterpillar took the hookah out of its mouth, and yawned once or twice, and shook itself.

"One side of *what*? The other side of *what*?" thought Alice to herself.

"Of the mushroom," said the Caterpillar, just as if she had asked it aloud; and in another moment it was out of sight.

Alice remained looking thoughtfully at the mushroom for a minute, trying to make out which were the two sides of it; and, as it was perfectly round, she found this a very difficult question. However, at last she stretched her arms round it as far as they would go, and broke off a bit of the edge with each hand.

"And now which is which?" she said to herself, and nibbled a little of the right-hand bit to try the effect. The next moment she felt a violent blow underneath her chin: it had struck her foot!

She was a good deal frightened by this very sudden change, but she felt that there was no time to be lost, as she was shrinking rapidly: so she set to work at once to eat some of the other bit. Her chin was pressed so closely against her foot, that there was hardly room to open her mouth; but she did it at last, and managed to swallow a morsel of the left-hand bit.

"Come, my head's free at last!" said Alice in a tone of delight, which changed into alarm in another moment, when she found that her shoulders were nowhere to be found: all she could see, when she looked down, was an immense length of neck, which seemed to rise like a stalk out of a sea of green leaves that lay far below her.

"What *can* all that green stuff be?" said Alice. "And where *have* my shoulders got to? And oh, my poor hands, how is it I can't see you?" She was moving them about as she spoke, but no result seemed to follow, except a little shaking among the distant green leaves.

As there seemed to be no chance of getting her hands up to her head, she tried to get her head down to them, and was delighted to find that her neck would bend about easily in any direction, like a serpent. She had just succeeded in curving it down into a graceful zigzag, and was going to dive in among the leaves, which she found to be nothing but the tops of the trees under which she had been wandering, when a sharp hiss made her draw back in a hurry: a large pigeon had flown into her face, and was beating her violently with its wings.

"Serpent!" screamed the Pigeon.

"I'm *not* a serpent!" said Alice indignantly. "Let me alone!"

"Serpent, I say again!" repeated the Pigeon, but in a more subdued tone, and added with a kind of sob, "I've tried every way, but nothing seems to suit them!"

"I haven't the least idea what you're talking about," said Alice.

"I've tried the roots of trees, and I've tried banks, and I've tried hedges," the Pigeon when on, without attending to her; "but those serpents! There's no pleasing them!"

Alice was more and more puzzled, but she thought there was no use in saying anything more till the Pigeon had finished.

"As if it wasn't trouble enough hatching the eggs," said the Pigeon; "but I must be on the look-out for serpents night and day! Why, I haven't had a wink of sleep these three weeks!"

"I'm very sorry you've been annoyed," said Alice, who was beginning to see its meaning.

"And just as I'd taken the highest tree in the wood," continued the Pigeon, raising its voice to a shriek, "and just as I was thinking I should be free of them at last, they must needs come wriggling down from the sky! Ugh, Serpent!"

"But I'm *not* a serpent, I tell you!" said Alice. "I'm a – I'm a –"

"Well! *What* are you?" said the Pigeon. "I can see you're trying to invent something!"

"I – I'm a little girl," said Alice, rather doubtfully, as she remembered the number of changes she had gone through that day.

"A likely story indeed!" said the Pigeon, in a tone of the deepest contempt. "I've seen a good many little girls in my time, but never *one* with such a neck as that! No, no! You're a serpent; and there's no use denying it. I suppose you'll be telling me next that you never tasted an egg!"

"I *have* tasted eggs, certainly," said Alice, who was a very truthful child; "but little girls eat eggs quite as much as serpents do, you know."

"I don't believe it," said the Pigeon, "but if they do, why then they're a kind of serpent: that's all I can say."

This was such a new idea to Alice, that she was quite silent for a minute or two, which gave the Pigeon the opportunity of adding, "You're looking for eggs, I know *that* well enough; and what does it matter to me whether you're a little girl or a serpent?"

"It matters a good deal to *me*," said Alice hastily; "but I'm not looking for eggs, as it happens; and if I was, I shouldn't want *yours*: I don't like them raw."

"Well, be off, then!" said the Pigeon in a sulky tone, as it settled down again into its nest. Alice crouched down among the trees as well as she could, for her neck kept getting entangled among the branches, and every now and then she had to stop and untwist it. After a while she remembered that she still held the pieces of mushroom in her hands, and she set to work very carefully, nibbling first at one and then at the other, and growing sometimes taller, and sometimes shorter, until she had succeeded in bringing herself down to her usual height.

It was so long since she had been anything near the right size, that it felt quite strange at first; but she got used to it in a few minutes, and began talking to herself, as usual, "Come, there's half my plan done now! How puzzling all these changes are! I'm never sure what I'm going to be, from one minute to another! However, I've got back to my right size: the next thing is, to get into that beautiful garden – how *is* that to be done, I wonder?" As she said this, she came suddenly upon an open place, with a little house in it about four feet high. "Whoever lives there," thought Alice, "it'll never do to come upon them *this* size: why, I should frighten them out of their wits!" So she began nibbling at the right-hand bit again, and did not venture to go near the house till she had brought herself down to nine inches high.

Chapter Six

♥ Pig and Pepper ♥

For a minute or two she stood looking at the house, and wondering what to do next, when suddenly a footman in livery came running out of the wood – (she considered him to be a footman because he was in livery: otherwise, judging by his face only, she would have called him a fish) – and rapped loudly at the door with his knuckles. It was opened by another footman in livery, with a round face, and large eyes like a frog; and both footmen, Alice noticed, had powdered hair that curled all over their heads. She felt very curious to know what it was all about, and crept a little way out of the wood to listen.

The Fish-Footman began by producing from under his arm a great letter, nearly as large as himself, and this he handed over to the other, saying, in a solemn tone, "For the Duchess. An invitation from the Queen to play croquet." The Frog-Footman repeated, in the same solemn tone, only changing the order of the words a little, "From the Queen. An invitation for the Duchess to play croquet."

Then they both bowed low, and their curls got entangled together.

Alice laughed so much at this, that she had to run back into the wood for fear of their hearing her; and, when she next peeped out, the Fish-Footman was gone, and the other was sitting on the ground near the door, staring stupidly up into the sky.

Alice went timidly up to the door, and knocked.

"There's no sort of use in knocking," said the Footman, "and that for two reasons. First, because I'm on the same side of the door as you are: secondly, because they're making such a noise inside, no one could possibly hear you." And certainly there *was* a most extraordinary noise going on within – a constant howling and sneezing, and every now and then a great crash, as if a dish or kettle had been broken to pieces.

"Please, then," said Alice, "how am I to get in?"

"There might be some sense in your knocking," the Footman went on, without attending to her, "if we had the door between us. For instance, if you were *inside*, you might knock, and I could let you out, you know." He was looking up into the sky all the time he was speaking, and this Alice thought decidedly uncivil. "But perhaps he can't help it," she said to herself; "his eyes are so *very* nearly at the top of his head. But at any rate he might answer questions. How am I to get in?" she repeated, aloud.

"I shall sit here," the Footman remarked, "till to-morrow–"

At this moment the door of the house opened, and a large plate came skimming out, straight at the Footman's head: it just grazed his nose, and broke to pieces against one of the trees behind him.

"– or next day, maybe," the Footman continued in the same tone, exactly as if nothing had happened.

"How am I to get in?" asked Alice again, in a louder tone.

"*Are* you to get in at all?" said the Footman. "That's the first question, you know."

It was, no doubt: only Alice did not like to be told so. "It's really dreadful," she muttered to herself, "the way all the creatures argue. It's enough to drive one crazy!"

The Footman seemed to think this a good opportunity of repeating his remark, with variations. "I shall sit here," he said, "on and off, for days and days."

"But what am *I* to do?" said Alice.

"Anything you like," said the Footman, and began whistling.

"Oh, there's no use in talking to him," said Alice desperately: "he's perfectly idiotic!" And she opened the door and went in.

The door led right into a large kitchen, which was full of smoke from one end to the other: the Duchess was sitting on a three-legged stool in the middle, nursing a baby; the cook was leaning over the fire, stirring a large cauldron which seemed to be full of soup.

"There's certainly too much pepper in that soup!" Alice said to herself, as well as she could for sneezing.

There was certainly too much of it in the *air*. Even the Duchess sneezed occasionally; and as for the baby it was sneezing and howling alternately without a moment's pause. The only two creatures in the kitchen that did *not* sneeze, were the cook, and a large cat, which was sitting on the hearth and grinning from ear to ear.

*... the Duchess was sitting on a three-legged stool
in the middle, nursing a baby ...*

"Please, would you tell me," said Alice a little timidly, for she was not quite sure whether it was good manners for her to speak first, "why your cat grins like that?"

"It's a Cheshire-Cat," said the Duchess, "and that's why. Pig!"

She said the last word with such sudden violence that Alice quite jumped; but she saw in another moment that it was addressed to the baby, and not to her, so she took courage, and went on again:

"I didn't know that Cheshire-Cats always grinned; in fact, I didn't know that cats *could* grin."

"They all can," said the Duchess; "and most of 'em do."

"I don't know of any that do," Alice said very politely, feeling quite pleased to have got into a conversation.

"You don't know much," said the Duchess; "and that's a fact."

Alice did not at all like the tone of this remark, and thought it would be as well to introduce some other subject of conversation. While she was trying to fix on one, the cook took the cauldron of soup off the fire, and at once set to work throwing everything within her reach at the Duchess and the baby – the fire-irons came first; then followed a shower of saucepans, plates, and dishes. The Duchess took no notice of them even when they hit her; and the baby was howling so much already, that it was quite impossible to say whether the blows hurt it or not.

"Oh, *please* mind what you're doing!" cried Alice, jumping up and down in an agony of terror. "Oh, there goes his *precious* nose!", as an unusually large saucepan few close by it, and very nearly carried it off.

"If everybody minded their own business," said the Duchess in a hoarse growl, "the world would go round a deal faster than it does."

"Which would *not* be an advantage," said Alice, who felt very glad to get an opportunity of showing off a little of her knowledge. "Just think what work it would make with the day and night! You see the earth takes twenty-four hours to turn round on its axis –"

"Talking of axes," said the Duchess, "chop off her head!"

Alice glanced rather anxiously at the cook, to see if she meant to take the hint; but the cook was busily stirring the soup, and seemed not to be listening, so she went on again: "Twenty-four hours, I *think*; or is it twelve? I –"

"Oh, don't bother *me*," said the Duchess; "I never could abide figures!" And with that she began nursing her child again, singing a sort of lullaby to it as she did so, and giving it a violent shake at the end of every line:

> *"Speak roughly to your little boy,*
> *And beat him when he sneezes;*
> *He only does it to annoy,*
> *Because he knows it teases."*

> *CHORUS*
> *(In which the cook and the baby joined):*
> *"Wow! wow! wow!"*

While the Duchess sang the second verse of the song, she kept tossing the baby violently up and down, and the poor little thing howled so, that Alice could hardly hear the words:

"I speak severely to my boy,
I beat him when he sneezes;
For he can thoroughly enjoy
The pepper when he pleases!"

CHORUS
"Wow! wow! wow!"

"Here! You may nurse it a bit, if you like!" said the Duchess to Alice, flinging the baby at her as she spoke. "I must go and get ready to play croquet with the Queen," and she hurried out of the room. The cook threw a frying-pan after her as she went, but it just missed her.

Alice caught the baby with some difficulty, as it was a queer-shaped little creature, and held out its arms and legs in all directions, "just like a star-fish," thought Alice. The poor little thing was snorting like a steam-engine when she caught it, and kept doubling itself up and straightening itself out again, so that altogether, for the first minute or two, it was as much as she could do to hold it.

As soon as she had made out the proper way of nursing it (which was to twist it up into a sort of knot, and then keep tight hold of its right ear and left foot, so as to prevent its undoing itself), she carried it out into the open air. "If I don't take this child away with me," thought Alice, "they're sure to kill it in a day or two. Wouldn't it be murder to leave it behind?" She said the last words out loud, and the little thing grunted in reply (it had left off sneezing by this time). "Don't grunt," said Alice; "that's not at all a proper way of expressing yourself."

The baby grunted again, and Alice looked very anxiously

into its face to see what was the matter with it. There could be no doubt that it had a *very* turn-up nose, much more like a snout than a real nose; also its eyes were getting extremely small for a baby: altogether Alice did not like the look of the thing at all. "But perhaps it was only sobbing," she thought, and looked into its eyes again, to see if there were any tears.

No, there were no tears. "If you're going to turn into a pig, my dear," said Alice, seriously, "I'll have nothing more to do with you. Mind now!" The poor little thing sobbed again (or grunted, it was impossible to say which), and they went on for some while in silence.

Alice was just beginning to think to herself, "Now, what am I to do with this creature, when I get it home?" when it grunted again, so violently, that she looked down into its face in some alarm. This time there could be *no* mistake about it: it was neither more nor less than a pig, and she felt that it would be quite absurd for her to carry it any further.

So she set the little creature down, and felt quite relieved to see it trot away quietly into the wood. "If it had grown up," she said to herself, "it would have made a dreadfully ugly child: but it makes rather a handsome pig, I think." And she began thinking over other children she knew, who might do very well as pigs, and was just saying to herself, "if one only knew the right way to change them –" when she was a little startled by seeing the Cheshire-Cat sitting on a bough of a tree a few yards off.

The Cat only grinned when it saw Alice. It looked goodnatured, she thought: still it had *very* long claws and a great many teeth, so she felt it ought to be treated with respect.

"Cheshire-Puss," she began, rather timidly, as she did not at all know whether it would like the name: however, it only grinned a little wider. "Come, it's pleased so far," thought Alice, and she went on, "Would you tell me, please, which way I ought to walk from here?"

"That depends a good deal on where you want to get to," said the Cat.

"I don't much care where –" said Alice.

"Then it doesn't matter which way you walk," said the Cat.

"– so long as I get *somewhere*," Alice added as an explanation.

"Oh, you're sure to do that," said the Cat, "if you only walk long enough."

Alice felt that this could not be denied, so she tried another question. "What sort of people live about here?"

"In *that* direction," the Cat said, waving its right paw round, "lives a Hatter: and in *that* direction," waving the other paw, "lives a March Hare. Visit either you like: they're both mad."

"But I don't want to go among mad people," Alice remarked.

"Oh, you can't help that," said the Cat: "we're all mad here. I'm mad. You're mad."

"How do you know I'm mad?" said Alice.

"You must be," said the Cat, "or you wouldn't have come here."

Alice didn't think that proved it at all; however, she went on: "And how do you know that you're mad?"

"To begin with," said the Cat, "a dog's not mad. You grant that?"

"I suppose so," said Alice.

"Well, then," the Cat went on, "you see a dog growls when it's angry, and wags its tail when it's pleased. Now *I* growl when I'm pleased, and wag my tail when I'm angry. Therefore I'm mad."

"*I* call it purring, not growling," said Alice.

"Call it what you like," said the Cat. "Do you play croquet with the Queen to-day?"

"I should like it very much," said Alice, "but I haven't been invited yet."

"You'll see me there," said the Cat, and vanished.

Alice was not much surprised at this, she was getting so well used to queer things happening. While she was looking at the place where it had been, it suddenly appeared again.

"By-the-bye, what became of the baby?" said the Cat. "I'd nearly forgotten to ask."

"It turned into a pig," Alice answered very quietly, just as if the Cat had come back in a natural way.

"I thought it would," said the Cat, and vanished again.

Alice waited a little, half expecting to see it again, but it did not appear, and after a minute or two she walked on in the direction in which the March Hare was said to live. "I've seen hatters before," she said to herself: "the March Hare will be much the most interesting, and perhaps as this is May it won't be raving mad – at least not so mad as it was in March." As she said this, she looked up, and there was the Cat again, sitting on a branch of a tree.

"Did you say 'pig', or 'fig'?" said the Cat.

"I said 'pig'," replied Alice; "and I wish you wouldn't keep appearing and vanishing so suddenly: you make one quite giddy!"

"All right," said the Cat; and this time it vanished quite slowly, beginning with the end of the tail, and ending with the grin, which remained some time after the rest of it had gone.

"Well! I've often seen a cat without a grin," thought Alice; "but a grin without a cat! It's the most curious thing I ever saw in all my life!"

She had not gone much farther before she came in sight of the house of the March Hare: she thought it must be the right house, because the chimneys were shaped like ears and the roof was thatched with fur. It was so large a house, that she did not like to go nearer till she had nibbled some more of the left-hand bit of mushroom, and raised herself to about two feet high: even then she walked up towards it rather timidly, saying to herself, "Suppose it should be raving mad after all! I almost wish I'd gone to see the Hatter instead!"

Chapter Seven

♥ A Mad Tea-Party ♥

There was a table set out under a tree in front of the house, and the March Hare and the Hatter were having tea at it: a Dormouse was sitting between them, fast asleep, and the other two were using it as a cushion, resting their elbows on it, and talking over its head. "Very uncomfortable for the Dormouse," thought Alice; "only as it's asleep, I suppose it doesn't mind."

The table was a large one, but the three were all crowded together at one corner of it. "No room! No room!" they cried out when they saw Alice coming. "There's *plenty* of room!" said Alice indignantly, and she sat down in a large arm-chair at one end of the table.

"Have some wine," the March Hare said in an encouraging tone.

Alice looked all round the table, but there was nothing on it but tea. "I don't see any wine," she remarked.

"There isn't any," said the March Hare.

"Then it wasn't very civil of you to offer it," said Alice angrily.

"It wasn't very civil of you to sit down without being invited," said the March Hare.

"I didn't know it was *your* table," said Alice; "it's laid for a great many more than three."

"Your hair wants cutting," said the Hatter. He had been looking at Alice for some time with great curiosity, and this was his first speech.

"You should learn not to make personal remarks," Alice said with some severity; "it's very rude."

The Hatter opened his eyes very wide on hearing this; but all he *said* was, "Why is a raven like a writing-desk?"

"Come, we shall have some fun now!" thought Alice. "I'm glad they've begun asking riddles – I believe I can guess that," she added aloud.

"Do you mean that you think you can find out the answer to it?" said the March Hare.

"Exactly so," said Alice.

"Then you should say what you mean," the March Hare went on.

"I do," Alice hastily replied; "at least – at least I mean what I say – that's the same thing, you know."

"Not the same thing a bit!" said the Hatter. "Why, you might just as well say that 'I see what I eat' is the same as 'I eat what I see'!"

"You might just as well say," added the March Hare, "that 'I like what I get' is the same thing as 'I get what I like'!"

"You might just as well say," added the Dormouse, who

seemed to be talking in its sleep, "that 'I breathe when I sleep' is the same thing as 'I sleep when I breathe'!"

"It *is* the same thing with you," said the Hatter, and here the conversation dropped, and the party sat silent for a minute, while Alice thought over all she could remember about ravens and writing-desks, which wasn't much.

The Hatter was the first to break the silence. "What day of the month is it?" he said, turning to Alice: he had taken his watch out of his pocket, and was looking at it uneasily, shaking it every now and then, and holding it to his ear.

Alice considered a little, and then said, "The fourth."

"Two days wrong!" sighed the Hatter. "I told you butter wouldn't suit the works!" he added, looking angrily at the March Hare.

"It was the *best* butter," the March Hare meekly replied.

"Yes, but some crumbs must have got in as well," the Hatter grumbled: "you shouldn't have put it in with the bread-knife."

The March Hare took the watch and looked at it gloomily: then he dipped it into his cup of tea, and looked at it again: but he could think of nothing better to say than his first remark, "It was the *best* butter, you know."

Alice had been looking over his shoulder with some curiosity. "What a funny watch!" she remarked.

"It tells the day of the month, and doesn't tell what o'clock it is!"

"Why should it?" muttered the Hatter. "Does *your* watch tell you what year it is?"

"Of course not," Alice replied very readily: "but that's because it stays the same year for such a long time together."

"Which is just the case with *mine*," said the Hatter.

Alice felt dreadfully puzzled. The Hatter's remark seemed to her to have no sort of meaning in it, and yet it was certainly English. "I don't quite understand you," she said, as politely as she could.

"The Dormouse is asleep again," said the Hatter, and he poured a little hot tea on to its nose.

The Dormouse shook its head impatiently, and said, without opening its eyes, "Of course, of course: just what I was going to remark myself."

"Have you guessed the riddle yet?" the Hatter said, turning to Alice again.

"No, I give it up," Alice replied. "What's the answer?"

"I haven't the slightest idea," said the Hatter.

"Nor I," said the March Hare.

Alice sighed wearily. "I think you might do something better with the time," she said, "than waste it in asking riddles that have no answers."

"If you knew Time as well as I do," said the Hatter, "you wouldn't talk about wasting *it*. It's *him*."

"I don't know what you mean," said Alice.

"Of course you don't!" the Hatter said, tossing his head contemptuously. "I dare say you never even spoke to Time!"

"Perhaps not," Alice cautiously replied; "but I know I have to beat time when I learn music."

*"The Dormouse is asleep again," said the Hatter,
and he poured a little hot tea on to its nose.*

"Ah! that accounts for it," said the Hatter. "He won't stand beating. Now, if you only kept on good terms with him, he'd do almost anything you liked with the clock. For instance, suppose it were nine o'clock in the morning, just time to begin lessons: you'd only have to whisper a hint to Time, and round goes the clock in a twinkling! Half-past one, time for dinner!"

("I only wish it was," the March Hare said to itself in a whisper.)

"That would be grand, certainly," said Alice thoughtfully: "but then – I shouldn't be hungry for it, you know."

"Not at first, perhaps," said the Hatter: "but you could keep it to half-past one as long as you liked."

"Is that the way *you* manage?" Alice asked.

The Hatter shook his head mournfully. "Not I!" he replied. "We quarrelled last March – just before *he* went mad, you know –" (pointing with his teaspoon at the March Hare) "– it was at the great concert given by the Queen of Hearts, and I had to sing

> *'Twinkle, twinkle little bat!*
> *How I wonder what you're at!'*

You know the song, perhaps?"

"I've heard something like it," said Alice.

"It goes on, you know," the Hatter continued, "in this way:

> *'Up above the world you fly,*
> *Like a tea-tray in the sky.*
> *Twinkle, twinkle –'"*

Here the Dormouse shook itself, and began singing in its sleep "*Twinkle, twinkle, twinkle, twinkle –*" and went on so long that they had to pinch it to make it stop.

"Well, I'd hardly finished the first verse," said the Hatter, "when the Queen bawled out, 'He's murdering the time! Off with his head!'"

"How dreadfully savage!" exclaimed Alice.

"And ever since that," the Hatter went on in a mournful tone, "he won't do a thing I ask! It's always six o'clock now."

A bright idea came into Alice's head. "Is that the reason so many tea-things are put out here?" she asked.

"Yes, that's it," said the Hatter with a sigh: "it's always tea-time, and we've no time to wash the things between whiles."

"Then you keep moving round, I suppose?" said Alice.

"Exactly so," said the Hatter: "as the things get used up."

"But what happens when you come to the beginning again?" Alice ventured to ask.

"Suppose we change the subject," the March Hare interrupted, yawning. "I'm getting tired of this. I vote the young lady tells us a story."

"I'm afraid I don't know one," said Alice, rather alarmed at the proposal.

"Then the Dormouse shall!" they both cried. "Wake up, Dormouse!" And they pinched it on both sides at once.

The Dormouse slowly opened his eyes. "I wasn't asleep," he said in a hoarse, feeble voice: "I heard every word you fellows were saying."

"Tell us a story!" said the March Hare.

"Yes, please do!" pleaded Alice.

"And be quick about it," added the Hatter, "or you'll be asleep again before it's done."

"Once upon a time there were three little sisters," the Dormouse began in a great hurry; "and their names were Elsie, Lacie, and Tillie; and they lived at the bottom of a well –"

"What did they live on?" said Alice, who always took a great interest in questions of eating and drinking.

"They lived on treacle," said the Dormouse, after thinking a minute or two.

"They couldn't have done that, you know," Alice gently remarked. "They'd have been ill."

"So they were," said the Dormouse; "*very* ill."

Alice tried to fancy to herself what such an extraordinary way of living would be like, but it puzzled her too much: so she went on: "But why did they live at the bottom of a well?"

"Take some more tea," the March Hare said to Alice, very earnestly.

"I've had nothing yet," Alice replied in an offended tone, "so I can't take more."

"You mean you can't take *less*," said the Hatter: "it's very easy to take *more* than nothing."

"Nobody asked *your* opinion," said Alice.

"Who's making personal remarks now?" the Hatter asked triumphantly.

Alice did not quite know what to say to this: so she helped herself to some tea and bread-and-butter, and then turned to the Dormouse, and repeated her question. "Why did they live at the bottom of a well?"

The Dormouse again took a minute or two to think about it, and then said, "It was a treacle-well."

"There's no such thing!" Alice was beginning very angrily, but the Hatter and the March Hare went, "Sh! Sh!" and the Dormouse sulkily remarked, "If you can't be civil, you'd better finish the story for yourself."

"No, please go on!" Alice said very humbly. "I won't interrupt you again. I dare say there may be *one*."

"One, indeed!" said the Dormouse indignantly. However, he consented to go on. "And so these three little sisters – they were learning to draw, you know –"

"What did they draw?" said Alice, quite forgetting her promise.

"Treacle," said the Dormouse, without considering at all this time.

"I want a clean cup," interrupted the Hatter: "let's all move one place on."

He moved on as he spoke, and the Dormouse followed him: the March Hare moved into the Dormouse's place, and Alice rather unwillingly took the place of the March Hare. The Hatter was the only one who got any advantage from the change; and Alice was a good deal worse off than before, as the March Hare had just upset the milk-jug into his plate.

Alice did not wish to offend the Dormouse again, so she began very cautiously: "But I don't understand. Where did they draw the treacle from?"

"You can draw water out of a water-well," said the Hatter; "so I should think you could draw treacle out of a treacle-well – eh, stupid?"

"But they were *in* the well," Alice said to the Dormouse, not choosing to notice this last remark.

"Of course they were," said the Dormouse: "well in."

This answer so confused poor Alice, that she let the Dormouse go on for some time without interrupting it.

"They were learning to draw," the Dormouse went on, yawning and rubbing its eyes, for it was getting very sleepy; "and they drew all manner of things – everything that begins with an M –"

"Why with an M?" said Alice.

"Why not?" said the March Hare.

Alice was silent.

The Dormouse had closed its eyes by this time, and was going off into a doze; but, on being pinched by the Hatter, it woke up again with a little shriek, and went on: "– that begins with an M, such as mouse traps, and the moon, and memory, and muchness – you know you say things are 'much of a muchness' – did you ever see such a thing as a drawing of a muchness?"

"Really, now you ask me," said Alice, very much confused, "I don't think –"

"Then you shouldn't talk," said the Hatter.

This piece of rudeness was more than Alice could bear: she got up in great disgust, and walked off: the Dormouse fell asleep instantly, and neither of the others took the least notice of her going, though she looked back once or twice, half hoping that they would call after her: the last time she saw them, they were trying to put the Dormouse into the teapot.

"At any rate I'll never go *there* again!" said Alice as she picked her way through the wood. "It's the stupidest tea-party I ever was at in all my life!"

Just as she said this, she noticed that one of the trees had a door leading right into it. "That's very curious!" she thought. "But everything's curious to-day. I think I may as well go in at once." And in she went.

Once more she found herself in the long hall, and close to the little glass table. "Now, I'll manage better this time," she said to herself, and began by taking the little golden key, and unlocking the door that led into the garden. Then she set to work nibbling at the mushroom (she had kept a piece of it in her pocket) till she was about a foot high: then she walked down the little passage: and *then* – she found herself at last in the beautiful garden, among the bright flower-beds and the cool fountains.

CHAPTER EIGHT

♥ The Queen's Croquet-Ground ♥

A large rose-tree stood near the entrance of the garden: the roses growing on it were white, but there were three gardeners at it, busily painting them red. Alice thought this a very curious thing, and she went nearer to watch them, and, just as she came up to them, she heard one of them say, "Look out now, Five! Don't go splashing paint over me like that!"

"I couldn't help it," said Five, in a sulky tone. "Seven jogged my elbow."

On which Seven looked up and said, "That's right, Five! Always lay the blame on others!"

"*You'd* better not talk!" said Five. "I heard the Queen say only yesterday you deserved to be beheaded!"

"What for?" said the one who had spoken first.

"That's none of *your* business, Two!" said Seven.

"Yes, it *is* his business!" said Five. "And I'll tell him – it was for bringing the cook tulip-roots instead of onions."

Seven flung down his brush, and had just begun, "Well, of all the unjust things –" when his eye chanced to fall upon Alice, as she stood watching them, and he checked himself suddenly: the others looked round also, and all of them bowed low.

"Would you tell me," said Alice, a little timidly, "why you are painting those roses?"

Five and Seven said nothing, but looked at Two. Two began, in a low voice, "Why, the fact is, you see, Miss, this here ought to have been a *red* rose-tree, and we put a white one in by mistake; and, if the Queen was to find it out, we should all have our heads cut off, you know. So you see, Miss, we're doing our best, afore she comes, to –" At this moment Five, who had been anxiously looking across the garden, called out, "The Queen! The Queen!", and the three gardeners instantly threw themselves flat upon their faces. There was a sound of many footsteps, and Alice looked round, eager to see the Queen.

First came ten soldiers carrying clubs: these were all shaped like the three gardeners, oblong and flat, with their hands and feet at the corners: next the ten courtiers: these were ornamented all over with diamonds, and walked two and two, as the soldiers did. After these came the royal children; there were ten of them, and the little dears came jumping merrily along, hand in hand, in couples: they were all ornamented with hearts. Next came the guests, mostly Kings and Queens, and among them Alice recognized the White Rabbit: it was talking in a hurried nervous manner, smiling at everything that was said, and went by without noticing her. Then followed the Knave of Hearts, carrying the King's crown on a crimson velvet cushion; and last of all this grand procession, came

THE KING AND QUEEN OF HEARTS.

Alice was rather doubtful whether she ought not to lie down on her face like the three gardeners, but she could not remember ever having heard of such a rule at processions; "and besides, what would be the use of a procession," thought she, "if people had all to lie down on their faces, so that they couldn't see it?" So she stood where she was, and waited.

When the procession came opposite to Alice, they all stopped and looked at her, and the Queen said severely, "Who is this?" She said it to the Knave of Hearts, who only bowed and smiled in reply.

"Idiot!" said the Queen, tossing her head impatiently; and, turning to Alice, she went on, "What's your name, child?"

"My name is Alice, so please your Majesty," said Alice very politely; but she added, to herself, "Why, they're only a pack of cards, after all. I needn't be afraid of them!"

"And who are *these*?" said the Queen, pointing to the three gardeners who were lying round the rose-tree; for, you see, as they were lying on their faces, and the pattern on their backs was the same as the rest of the pack, she could not tell whether they were gardeners, or soldiers, or courtiers, or three of her own children.

"How should *I* know?" said Alice, surprised at her own courage. "It's no business of *mine*."

The Queen turned crimson with fury, and, after glaring at her for a moment like a wild beast, began screaming, "Off with her head! Off with –"

"Nonsense!" said Alice, very loudly and decidedly, and the Queen was silent.

The King laid his hand upon her arm, and timidly said,

"Consider, my dear: she is only a child!"

The Queen turned angrily away from him, and said to the Knave, "Turn them over!" The Knave did so, very carefully, with one foot.

"Get up!" said the Queen in a shrill, loud voice, and the three gardeners instantly jumped up, and began bowing to the King, the Queen, the royal children, and everybody else.

"Leave off that!" screamed the Queen. "You make me giddy." And then, turning to the rose-tree, she went on, "What *have* you been doing here?"

"May it please your Majesty," said Two, in a very humble tone, going down on one knee as he spoke, "we were trying –"

"*I* see!" said the Queen, who had meanwhile been examining the roses. "Off with their heads!" and the procession moved on, three of the soldiers remaining behind to execute the unfortunate gardeners, who ran to Alice for protection.

"You shan't be beheaded!" said Alice, and she put them into a large flower-pot that stood near. The three soldiers wandered about for a minute or two, looking for them, and then quietly marched off after the others.

"Are their heads off?" shouted the Queen.

"Their heads are gone, if it please your Majesty!" the soldiers shouted in reply.

"That's right!" shouted the Queen. "Can you play croquet?"

The soldiers were silent, and looked at Alice, as the question was evidently meant for her.

"Yes!" shouted Alice.

"Come on, then!" roared the Queen, and Alice joined the procession, wondering very much what would happen next.

"It's – it's a very fine day!" said a timid voice at her side. She was walking by the White Rabbit, who was peeping anxiously into her face.

"Very," said Alice. "Where's the Duchess?"

"Hush! Hush!" said the Rabbit in a low hurried tone. He looked anxiously over his shoulder as he spoke, and then raised himself up on tiptoe, put his mouth close to her ear, and whispered, "She's under sentence of execution."

"What for?" said Alice.

"Did you say 'What a pity!'?" the Rabbit asked.

"No, I didn't," said Alice: "I don't think it's at all a pity. I said 'What for?'"

"She boxed the Queen's ears –" the Rabbit began. Alice gave a little scream of laughter. "Oh, hush!" the Rabbit whispered in a frightened tone. "The Queen will hear you! You see she came rather late, and the Queen said –"

"Get to your places!" shouted the Queen in a voice of thunder, and people began running about in all directions, tumbling up against each other: however, they got settled down in a minute or two, and the game began.

Alice thought she had never seen such a curious croquet-ground in all her life: it was all ridges and furrows: the croquet balls were live hedgehogs, the mallets live flamingoes, and the soldiers had to double themselves up and stand on their hands and feet, to make the arches.

The chief difficulty Alice found at first was in managing her flamingo: she succeeded in getting its body tucked away, comfortably enough, under her arm, with its legs hanging down, but generally, just as she had got its neck nicely straightened out, and was going to give the hedgehog a blow with its head, it *would* twist itself round and look up in her face, with such a puzzled expression that she could not help bursting out laughing; and when she had got its head down, and was going to begin again, it was very provoking to find that the hedgehog had unrolled itself, and was in the act of crawling away: besides all this, there was generally a ridge or a furrow in the way wherever she wanted to send the hedgehog to, and, as the doubled-up soldiers were always getting up and walking off to other parts of the ground, Alice soon came to the conclusion that it was a very difficult game indeed.

The players all played at once without waiting for turns, quarrelling all the while, and fighting for the hedgehogs; and in a very short time the Queen was in a furious passion, and went stamping about, and shouting, "Off with his head!" or "Off with her head!" about once in a minute.

Alice began to feel very uneasy: to be sure, she had not as yet had any dispute with the Queen, but she knew that it might happen any minute, "and then," thought she, "what would become of me? They're dreadfully fond of beheading people here: the great wonder is, that there's anyone left alive!"

She was looking about for some way of escape, and wondering whether she could get away without being seen, when she noticed a curious appearance in the air: it puzzled her very much at first, but after watching it a minute or two, she made it out to be a grin, and she said to herself, "It's the Cheshire-Cat: now I shall have somebody to talk to."

"How are you getting on?" said the Cat, as soon as there was mouth enough for it to speak with.

Alice waited till the eyes appeared, and then nodded. "It's no use speaking to it," she thought, "till its ears have come, or at least one of them." In another minute the whole head appeared, and then Alice put down her flamingo, and began an account of the game, feeling very glad she had someone to listen to her. The Cat seemed to think that there was enough of it now in sight, and no more of it appeared.

"I don't think they play at all fairly," Alice began, in rather a complaining tone, "and they all quarrel so dreadfully one can't hear oneself speak – and they don't seem to have any rules in particular: at least, if there are, nobody attends to them – and you've no idea how confusing it is all the things being alive: for instance, there's the arch I've got to go through next walking about at the other end of the ground – and I should have croqueted the Queen's hedgehog just now, only it ran away when it saw mine coming!"

"How do you like the Queen?" said the Cat in a low voice.

"Not at all," said Alice. "She's so extremely –" Just then she noticed that the Queen was close behind her listening: so she went on, "– likely to win, that it's hardly worth while finishing the game."

The Queen smiled and passed on.

THE QUEEN'S CROQUET-GROUND

*Alice thought she had never seen such
a curious croquet-ground in all her life ...*

"Who *are* you talking to?" said the King, coming up to Alice, and looking at the Cat's head with great curiosity.

"It's a friend of mine – a Cheshire-Cat," said Alice: "allow me to introduce it."

"I don't like the look of it at all," said the King: "however, it may kiss my hand if it likes."

"I'd rather not," the Cat remarked.

"Don't be impertinent," said the King, "and don't look at me like that!" He got behind Alice as he spoke.

"A cat may look at a king," said Alice. "I've read that in some book, but I don't remember where."

"Well, it must be removed," said the King very decidedly; and he called to the Queen, who was passing at the moment, "My dear! I wish you would have this cat removed!"

The Queen had only one way of settling all difficulties, great or small. "Off with his head!" she said without even looking round.

"I'll fetch the executioner myself," said the King eagerly, and he hurried off.

Alice thought she might as well go back and see how the game was going on, as she heard the Queen's voice in the distance, screaming with passion. She had already heard her sentence three of the players to be executed for having missed their turns, and she did not like the look of things at all, as the game was in such confusion that she never knew whether it was her turn or not. So she went off in search of her hedgehog.

The hedgehog was engaged in a fight with another hedgehog, which seemed to Alice an excellent opportunity for croqueting one of them with the other: the only difficulty was, that her flamingo was gone across to the other side of the garden, where Alice could see it trying in a helpless sort of way to fly up into a tree.

By the time she had caught the Flamingo and brought it back, the fight was over, and both the hedgehogs were out of sight: "but it doesn't matter much," thought Alice, "as all the arches are gone from this side of the ground." So she tucked it away under her arm, that it might not escape again, and went back to have a little more conversation with her friend.

When she got back to the Cheshire-Cat, she was surprised to find quite a large crowd collected round it: there was a dispute going on between the executioner, the King, and the Queen, who were all talking at once, while all the rest were quite silent, and looked very uncomfortable.

The moment Alice appeared, she was appealed to by all three to settle the question, and they repeated their arguments to her, though, as they all spoke at once, she found it very hard to make out exactly what they said.

The executioner's argument was, that you couldn't cut off a head unless there was a body to cut it off from: that he had never had to do such a thing before, and he wasn't going to begin at *his* time of life.

The King's argument was that anything that had a head could be beheaded, and that you weren't to talk nonsense.

The Queen's argument was that, if something wasn't done about it in less than no time, she'd have everybody executed, all round. (It was this last remark that had made the whole party look so grave and anxious.)

Alice could think of nothing else to say but, "It belongs to the Duchess: you'd better ask *her* about it."

"She's in prison," the Queen said to the executioner: "fetch her here." And the executioner went off like an arrow.

The Cat's head began fading away the moment he was gone, and, by the time he had come back with the Duchess, it had entirely disappeared: so the King and the executioner ran wildly up and down, looking for it, while the rest of the party went back to the game.

CHAPTER NINE

♥ The Mock Turtle's Story ♥

"You can't think how glad I am to see you again, you dear old thing!" said the Duchess, as she tucked her arm affectionately into Alice's, and they walked off together.

Alice was very glad to find her in such a pleasant temper, and thought to herself that perhaps it was only the pepper that had made her so savage when they met in the kitchen. "When *I'm* a Duchess," she said to herself (not in a very hopeful tone, though), "I won't have any pepper in my kitchen at *all*. Soup does very well without – Maybe it's always pepper that makes people hot-tempered," she went on, very much pleased at having found out a new kind of rule, "and vinegar that makes them sour – and camomile that makes them bitter – and – and barley-sugar and such things that make children sweet-tempered. I only wish people knew *that*: then they wouldn't be so stingy about it, you know –"

She had quite forgotten the Duchess by this time, and was

a little startled when she heard her voice close to her ear. "You're thinking about something, my dear, and that makes you forget to talk. I can't tell you just now what the moral of that is, but I shall remember it in a bit."

"Perhaps it hasn't one," Alice ventured to remark.

"Tut, tut, child!" said the Duchess. "Everything's got a moral, if only you can find it." And she squeezed herself up closer to Alice's side as she spoke.

Alice did not much like her keeping so close to her: first, because the Duchess was *very* ugly; and secondly, because she was exactly the right height to rest her chin on Alice's shoulder, and it was an uncomfortably sharp chin. However, she did not like to be rude: so she bore it as well as she could.

"The game's going on rather better now," she said, by way of keeping up the conversation a little.

"'Tis so," said the Duchess: "and the moral of that is – 'Oh, 'tis love, 'tis love, that makes the world go round!'"

"Somebody said," Alice whispered, "that it's done by everybody minding their own business!"

"Ah well! It means much the same thing," said the Duchess, digging her sharp little chin into Alice's shoulder as she added, "and the moral of *that* is – 'Take care of the sense, and the sounds will take care of themselves.'"

"How fond she is of finding morals in things!" Alice thought to herself.

"I dare say you're wondering why I don't put my arm round your waist," the Duchess said after a pause: "the reason is, that I'm doubtful about the temper of your flamingo. Shall I try the experiment?"

"He might bite," Alice cautiously replied, not feeling at all anxious to have the experiment tried.

"Very true," said the Duchess: "flamingoes and mustard both bite. And the moral of that is – 'Birds of a feather flock together.'"

"Only mustard isn't a bird," Alice remarked.

"Right as usual," said the Duchess: "what a clear way you have of putting things!"

"It's a mineral, I *think*," said Alice.

"Of course it is," said the Duchess, who seemed ready to agree to everything that Alice said. "There's a large mustard-mine near here. And the moral of that is – 'The more there is of mine, the less there is of yours.'"

"Oh, I know!" exclaimed Alice, who had not attended to this last remark. "It's a vegetable. It doesn't look like one, but it is."

"I quite agree with you," said the Duchess; "and the moral of that is – 'Be what you would seem to be' – or if you'd like it put more simply – 'Never imagine yourself not to be otherwise than what it might appear to others that what you were or might have been was not otherwise than what you had been would have appeared to them to be otherwise.'"

"I think I should understand that better," Alice said very politely, "if I had it written down: but I can't quite follow it as you say it."

"That's nothing to what I could say if I chose," the Duchess replied, in a pleased tone.

"Pray, don't trouble yourself to say it any longer than that," said Alice.

"Oh, don't talk about trouble!" said the Duchess. "I make you a present of everything I've said as yet."

"A cheap sort of present!" thought Alice. "I'm glad they don't give birthday-presents like that!" But she did not venture to say it out loud.

"Thinking again?" the Duchess asked, with another dig of her sharp little chin.

"I've a right to think," said Alice sharply, for she was beginning to feel a little worried.

"Just about as much right," said the Duchess, "as pigs have to fly: and the m —"

But here, to Alice's great surprise, the Duchess's voice died away, even in the middle of her favourite word "moral", and the arm that was linked to hers began to tremble. Alice looked up, and there stood the Queen in front of them, with her arms folded, frowning like a thunderstorm.

"A fine day, your Majesty!" the Duchess began in a low, weak voice.

"Now, I give you fair warning," shouted the Queen, stamping on the ground as she spoke; "either you or your head must be off, and that in about half no time! Take your choice!"

The Duchess took her choice, and was gone in a moment.

"Let's go on with the game," the Queen said to Alice; and Alice was too much frightened to say a word, but slowly followed her back to the croquet-ground.

The other guests had taken advantage of the Queen's absence, and were resting in the shade: however, the moment they saw her, they hurried back to the game, the Queen merely remarking that a moment's delay would cost them their lives.

All the time they were playing the Queen never left off quarrelling with the other players, and shouting, "Off with his head!" or "Off with her head!" Those whom she sentenced

*"Let's go on with the game," the Queen said to Alice; and
Alice was too much frightened to say a word ...*

were taken into custody by the soldiers, who of course had to leave off being arches to do this, so that by the end of half an hour or so, there were no arches left, and all the players, except the King, the Queen, and Alice were in custody and under sentence of execution.

Then the Queen left off, quite out of breath, and said to Alice, "Have you seen the Mock Turtle yet?"

"No," said Alice. "I don't even know what a Mock Turtle is."

"It's the thing Mock Turtle Soup is made from," said the Queen.

"I never saw one, or heard of one," said Alice.

"Come on, then," said the Queen, "and he shall tell you his history."

As they walked off together, Alice heard the King say in a low voice, to the company generally, "You are all pardoned." "Come, *that's* a good thing!" she said to herself, for she had felt quite unhappy at the number of executions the Queen had ordered.

They very soon came upon a Gryphon, lying fast asleep in the sun. (If you don't know what a Gryphon is, look at the picture.) "Up, lazy thing!" said the Queen, "and take this young lady to see the Mock Turtle, and to hear his history. I must go back and see after some executions I have ordered;" and she walked off, leaving Alice alone with the Gryphon. Alice did not quite like the look of the creature, but on the whole she thought it would be quite as safe to stay with it as to go after that savage Queen: so she waited.

The Gryphon sat up and rubbed its eyes: then it watched the Queen till she was out of sight: then it chuckled. "What fun!" said the Gryphon, half to itself, half to Alice.

"What *is* the fun?" said Alice.

"Why, *she*," said the Gryphon. "It's all her fancy, that: they never executes nobody, you know. Come on!"

"Everybody says 'come on!' here," thought Alice, as she went slowly after it: "I never was so ordered about in all my life, never!"

They had not gone far before they saw the Mock Turtle in the distance, sitting sad and lonely on a little ledge of rock and, as they came nearer, Alice could hear him sighing as if his heart would break. She pitied him deeply. "What is his sorrow?" she asked the Gryphon, and the Gryphon answered very nearly in the same words as before, "It's all his fancy, that: he hasn't got no sorrow, you know. Come on!"

So they went up to the Mock Turtle, who looked at them with large eyes full of tears, but said nothing.

"This here young lady," said the Gryphon, "she wants for to know your history, she do."

"I'll tell it her," said the Mock Turtle, in a deep, hollow tone.

"Sit down both of you, and don't speak a word till I've finished."

So they sat down, and nobody spoke for some minutes. Alice thought to herself, "I don't see how he can *ever* finish, if he doesn't begin." But she waited patiently.

"Once," said the Mock Turtle at last, with a deep sigh, "I was a real Turtle."

These words were followed by a very long silence, broken only by an occasional exclamation of "Hjckrrh!" from the Gryphon, and the constant heavy sobbing of the Mock Turtle. Alice was very nearly getting up and saying, "Thank you, Sir, for your interesting story," but she could not help thinking there *must* be more to come, so she sat still and said nothing.

"When we were little," the Mock Turtle went on at last, more calmly, though still sobbing a little now and then, "we went to school in the sea. The master was an old Turtle – we used to called him Tortoise –"

"Why did you call him Tortoise, if he wasn't one?" Alice asked.

"We called him Tortoise because he taught us," said the Mock Turtle angrily. "Really you are very dull!"

"You ought to be ashamed of yourself for asking such a simple question," added the Gryphon; and then they both sat silent and looked at poor Alice, who felt ready to sink into the earth. At last the Gryphon said to the Mock Turtle, "Drive on, old fellow! Don't be all day about it!", and he went on in these words.

"Yes, we went to school in the sea, though you mayn't believe it –"

"I never said I didn't!" interrupted Alice.

"You did," said the Mock Turtle.

"Hold your tongue!" added the Gryphon, before Alice could speak again. The Mock Turtle went on.

"We had the best of educations – in fact, we went to school every day –"

"*I've* been to a day-school, too," said Alice, "you needn't be so proud as all that."

"With extras?" asked the Mock Turtle, a little anxiously.

"Yes," said Alice: "we learned French and music."

"And washing?" said the Mock Turtle.

"Certainly not!" said Alice indignantly.

"Ah! then yours wasn't a really good school," said the Mock Turtle in a tone of great relief. "Now at *ours*, they had, at the end of the bill, 'French, music, *and washing* – extra.'"

"You couldn't have wanted it much," said Alice; "living at the bottom of the sea."

I couldn't afford to learn it," said the Mock Turtle with a sigh. "I only took the regular course."

"What was that?" enquired Alice.

"Reeling and Writhing, of course, to begin with," the Mock Turtle replied; "and then the different branches of Arithmetic – Ambition, Distraction, Uglification, and Derision."

"I never heard of 'Uglification'," Alice ventured to say. "What is it?"

The Gryphon lifted up both of its paws in surprise. "Never heard of uglifying!" it exclaimed. "You know what to beautify is, I suppose?"

"Yes," said Alice doubtfully: "it means – to – make – anything – prettier."

"Well, then," the Gryphon went on, "if you don't know what to uglify is, you are a simpleton."

Alice did not feel encouraged to ask any more questions about it: so she turned to the Mock Turtle, and said, "What else had you to learn?"

"Well, there was Mystery," the Mock Turtle replied, counting off the subjects on his flippers, "Mystery, ancient and modern, with Seaography. Then Drawling – the Drawling-master was an old conger-eel, that used to come once a week: *he* taught us Drawling, Stretching, and Fainting in Coils."

"What was *that* like?" said Alice.

"Well, I can't show it you myself," the Mock Turtle said: "I'm too stiff. And the Gryphon never learnt it."

"Hadn't time," said the Gryphon: "I went to the Classical master, though. He was an old crab, *he* was."

"I never went to him," the Mock Turtle said with a sigh. "He taught Laughing and Grief, they used to say."

"So he did, so he did," said the Gryphon, sighing in his turn; and both creatures hid their faces in their paws.

"And how many hours a day did you do lessons?" said Alice, in a hurry to change the subject.

"Ten hours the first day," said the Mock Turtle, "nine the next, and so on."

"What a curious plan!" exclaimed Alice.

"That's the reason they're called lessons," the Gryphon remarked: "because they lessen from day to day."

This was quite a new idea to Alice, and she thought it over a little before she made her next remark. "Then the eleventh day must have been a holiday?"

"Of course it was," said the Mock Turtle.

THE MOCK TURTLE'S STORY

"And how did you manage on the twelfth?" Alice went on eagerly.

"That's enough about lessons," the Gryphon interrupted in a very decided tone. "Tell her something about the games now."

CHAPTER TEN

🩶 The Lobster-Quadrille 🩶

The Mock Turtle sighed deeply, and drew the back of one flipper across his eyes. He looked at Alice and tried to speak, but, for a minute or two, sobs choked his voice. "Same as if he had a bone in his throat," said the Gryphon; and it set to work shaking him and punching him in the back. At last the Mock Turtle recovered his voice, and, with tears running down his cheeks, went on again:

"You may not have lived much under the sea –" ("I haven't," said Alice) "and perhaps you were never even introduced to a lobster –" (Alice began to say "I once tasted –" but checked herself hastily, and said, "No, never") "– so you can have no idea what a delightful thing a Lobster-Quadrille is?"

"No, indeed," said Alice. "What sort of a dance is it?"

"Why," said the Gryphon, "you first form into a line along the sea-shore –"

"Two lines!" cried the Mock Turtle. "Seals, turtles, salmon and so on: then, when you've cleared all the jelly-fish out of the way –"

"*That* generally takes some time," interrupted the Gryphon.

"– you advance twice –"

"Each with a lobster as a partner!" cried the Gryphon.

"Of course," the Mock Turtle said: "advance twice, set to partners –"

"– change lobsters, and retire in same order," continued the Gryphon.

"Then, you know," the Mock Turtle went on, "you throw the –"

"The lobsters!" shouted the Gryphon, with a bound into the air.

"– as far out to sea as you can –"

"Swim after them!" screamed the Gryphon.

"Turn a somersault in the sea!" cried the Mock Turtle, capering wildly about.

"Change lobsters again!" yelled the Gryphon at the top of its voice.

"Back to land again, and – that's all the first figure," said the Mock Turtle, suddenly dropping his voice; and the two creatures, who had been jumping about like mad things all this time, sat down again very sadly and quietly, and looked at Alice.

"It must be a very pretty dance," said Alice timidly.

"Would you like to see a little of it?" said the Mock Turtle.

"Very much indeed," said Alice.

"Come, let's try the first figure!" said the Mock Turtle to

the Gryphon. "We can do without lobsters, you know. Which shall sing?"

"Oh, *you* sing," said the Gryphon. "I've forgotten the words."

So they began solemnly dancing round and round Alice, every now and then treading on her toes when they passed too close, and waving their fore-paws to mark the time, while the Mock Turtle sang this, very slowly and sadly:

> "Will you walk a little faster?" said a whiting to a snail,
>   "There's a porpoise close behind us, and he's treading
>   on my tail.
> See how eagerly the lobsters and the turtles all advance!
>   They are waiting on the shingle – will you come and
>   join the dance?
>   Will you, won't you, will you, won't you,
>   will you join the dance?
>   Will you, won't you, will you, won't you,
>   won't you join the dance?

> "You can really have no notion how delightful it will be
>   When they take us up and throw us, with the lobsters,
>   out to sea!"
> But the snail replied, "Too far, too far!" and gave a
>   look askance –
> Said he thanked the whiting kindly, but he would
>   not join the dance.
>   Would not, could not, would not, could not,
>   would not join the dance.
>   Would not, could not, would not, could not,
>   could not join the dance.

So they began solemnly dancing round and round Alice,
every now and then treading on her toes ...

"What matters it how far we go?" his scaly
   friend replied.
"There is another shore, you know, upon the other side.
   The further off from England the nearer is to France –
Then turn not pale, beloved snail, but come and
   join the dance.
      Will you, won't you, will you, won't you,
       will you join the dance?
      Will you, won't you, will you, won't you,
       won't you join the dance?"

"Thank you, it's a very interesting dance to watch," said Alice, feeling very glad that it was over at last: "and I do so like that curious song about the whiting!"

"Oh, as to the whiting," said the Mock Turtle, "they – you've seen them, of course?"

"Yes," said Alice, "I've often seen them at dinn–" she checked herself hastily.

"I don't know where Dinn may be," said the Mock Turtle, "but if you've seem them so often, of course you know what they're like?"

"I believe so," Alice replied thoughtfully. "They have their tails in their mouths – and they're all over crumbs."

"You're wrong about the crumbs," said the Mock Turtle: "crumbs would all wash off in the sea. But they *have* their tails in their mouths; and the reason is –" here the Mock Turtle yawned and shut his eyes. "Tell her about the reason and all that," he said to the Gryphon.

"The reason is," said the Gryphon, "that they *would* go with the lobsters to the dance. So they got thrown out to sea.

So they had to fall a long way. So they got their tails fast in their mouths. So they couldn't get them out again. That's all."

"Thank you," said Alice, "it's very interesting. I never knew so much about a whiting before."

"I can tell you more than that, if you like," said the Gryphon. "Do you know why it's called a whiting?"

"I never thought about it," said Alice. "Why?"

"*It does the boots and shoes,*" the Gryphon replied very solemnly.

Alice was thoroughly puzzled. "Does the boots and shoes!" she repeated in a wondering tone.

"Why, what are *your* boots and shoes done with?" said the Gryphon. "I mean, what makes them so shiny?"

Alice looked down at them, and considered a little before she gave her answer. "They're done with blacking, I believe."

"Boots and shoes under the sea," the Gryphon went on in a deep voice, "are done with whiting. Now you know."

"And what are they made of?" Alice asked in a tone of great curiosity.

"Soles and eels, of course," the Gryphon replied rather impatiently; "any shrimp could have told you that."

"If I'd been the whiting," said Alice, whose thoughts were still running on the song, "I'd have said to the porpoise, 'Keep back, please: we don't want *you* with us!'"

"They were obliged to have him with them," the Mock Turtle said. "No wise fish would go anywhere without a porpoise."

"Wouldn't it really?" said Alice in a tone of great surprise.

"Of course not," said the Mock Turtle. "Why, if a fish came to *me*, and told me he was going on a journey, I should say, 'With what porpoise?'"

"Don't you mean 'purpose'?" said Alice.

"I mean what I say," the Mock Turtle replied, in an offended tone. And the Gryphon added, "Come, let's hear some of *your* adventures."

"I could tell you my adventures – beginning from this morning," said Alice a little timidly; "but it's no use going back to yesterday, because I was a different person then."

"Explain all that," said the Mock Turtle.

"No, no! The adventures first," said the Gryphon in an impatient tone: "explanations take such a dreadful time."

So Alice began telling them her adventures from the time when she first saw the White Rabbit. She was a little nervous about it, just at first, the two creatures got so close to her, one on each side, and opened their eyes and mouths so *very* wide, but she gained courage as she went on. Her listeners were perfectly quiet till she got to the part about her repeating "*You are old, Father William*," to the Caterpillar, and the words all coming different, and then the Mock Turtle drew a long breath, and said, "That's very curious!"

"It's all about as curious as it can be," said the Gryphon.

"It all came different!" the Mock Turtle repeated thoughtfully. "I should like to hear her try and repeat something now. Tell her to begin." He looked at the Gryphon as if he thought it had some kind of authority over Alice.

"Stand up and repeat ''Tis the voice of the sluggard'," said the Gryphon.

"How the creatures order one about, and make one repeat lessons!" thought Alice. "I might just as well be at school at once." However, she got up, and began to repeat it, but her head was so full of the Lobster-Quadrille, that she hardly knew what she was saying; and the words came very queer indeed:

"'Tis the voice of the Lobster; I heard him declare
  'You have baked me too brown, I must sugar my hair.'
As a duck with its eyelids, so he with his nose
  Trims his belt and his buttons, and turns out his toes.

When the sands are all dry, he is gay as a lark,
  And will talk in contemptuous tones of the Shark;
But, when the tide rises and sharks are around
  His voice has a timid and tremulous sound."

"That's different from what I used to say when I was a child," said the Gryphon.

"Well, *I* never heard it before," said the Mock Turtle; "but it sounds uncommon nonsense."

Alice said nothing: she had sat down with her face in her hands, wondering if anything would *ever* happen in a natural way again.

"I should like to have it explained," said the Mock Turtle.

"She can't explain it," said the Gryphon hastily. "Go on with the next verse."

"But about his toes?" the Mock Turtle persisted. "How *could* he turn them out with his nose, you know?"

"It's the first position in dancing," Alice said; but she was dreadfully puzzled by the whole thing, and longed to change the subject.

"Go on with the next verse," the Gryphon repeated impatiently: "it begins with the words '*I passed by his garden*'."

Alice did not dare to disobey, though she felt sure it would all come wrong, and she went on in a trembling voice:

> *"I passed by his garden, and marked, with one eye,*
> *How the Owl and the Panther were sharing a pie:*
> *The Panther took pie-crust, and gravy, and meat,*
> *While the Owl had the dish as its share of the treat.*

> *When the pie was all finished, the Owl, as a boon,*
> *Was kindly permitted to picket the spoon:*
> *While the Panther received knife and fork with a growl,*
> *And concluded the banquet by –"*

"What *is* the use of repeating all that stuff," the Mock Turtle interrupted, "if you don't explain it as you go on? It's by far the most confusing thing *I* ever heard!"

"Yes, I think you'd better leave off," said the Gryphon, and Alice was only too glad to do so.

"Shall we try another figure of the Lobster-Quadrille?" the Gryphon went on. "Or would you like the Mock Turtle to sing you a song?"

"Oh, a song, please, if the Mock Turtle would be so kind," Alice replied, so eagerly that the Gryphon said, in a rather offended tone, "Hm! No accounting for tastes! Sing her '*Turtle Soup*', will you, old fellow?"

The Mock Turtle sighed deeply, and began, in a voice sometimes choked with sobs, to sing this:

"Beautiful Soup, so rich and green,
Waiting in a hot tureen!
Who for such dainties would not stoop?
Soup of the evening, beautiful Soup!
Soup of the evening, beautiful Soup!
Beau – ootiful Soo – oop!
Beau – ootiful Soo – oop!
Soo – oop of the e – e – evening,
Beautiful, beautiful Soup!

Beautiful Soup! Who cares for fish,
Game, or any other dish?
Who would not give all else for two
Pennyworth only of beautiful Soup?
Pennyworth only of beautiful Soup?
Beau – ootiful Soo –oop!
Beau – ootiful Soo – oop!
Soo – oop of the e – e – evening,
Beautiful, beauti – FUL – SOUP!"

"Chorus again!" cried the Gryphon, and the Mock Turtle had just begun to repeat it, when a cry of "The trial's beginning!" was heard in the distance.

"Come on!" cried the Gryphon, and, taking Alice by the hand, it hurried off, without waiting for the end of the song.

"What trial is it?" Alice panted as she ran; but the Gryphon only answered, "Come on!" and ran the faster, while more and more faintly came, carried on the breeze that followed them, the melancholy words:

"*Soo – oop of the e – e – evening,*
Beautiful, beautiful Soup!"

Chapter Eleven

♥ Who Stole the Tarts? ♥

The King and Queen of Hearts were seated on their throne when they arrived, with a great crowd assembled about them – all sorts of little birds and beasts, as well as the whole pack of cards: the Knave was standing before them, in chains, with a soldier on each side to guard him; and near the King was the White Rabbit, with a trumpet in one hand, and a scroll of parchment in the other. In the very middle of the court was a table, with a large dish of tarts upon it: they looked so good, that it made Alice quite hungry to look at them – "I wish they'd get the trial done," she thought, "and hand round the refreshments!" But there seemed to be no chance of this; so she began looking at everything about her to pass away the time.

Alice had never been in a court of justice before but she had read about them in books, and she was quite pleased to find that she knew the name of nearly everything there. "That's the judge," she said to herself, "because of his great wig."

The judge, by the way, was the King; and, as he wore his crown over the wig, he did not look at all comfortable, and it was certainly not becoming.

"And that's the jury-box," thought Alice; "and those twelve creatures" (she was obliged to say "creatures", you see, because some of them were animals, and some were birds) "I suppose they are the jurors." She said this last word two or three times over to herself, being rather proud of it: for she thought, and rightly too, that very few little girls of her age knew the meaning of it at all. However, "jurymen" would have done just as well.

The twelve jurors were all writing very busily on slates. "What are they doing?" Alice whispered to the Gryphon. "They can't have anything to put down yet, before the trial's begun."

"They're putting down their names," the Gryphon whispered in reply, "for fear they should forget them before the end of the trial."

"Stupid things!" Alice began in a loud indignant voice; but she stopped hastily, for the White Rabbit cried out, "Silence in the court!", and the King put on his spectacles and looked anxiously round, to make out who was talking.

Alice could see, as well as if she were looking over their shoulders, that all the jurors were writing down "Stupid things!" on their slates, and she could even make out that one of them didn't know how to spell "stupid", and that he had to ask his neighbour to tell him. "A nice muddle their slates'll be in before the trial's over!" thought Alice.

One of the jurors had a pencil that squeaked. This, of course, Alice could *not* stand, and she went round the court and got behind him, and very soon found an opportunity of taking it away. She did it so quickly that the poor little juror (it was Bill, the Lizard) could not make out at all what had become of it; so, after hunting all about for it, he was obliged to write with one finger for the rest of the day; and this was of very little use, as it left no mark on the slate.

"Herald, read the accusation!" said the King.

On this the White Rabbit blew three blasts on the trumpet, and then unrolled the parchment scroll, and read as follows:

"The Queen of Hearts, she made some tarts,
All on a summer day:
The Knave of Hearts, he stole those tarts
And took them quite away!"

"Consider your verdict," the King said to the jury.

"Not yet, not yet!" the Rabbit hastily interrupted. "There's a great deal to come before that!"

"Call the first witness," said the King; and the White Rabbit blew three blasts on the trumpet, and called out, "First witness!"

The first witness was the Hatter. He came in with a teacup in one hand and a piece of bread-and-butter in the other. "I beg pardon, your Majesty," he began, "for bringing these in but I hadn't quite finished my tea when I was sent for."

"You ought to have finished," said the King. "When did you begin?"

The Hatter looked at the March Hare, who had followed him into the court, arm-in-arm with the Dormouse. "Fourteenth of March, I *think* it was," he said.

"Fifteenth," said the March Hare.

"Sixteenth," added the Dormouse.

"Write that down," the King said to the jury; and the jury eagerly wrote down all three dates on their slates, and then added them up, and reduced the answer to shillings and pence.

"Take off your hat," the King said to the Hatter.

"It isn't mine," said the Hatter.

"*Stolen!*" the King exclaimed, turning to the jury, who instantly made a memorandum of the fact.

"I keep them to sell," the Hatter added as an explanation. "I've none of my own. I'm a hatter."

Here the Queen put on her spectacles, and began staring hard at the Hatter, who turned pale and fidgeted.

"Give your evidence," said the King; "and don't be nervous, or I'll have you executed on the spot."

"I beg pardon, your Majesty," he began," ... but I hadn't quite finished my tea when I was sent for."

This did not seem to encourage the witness at all: he kept shifting from one foot to the other, looking uneasily at the Queen, and in his confusion he bit a large piece out of his teacup instead of the bread-and-butter.

Just at this moment Alice felt a very curious sensation, which puzzled her a good deal until she made out what it was: she was beginning to grow larger again, and she thought at first she would get up and leave the court; but on second thoughts she decided to remain where she was as long as there was room for her.

"I wish you wouldn't squeeze so," said the Dormouse, who was sitting next to her. "I can hardly breathe."

"I can't help it," said Alice very meekly: "I'm growing."

"You've no right to *grow* here," said the Dormouse.

"Don't talk nonsense," said Alice more boldly: "you know you're growing too."

"Yes, but *I* grow at a reasonable pace," said the Dormouse, "not in that ridiculous fashion." And he got up very sulkily and crossed over to the other side of the court.

All this time the Queen had never left off staring at the Hatter, and, just as the Dormouse crossed the court, she said to one of the officers of the court, "Bring me the list of the singers in the last concert!" on which the wretched Hatter trembled so, that he shook off both his shoes.

"Give your evidence," the King repeated angrily, "or I'll have you executed, whether you're nervous or not."

"I'm a poor man, your Majesty," the Hatter began, in a trembling voice, "and I hadn't begun my tea – not above a week or so – and what with the bread-and-butter getting so thin – and the twinkling of the tea –"

"The twinkling of *what*?" said the King.

"It *began* with the tea," the Hatter replied.

"Of course twinkling *begins* with a T!" said the King sharply. "Do you take me for a dunce? Go on!"

"I'm a poor man," the Hatter went on, "and most things twinkled after that – only the March Hare said –"

"I didn't!" the March Hare interrupted in a great hurry.

"You did!" said the Hatter.

"I deny it!" said the March Hare.

"He denies it," said the King: "leave out that part."

"Well, at any rate, the Dormouse said –" the Hatter went on, looking anxiously round to see if he would deny it, too: but the Dormouse denied nothing, being fast asleep.

"After that," continued the Hatter, "I cut some more bread-and-butter –"

"But what did the Dormouse say?" one of the jury asked.

"That I can't remember," said the Hatter.

"You *must* remember," remarked the King, "or I'll have you executed."

The miserable Hatter dropped his teacup and bread-and-butter, and went down on one knee. "I'm a poor man, your Majesty," he began.

"You're a *very* poor *speaker*," said the King.

Here one of the guinea-pigs cheered, and was immediately suppressed by the officers of the court. (As that is rather a hard word, I will just explain to you how it was done. They had a large canvas bag, which tied up at the mouth with strings: into this they slipped the guinea-pig, head first, and then sat upon it.)

"I'm glad I've seen that done," thought Alice. "I've so often read in the newspapers, at the end of trials, 'There was some attempt at applause, which was immediately suppressed by the officers of the court', and I never understood what it meant till now."

"If that's all you know about it, you may stand down," continued the King.

"I can't go no lower," said the Hatter. "I'm on the floor, as it is."

"Then you may *sit* down," the King replied.

Here the other guinea-pig cheered, and was suppressed.

"Come, that finishes the guinea-pigs!" thought Alice. "Now we shall get on better."

"I'd rather finish my tea," said the Hatter, with an anxious look at the Queen, who was reading the list of singers.

"You may go," said the King, and the Hatter hurriedly left the court, without even waiting to put his shoes on.

"– and just take his head off outside," the Queen added to one of the officers; but the Hatter was out of sight before the officer could get to the door.

"Call the next witness!" said the King.

The next witness was the Duchess's cook. She carried the pepper-pot in her hand, and Alice guessed who it was, even before she got into the court, by the way the people near the door began sneezing all at once.

"Give your evidence," said the King.

"Shan't," said the cook.

The King looked anxiously at the White Rabbit, who said in a low voice, "Your Majesty must cross-examine *this* witness."

"Well, if I must, I must," the King said with a melancholy

air, and, after folding his arms and frowning
at the cook till his eyes were nearly out
of sight, he said, in a deep voice,
"What are tarts made of?"

"Pepper, mostly," said
the cook.

"Treacle," said a sleepy
voice behind her.

"Collar that Dormouse,"
the Queen shrieked out.
"Behead that Dormouse! Turn
that Dormouse out of court!
Suppress him! Pinch him! Off
with his whiskers!"

For some minutes the
whole court was in confusion,
getting the Dormouse turned
out, and, by the time they had
settled down again, the cook
had disappeared.

"Never mind!" said the King, with an air
of great relief. "Call the next witness." And, he added, in an
under-tone to the Queen, "Really, my dear, *you* must cross-
examine the next witness. It quite makes my forehead ache!"

Alice watched the White Rabbit as he fumbled over the
list, feeling very curious to see what the next witness would be
like, "– for they haven't got much evidence *yet*," she said to
herself. Imagine her surprise, when the White Rabbit read out,
at the top of his shrill little voice, the name "Alice!"

CHAPTER TWELVE

🖤 Alice's Evidence 🖤

"Here!" cried Alice, quite forgetting in the flurry of the moment how large she had grown in the last few minutes, and she jumped up in such a hurry that she tipped over the jury-box with the edge of her skirt, upsetting all the jury-men on to the heads of the crowd below, and there they lay sprawling about, reminding her very much of a globe of gold-fish she had accidentally upset the week before.

"Oh, I *beg* your pardon!" she exclaimed in a tone of great dismay, and began picking them up again as quickly as she could, for the accident of the gold-fish kept running in her head, and she had a vague sort of idea that they must be collected at once and put back into the jury-box, or they would die.

"The trial cannot proceed," said the King, in a very grave voice, "until all the jurymen are back in their proper places – *all*," he repeated with great emphasis, looking hard at Alice as he said so.

Alice looked at the jury-box, and saw that, in her haste, she had put the Lizard in head downwards, and the poor little thing was waving its tail about in a melancholy way, being quite unable to move. She soon got it out again, and put it right; "not that it signifies much," she said to herself; "I should think it would be *quite* as much use in the trial one way up as the other."

As soon as the jury had a little recovered from the shock of being upset, and their slates and pencils had been found and handed back to them, they set to work very diligently to write out a history of the accident, all except the Lizard, who seemed too much overcome to do anything but sit with its mouth open, gazing up into the roof of the court.

"What do you know about this business?" the King said to Alice.

"Nothing," said Alice.

"Nothing *whatever*?" persisted the King.

"Nothing whatever," said Alice.

"That's very important," the King said, turning to the jury. They were just beginning to write this down on their slates, when the White Rabbit interrupted: "*Un*important, your Majesty means, of course," he said in a very respectful tone, but frowning and making faces at him as he spoke.

"*Un*important, of course, I meant," the King hastily said, and went on to himself in an undertone, "important – unimportant – unimportant – important –" as if he were trying which word sounded best.

Some of the jury wrote it down "important", and some "unimportant". Alice could see this, as she was near enough to look over their slates; "but it doesn't matter a bit," she thought to herself.

At this moment the King, who had been for some time busily writing in his note-book, called out "Silence!", and read out from his book, "Rule Forty-two. *All persons more than a mile high to leave the court.*"

Everybody looked at Alice.

"*I'm* not a mile high," said Alice.

"You are," said the King.

"Nearly two miles high," added the Queen.

"Well, I shan't go, at any rate," said Alice: "besides, that's not a regular rule: you invented it just now."

"It's the oldest rule in the book," said the King.

"Then it ought to be Number One," said Alice.

The King turned pale, and shut his note-book hastily. "Consider your verdict," he said to the jury, in a low trembling voice.

"There's more evidence to come yet, please your Majesty," said the White Rabbit, jumping up in a great hurry: "this paper has just been picked up."

"What's in it?" said the Queen.

"I haven't opened it yet," said the White Rabbit, "but it seems to be a letter, written by the prisoner to – to somebody."

"It must have been that," said the King, "unless it was written to nobody, which isn't usual, you know."

"Who is it directed to?" said one of the jurymen.

"It isn't directed at all," said the White Rabbit: "in fact, there's nothing written on the *outside*." He unfolded the paper as he spoke, and added, "It isn't a letter, after all: it's a set of verses."

"Are they in the prisoner's handwriting?" asked another of the jurymen.

"No, they're not," said the White Rabbit, "and that's the queerest thing about it." (The jury all looked puzzled.)

"He must have imitated somebody else's hand," said the King. (The jury all brightened up again.)

"Please, your majesty," said the Knave, "I didn't write it, and they can't prove I did: there's no name signed at the end."

"If you didn't sign it," said the King, "that only makes the matter worse. You *must* have meant some mischief, or else you'd have signed your name like an honest man."

There was a general clapping of hands at this: it was the first really clever thing the King had said that day.

"That *proves* his guilt," said the Queen: "so, off with –"

"It doesn't prove anything of the sort!" said Alice. "Why, you don't even know what they're about!"

"Read them," said the King.

The White Rabbit put on his spectacles. "Where shall I begin, please your Majesty?" he asked.

"Begin at the beginning," the King said, gravely, "and go on till you come to the end: then stop."

There was dead silence in the court, whilst the White Rabbit read out these verses:

"They told me you had been to her,
  And mentioned me to him:
She gave me a good character,
  But said, I could not swim.

He sent them word I had not gone
  (We know it to be true):
If she should push the matter on,
  What would become of you?

I gave her one, they gave him two,
  You gave us three or more;
They all returned from him to you,
  Though they were mine before.

If I or she should chance to be
  Involved in this affair,
He trusts to you to set them free,
  Exactly as we were.

My notion was that you had been
  (Before she had this fit)
An obstacle that came between
  Him, and ourselves, and it.

Don't let him know she liked them best,
  For this must ever be
A secret, kept from all the rest,
  Between yourself and me."

"That's the most important piece of evidence we've heard yet," said the King, rubbing his hands; "so now let the jury –"

"If any one of them can explain it," said Alice (she had grown so large in the last few minutes that she wasn't a bit afraid of interrupting him), "I'll give him sixpence. *I* don't believe there's an atom of meaning in it."

The jury all wrote down on their slates, "*She* doesn't believe there's an atom of meaning in it," but none of them attempted to explain the paper.

"If there's no meaning in it," said the King, "that saves a world of trouble, you know, as we needn't try to find any. And yet I don't know," he went on, spreading out the verses on his knee, and looking at them with one eye; "I seem to see some meaning in them, after all. '– *said I could not swim –*' you can't swim, can you?" he added, turning to the Knave.

The Knave shook his head sadly. "Do I look like it?" he said. (Which he certainly did *not*, being made entirely of cardboard.)

"All right, so far," said the King, and he went on muttering over the verses to himself: "'*We know it to be true*' – that's the jury, of course. '*If she should push the matter on*' – that must be the queen – '*What would become of you?*' – What indeed! – '*I gave her one, they gave him two*' – why, that must be what he did with the tarts, you know –"

"But it goes on '*They all returned from him to you,*'" said Alice.

"Why, there they are!" said the King triumphantly, pointing to the tarts on the table. "Nothing can be clearer than *that*. Then again – '*before she had this fit*' – you never had fits, my dear, I think?" he said to the Queen.

"Never!" said the Queen furiously, throwing an inkstand

at the Lizard as she spoke. (The unfortunate little Bill had left off writing on his slate with one finger, as he found it made no mark; but he now hastily began again, using the ink, that was trickling down his face, as long as it lasted.)

"Then the words don't *fit* you," said the King, looking round the court with a smile. There was a dead silence.

"It's a pun!" the King added in an angry tone, and everybody laughed. "Let the jury consider their verdict," the King said, for about the twentieth time that day.

"No, no!" said the Queen. "Sentence first – verdict afterwards."

"Stuff and nonsense!" said Alice loudly. "The idea of having the sentence first!"

"Hold your tongue!" said the Queen, turning purple.

"I won't!" said Alice.

"Off with her head!" the Queen shouted at the top of her voice. Nobody moved.

"Who cares for *you*?" said Alice (she had grown to her full size by this time). "You're nothing but a pack of cards!"

At this the whole pack rose up into the air, and came flying down upon her; she gave a little scream, half of fright and half of anger, and tried to beat them off, and found herself lying on the bank, with her head in the lap of her sister, who was gently brushing away some dead leaves that had fluttered down from the trees on to her face.

"Wake up, Alice dear!" said her sister. "Why, what a long sleep you've had!"

"Oh, I've had such a curious dream!" said Alice, and she told her sister, as well as she could remember them, all these strange Adventures of hers that you have just been reading

"Who cares for you?" said Alice (she had grown to her full size by this time). "You're nothing but a pack of cards!"

about; and when she had finished, her sister kissed her, and said, "It *was* a curious dream, dear, certainly; but now run in to your tea; it's getting late." So Alice got up and ran off, thinking while she ran, as well she might, what a wonderful dream it had been.

But her sister sat still just as she left her, leaning her head on her hand, watching the setting sun, and thinking of little Alice and all her wonderful Adventures, till she too began dreaming after a fashion, and this was her dream:

First, she dreamed of little Alice herself: once again the tiny hands were clasped upon her knee, and the bright eager eyes were looking up into hers – she could hear the very tones of her voice, and see that queer little toss of her head, to keep back the wandering hair that *would* always get into her eyes – and still as she listened, or seemed to listen, the whole place around her became alive with the strange creatures of her little sister's dream.

The long grass rustled at her feet as the White Rabbit hurried by – the frightened Mouse splashed his way through the neighbouring pool – she could hear the rattle of the teacups as the March Hare and his friends shared their never-ending meal, and the shrill voice of the Queen ordering off her unfortunate guests to execution – once more the pig-baby was sneezing on the Duchess's knee, while plates and dishes crashed around it – once more the shriek of the Gryphon, the squeaking of the Lizard's slate-pencil, and the choking of the suppressed guinea-pigs, filled the air, mixed up with the distant sobs of the miserable Mock Turtle.

So she sat on, with closed eyes, and half believed herself in Wonderland, though she knew she had but to open them again and all would change to dull reality – the grass would be only rustling in the wind, and the pool rippling to the waving of the reeds – the rattling teacups would change to tinkling sheep-bells, and the Queen's shrill cries to the voice of the shepherd boy – and the sneeze of the baby, the shriek of the Gryphon, and all the other queer noises, would change (she knew) to the confused clamour of the busy farm-yard – while the lowing of the cattle in the distance would take the place of the Mock Turtle's heavy sobs.

Lastly, she pictured to herself how this same little sister of hers would, in the after-time, be herself a grown woman; and how she would keep, through all her riper years, the simple and loving heart of her childhood; and how she would gather about her other little children, and make *their* eyes bright and eager with many a strange tale, perhaps even with the dream of Wonderland of long ago, and how she would feel with all their simple sorrows, and find a pleasure in all their simple joys, remembering her own child-life, and the happy summer days.

DEAR CHILDREN

At Christmas-time a few grave words are not quite out of place, I hope, even at the end of a book of nonsense – and I want to take this opportunity of thanking the thousands of children who have read "Alice's Adventures in Wonderland", for the kindly interest they have taken in my little dream-child.

The thought of the many English firesides where happy faces have smiled her a welcome, and of the many English children to whom she brought an hour of (I trust) innocent amusement, is one of the brightest and pleasantest thoughts of my life. I have a host of young friends already, whose names and whose faces I know – but I cannot help feeling as if, through "Alice's Adventures", I had made friends with many other dear children whose faces I shall never see.

To all my little friends, known and unknown, I wish with all my heart, "A Merry Christmas and a Happy New Year". May God bless you, dear children, and make each Christmas-tide, as it comes round to you, more bright and beautiful than the last – bright with the presence of that unseen Friend, Who once on earth blessed little children – and beautiful with memories of a loving life, which has sought and found that truest kind of happiness, the only kind that is really worth the having, the happiness of making others happy too!

Your affectionate Friend
LEWIS CARROLL

Christmas, 1871

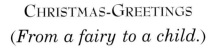

CHRISTMAS-GREETINGS

(From a fairy to a child.)

Lady dear, if Fairies may
* For a moment lay aside*
Cunning tricks and elfish play,
* 'Tis at happy Christmas-tide.*

We have heard the children say —
* Gentle children, whom we love —*
Long ago, on Christmas-Day,
* Came a message from above.*

Still, as Christmas-tide comes round,
* They remember it again —*
Echo still the joyful sound
* "Peace on earth, good-will to men!"*

Yet the hearts must child-like be
* Where such heavenly guests abide;*
Unto children, in their glee,
* All the year is Christmas-tide!*

Thus, forgetting tricks and play
* For a moment, Lady dear,*
We would wish you, if we may,
* Merry Christmas, glad New Year!*

Christmas, 1867

Through the
Looking-Glass

And what Alice found there

🩷 DRAMATIS PERSONÆ 🩷

(As arranged before commencement of game.)

WHITE   RED

PIECES	PAWNS	PAWNS	PIECES
Tweedledee	Daisy	Daisy	Humpty Dumpty
Unicorn	Haigha	Messenger	Carpenter
Sheep	Oyster	Oyster	Walrus
W. Queen	"Lily"	Tiger-lily	R. Queen
W. King	Fawn	Rose	R. King
Aged man	Oyster	Oyster	Crow
W. Knight	Hatta	Frog	R. Knight
Tweedledum	Daisy	Daisy	Lion

White Pawn (Alice) to play, and win in eleven moves.

From the Author's Preface
to the Sixty-First Thousand
of the 6/- Edition, 1897

As the chess problem, given on a previous page, has puzzled some of my readers, it may be well to explain that it is correctly worked out, so far as the moves are concerned. The alternation of Red and White is perhaps not so strictly observed as it might be, and the "castling" of the three Queens is merely a way of saying that they entered the palace: but the "check" of the White King at move 6, the capture of the Red Knight at move 7, and the final "checkmate" of the Red King, will be found, by anyone who will take the trouble to set the pieces and play the moves as directed, to be strictly in accordance with the laws of the game.

The new words, in the poem "Jabberwocky" (see pp. 153–156), have given rise to some differences of opinion as to their pronunciation: so it may be well to give instructions on that point also. Pronounce "slithy" as if it were the two words "sly, the": make the "g" hard in "gyre" and "gimble": and pronounce "rath" to rhyme with "bath".

Christmas, 1896

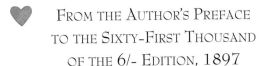

"Oh, Kitty, how nice it would be if we could only get through into Looking-glass House!"

Child of the pure unclouded brow
And dreaming eyes of wonder!
Though time be fleet, and I and thou
Are half a life asunder,
Thy loving smile will surely hail
The love-gift of a fairy-tale.

I have not seen thy sunny face,
Nor heard thy silver laughter:
No thought of me shall find a place
In thy young life's hereafter –
Enough that now thou wilt not fail
To listen to my fairy-tale.

A tale begun in other days,
When summer suns were glowing –
A simple chime, that served to time
The rhythm of our rowing –
Whose echoes live in memory yet,
Though envious years would say "forget".

Come, hearken then, ere voice of dread,
    With bitter tidings laden,
Shall summon to unwelcome bed
    A melancholy maiden!
We are but older children, dear,
    Who fret to find our bedtime near.

Without, the frost, the blinding snow,
    The storm-wind's moody madness –
Within, the firelight's ruddy glow,
    And childhood's nest of gladness.
The magic words shall hold thee fast:
    Thou shalt not heed the raving blast.

And, though the shadow of a sigh
    May tremble through the story,
For "happy summer days" gone by,
    And vanish'd summer glory –
It shall not touch, with breath of bale,
    The pleasance of our fairy-tale.

♥ ♥ ♥

CHAPTER ONE
♥ Looking-Glass House ♥

One thing was certain, that the *white* kitten had had nothing to do with it: – it was the black kitten's fault entirely. For the white kitten had been having its face washed by the old cat for the last quarter of an hour (and bearing it pretty well, considering): so you see that it *couldn't* have had any hand in the mischief.

The way Dinah washed her children's faces was this: first she held the poor thing down by its ear with one paw, and then with the other paw she rubbed its face all over, the wrong way, beginning at the nose: and just now, as I said, she was hard at work on the white kitten, which was lying quite still and trying to purr – no doubt feeling that it was all meant for its good.

But the black kitten had been finished with earlier in the afternoon, and so, while Alice was sitting curled up in a corner of the great arm-chair, half talking to herself and half asleep, the kitten had been having a grand game of romps with the ball of worsted Alice had been trying to wind up, and had been rolling it up and down till it had all come undone again; and there it was, spread over the hearth-rug, all knots and tangles, with the kitten running after its own tail in the middle.

"Oh, you wicked little thing!" cried Alice, catching up the kitten, and giving it a little kiss to make it understand that it was in disgrace. "Really, Dinah ought to have taught you better manners! You *ought*, Dinah, you know you ought!" she added, looking reproachfully at the old cat, and speaking in as cross a voice as she could manage – and then she scrambled back into the arm-chair, taking the kitten and the worsted with her, and began winding up the ball again. But she didn't get on very fast, as she was talking all the time, sometimes to the kitten, and sometimes to herself. Kitty sat very demurely on her knee, pretending to watch the progress of the winding, and now and then putting out one paw and gently touching the ball, as if it would be glad to help if it might.

"Do you know what to-morrow is, Kitty?" Alice began. "You'd have guessed if you'd been up in the window with me – only Dinah was making you tidy, so you couldn't. I was watching the boys getting in sticks for the bonfire – and it wants plenty of sticks, Kitty! Only it got so cold, and it snowed so, they had to leave off. Never mind, Kitty, we'll go and see the bonfire to-morrow." Here Alice wound two or three turns of the worsted round the kitten's neck, just to see how it would look: this led to a scramble, in which the ball rolled down upon the floor, and yards and yards of it got unwound again.

"Do you know, I was so angry, Kitty," Alice went on, as soon as they were comfortably settled again, "when I saw all the mischief you had been doing, I was very nearly opening the window, and putting you out into the snow! And you'd have deserved it, you little mischievous darling! What have you got to say for yourself? Now don't interrupt me!" she went on, holding up one finger. "I'm going to tell you all your faults. Number one: you squeaked twice while Dinah was washing your face this morning. Now you can't deny it, Kitty: I heard you! What's that you say?" (pretending that the kitten was speaking). "Her paw went into your eye? Well, that's *your* fault, for keeping your eyes open – if you'd shut them tight up, it wouldn't have happened. Now don't make any more excuses, but listen! Number two: you pulled Snowdrop away by the tail just as I had put down the saucer of milk before her! What, you were thirsty, were you? How do you know she wasn't thirsty too? Now for number three: you unwound every bit of the worsted while I wasn't looking!

"That's three faults, Kitty, and you've not been punished for any of them yet. You know I'm saving up all your punishments for Wednesday week – suppose they had saved up all *my* punishments!" she went on, talking more to herself than the kitten. "What *would* they do at the end of the year? I should be sent to prison, I suppose, when the day came. Or –

let me see – suppose each punishment was to be going without a dinner: then, when the miserable day came, I should have to go without fifty dinners at once! Well, I shouldn't mind that much! I'd far rather go without them than eat them!

"Do you hear the snow against the window-panes, Kitty? How nice and soft it sounds! Just as if some one was kissing the window all over outside. I wonder if the snow *loves* the trees and fields, it kisses them so gently? And then it covers them up snug, you know, with a white quilt; and perhaps it says, 'Go to sleep, darlings, till the summer comes again.' And when they wake up in the summer, Kitty, they dress themselves all in green, and dance about – whenever the wind blows – oh, that's very pretty!" cried Alice, dropping the ball of worsted to clap her hands. "And I do so *wish* it was true! I'm sure the woods look sleepy in the autumn, when the leaves are getting brown.

"Kitty, can you play chess? Now, don't smile, my dear, I'm asking it seriously. Because, when we were playing just now, you watched just as if you understood it: and when I said 'Check!' you purred! Well, it *was* a nice check, Kitty, and really I might have won, if it hadn't been for that nasty Knight, that came wriggling down among my pieces. Kitty, dear, let's pretend –" And here I wish I could tell you half the things Alice used to say, beginning with her favourite phrase "Let's pretend." She had had quite a long argument with her sister only the day before – all because Alice had begun with "Let's pretend we're kings and queens;" and her sister, who liked being very exact, had argued that they couldn't, because there were only two of them, and Alice had been reduced at last to say, "Well, *you* can be one of them then, and *I'll* be all the rest." And once she had really frightened her old nurse by shouting suddenly in her ear, "Nurse! Do let's pretend that I'm a hungry hyena, and you're a bone!"

But this is taking us away from Alice's speech to the kitten. "Let's pretend that you're the Red Queen, Kitty! Do you know, I think if you sat up and folded your arms, you'd look exactly like her. Now do try, there's a dear!" And Alice got the Red Queen off the table, and set it up before the kitten as a model for it to imitate: however, the thing didn't succeed, principally, Alice said, because the kitten wouldn't fold its arms properly. So, to punish it, she held it up to the looking-glass, that it might see how sulky it was – "and if you're not good directly," she added, "I'll put you through into Looking-glass House. How would you like *that*?

"Now, if you'll only attend, Kitty, and not talk so much, I'll tell you all my ideas about Looking-glass House. First, there's the room you can see through the glass – that's just the same as our drawing room, only the things go the other way. I can see all of it when I get upon a chair – all but the bit just behind the fireplace. Oh! I do so wish I could see *that* bit! I want so much to know whether they've a fire in the winter: you never *can* tell, you know, unless our fire smokes, and then smoke comes up in that room too – but that may be only pretence, just to make it look as if they had a fire. Well then, the books are something like our books, only the words go the wrong way; I know *that*, because I've held up one of our books to the glass, and then they hold up one in the other room.

"How would you like to live in Looking-glass House, Kitty? I wonder if they'd give you milk in there? Perhaps Looking-glass milk isn't good to drink – But oh, Kitty! now we come to the passage. You can just see a little *peep* of the passage in Looking-glass House, if you leave the door of our drawing-room wide open: and it's very like our passage as far as you can see, only you know it may be quite different on beyond. Oh, Kitty, how nice it would be if we could only get through into Looking-glass House! I'm sure it's got, oh! such beautiful things in it! Let's pretend there's a way of getting through into it, somehow, Kitty. Let's pretend the glass has got all soft like gauze, so that we can get through. Why, it's turning into a sort of mist now, I declare! It'll be easy enough to get through –" She was up on the chimney-piece while she said this, though she hardly knew how she had got there. And certainly the glass *was* beginning to melt away, just like a bright silvery mist.

In another moment Alice was through the glass, and had jumped lightly down into the Looking-glass room. The very first thing she did was to look whether there was a fire in the fireplace, and she was quite pleased to find that there was a real one, blazing away as brightly as the one she had left behind. "So I shall be as warm here as I was in the old room," thought Alice: "warmer, in fact, because there'll be no one here to scold me away from the fire. Oh, what fun it'll be, when they see me through the glass in here, and can't get at me!"

Then she began looking about, and noticed that what could be seen from the old room was quite common and uninteresting, but that all the rest was as different as possible.

*Alice was through the glass, and had jumped lightly down
into the Looking-glass room.*

For instance, the pictures on the wall next the fire seemed to be all alive, and the very clock on the chimney-piece (you know you can only see the back of it in the Looking-glass) had got the face of a little old man, and grinned at her.

"They don't keep this room so tidy as the other," Alice thought to herself, as she noticed several of the chessmen down in the hearth among the cinders: but in another moment, with a little "Oh!" of surprise, she was down on her hands and knees watching them. The chessmen were walking about, two and two!

"Here are the Red King and the Red Queen," Alice said (in a whisper, for fear of frightening them), "and there are the White King and the White Queen sitting on the edge of the shovel – and here are two castles walking arm in arm – I don't think they can hear me," she went on, as she put her head closer down, "and I'm nearly sure they can't see me. I feel somehow as if I was getting invisible –"

Here something began squeaking on the table behind Alice, and made her turn her head just in time to see one of the White Pawns roll over and begin kicking: she watched it with great curiosity to see what would happen next.

"It is the voice of my child!" the White Queen cried out, as she pushed past the King, so violently that she knocked him over among the cinders. "My precious Lily! My imperial kitten!" and she began scrambling wildly up the side of the fender.

"Imperial fiddlestick!" said the King, rubbing his nose, which had been hurt by the fall. He had a right to be a *little* annoyed with the Queen, for he was covered with ashes from head to foot.

Alice was very anxious to be of use, and, as the poor little Lily was nearly screaming herself into a fit, she hastily picked up the Queen and set her on the table by the side of her noisy little daughter.

The Queen gasped, and sat down: the rapid journey through the air had quite taken away her breath, and for a minute or two she could do nothing but hug the little Lily in silence. As soon as she had recovered her breath a little, she called out to the White King, who was sitting sulkily among the ashes, "Mind the volcano!"

"What volcano?" said the King, looking up anxiously into the fire, as if he thought that the most likely place to find one.

"Blew – me – up," panted the Queen, who was still a little out of breath. "Mind you come up – the regular way – don't get blown up!"

Alice watched the White King as he slowly struggled up from bar to bar, till at last she said, "Why, you'll be hours and hours getting to the table, at that rate. I'd far better help you, hadn't I?" But the King took no notice of the question: it was quite clear that he could neither hear her nor see her.

So Alice picked him up very gently, and lifted him across more slowly than she had lifted the Queen, that she mightn't take his breath away: but, before she put him on the table, she thought she might as well dust him a little, he was so covered with ashes.

She said afterwards that she had never seen in all her life such a face as the King made, when he found himself held in the air by an invisible hand, and being dusted: he was far too much astonished to cry out, but his eyes and his mouth went on getting larger and larger, and rounder and rounder, till her hand shook so with laughing that she nearly let him drop upon the floor.

"Oh! *please* don't make such faces, my dear!" she cried out, quite forgetting that the King couldn't hear her. "You make me laugh so that I can hardly hold you! And don't keep your mouth so wide open! All the ashes will get into it – there, now I think you're tidy enough!" she added, as she smoothed his hair, and set him upon the table near the Queen.

The King immediately fell flat on his back, and lay perfectly still: and Alice was a little alarmed at what she had done, and went round the room to see if she could find any water to throw over him. However, she could find nothing but a bottle of ink, and when she got back with it she found he had recovered, and he and the Queen were talking together in a frightened whisper – so low, that Alice could hardly hear what they said.

The King was saying, "I assure you, my dear, I turned cold to the very ends of my whiskers!"

To which the Queen replied, "You haven't got any whiskers."

"The horror of that moment," the King went on, "I shall never, *never* forget!"

"You will, though," the Queen said, "if you don't make a memorandum of it."

Alice looked on with great interest as the King took an enormous memorandum-book out of his pocket, and began writing. A sudden thought struck her, and she took hold of the end of the pencil, which came some way over his shoulder, and began writing for him.

The poor King look puzzled and unhappy, and struggled with the pencil for some time without saying anything; but Alice was too strong for him, and at last he panted out, "My dear! I really must get a thinner pencil. I can't manage this one a bit; it writes all manner of things that I don't intend —"

"What manner of things?" said the Queen, looking over the book (in which Alice had put *"The White Knight is sliding down the poker. He balances very badly"*). "That's not a memorandum of *your* feelings!"

There was a book lying near Alice on the table, and while she sat watching the White King (for she was still a little anxious about him, and had the ink all ready to throw over him, in case he fainted again), she turned over the leaves, to find some part that she could read, "– for it's all in some language I don't know," she said to herself.

It was like this.

ЈАВВЕRWOCKY

'Twas brillig, and the slithy toves
Did gyre and gimble in the wabe;
All mimsy were the borogoves,
And the mome raths outgrabe.

She puzzled over this for some time, but at last a bright thought struck her. "Why, it's a Looking-glass book, of course!

And if I hold it up to a glass, the words will all go the right way again."

This was the poem that Alice read.

JABBERWOCKY

'Twas brillig, and the slithy toves
Did gyre and gimble in the wabe;
All mimsy were the borogoves,
And the mome raths outgrabe.

"Beware the Jabberwock, my son!
The jaws that bite, the claws that catch!
Beware the Jubjub bird, and shun
The frumious Bandersnatch!"

He took his vorpal sword in hand:
Long time the manxome foe he sought –
So rested he by the Tumtum tree,
And stood awhile in thought.

And as in uffish thought he stood,
The Jabberwock, with eyes of flame,
Came whiffling through the tulgey wood,
And burbled as it came!

One, two! One, two! And through and through
The vorpal blade went snicker-snack!
He left it dead, and with its head
He went galumphing back.

"Beware the Jabberwock, my son!
The jaws that bite, the claws that catch!"

"And has thou slain the Jabberwock?
  Come to my arms, my beamish boy!
O frabjous day! Callooh! Callay!"
  He chortled in his joy.

'Twas brillig, and the slithy toves
  Did gyre and gimble in the wabe;
All mimsy were the borogoves,
  And the mome raths outgrabe.

"It seems very pretty," she said when she had finished it, "but it's *rather* hard to understand!" (You see she didn't like to confess, even to herself, that she couldn't make it out at all.) "Somehow it seems to fill my head with ideas – only I don't exactly know what they are! However, *somebody* killed *something*: that's clear, at any rate –"

"But oh!" thought Alice, suddenly jumping up, "if I don't make haste I shall have to go back through the Looking-glass, before I've seen what the rest of the house is like! Let's have a look at the garden first!" She was out of the room in a moment, and ran down stairs – or, at least, it wasn't exactly running, but a new invention of hers for getting downstairs quickly and easily, as Alice said to herself. She just kept the tips of her fingers on the hand-rail, and floated gently down without even touching the stairs with her feet; then she floated on through the hall, and would have gone straight out at the door in the same way, if she hadn't caught hold of the door-post. She was getting a little giddy with so much floating in the air, and was rather glad to find herself walking again in the natural way.

CHAPTER TWO

♥ The Garden of Live Flowers ♥

"I should see the garden far better," said Alice to herself, "if I could get to the top of that hill: and here's a path that leads straight to it – at least, no, it doesn't do *that* –" (after going a few yards along the path, and turning several sharp corners), "but I suppose it will at last. But how curiously it twists! It's more like a corkscrew than a path! Well, *this* turn goes to the hill, I suppose – no, it doesn't! This goes straight back to the house! Well then, I'll try it the other way."

And so she did: wandering up and down, and trying turn after turn, but always coming back to the house, do what she would. Indeed, once, when she turned a corner rather more quickly than usual, she ran against it before she could stop herself.

"It's no use talking about it," Alice said, looking up at the house and pretending it was arguing with her. "I'm *not* going in again yet. I know I should have to get through the Looking-glass again – back into the old room – and there'd be an end of all my adventures!"

So, resolutely turning back upon the house, she set out once more down the path, determined to keep straight on till she got to the hill. For a few minutes all went on well, and she was just saying "I really *shall* do it this time –" when the path gave a sudden twist and shook itself (as she described it afterwards), and the next moment she found herself actually walking in at the door.

"Oh, it's too bad!" she cried. "I never saw such a house for getting in the way! Never!"

However, there was the hill full in sight, so there was nothing to be done but start again. This time she came upon a large flower-bed, with a border of daisies, and a willow-tree growing in the middle.

"O Tiger-lily!" said Alice, addressing herself to one that was waving gracefully about in the wind, "I *wish* you could talk!"

"We *can* talk," said the Tiger-lily: "when there's anybody worth talking to."

Alice was so astonished that she couldn't speak for a minute: it quite seemed to take her breath away. At length, as the Tiger-lily only went on waving about, she spoke again, in a timid voice – almost in a whisper. "And can *all* the flowers talk?"

"As well as *you* can," said the Tiger-lily. "And a great deal louder."

"It isn't manners for us to begin, you know," said the Rose, "and I really was wondering when you'd speak! Said I to myself, 'Her face has got *some* sense in it, though it's not a clever one!' Still, you're the right colour, and that goes a long way."

"I don't care about the colour," the Tiger-lily remarked.

"If only her petals curled up a little more, she'd be all right."

Alice didn't like being criticised, so she began asking questions. "Aren't you sometimes frightened at being planted out here, with nobody to take care of you?"

"There's the tree in the middle," said the Rose. "What else is it good for?"

"But what could it do, if any danger came?" Alice asked.

"It could bark," said the Rose.

"It says 'Bough-wough!'"cried a Daisy. "That's why its branches are called boughs!"

"Didn't you know *that*?" cried another Daisy. And here they all began shouting together, till the air seemed quite full of little shrill voices. "Silence, every one of you!" cried the Tiger-lily, waving itself passionately from side to side, and trembling with excitement. "They know I can't get at them!" it panted, bending its quivering head towards Alice, "or they wouldn't dare to do it!"

"Never mind!" Alice said in a soothing tone, and stooping down to the daisies, who were just beginning again, she whispered, "If you don't hold your tongues, I'll pick you!"

There was silence in a moment, and several of the pink daisies turned white.

"That's right!" said the Tiger-lily. "The daisies are worst of all. When one speaks, they all begin together, and it's enough to make one wither to hear the way they go on!"

"How is it you can all talk so nicely?" Alice said, hoping to get it into a better temper by a compliment. "I've been in many gardens before, but none of the flowers could talk."

"Put your hand down, and feel the ground," said the Tiger-lily. "Then you'll know why."

Alice did so. "It's very hard," she said, "but I don't see what that has to do with it."

"In most gardens," the Tiger-lily said, "they make the beds too soft – so that the flowers are always asleep."

This sounded a very good reason, and Alice was quite pleased to know it. "I never thought of that before!" she said.

"It's *my* opinion that you never think *at all*," the Rose said in a rather severe tone.

"I never saw anybody that looked stupider," a Violet said, so suddenly, that Alice quite jumped; for it hadn't spoken before.

"Hold *your* tongue!" cried the Tiger-lily. "As if *you* ever saw anybody! You keep your head under the leaves, and snore away there, till you know no more what's going on in the world, than if you were a bud!"

"Are there any more people in the garden besides me?" Alice said, not choosing to notice the Rose's last remark.

"There's one other flower in the garden that can move about like you," said the Rose. "I wonder how you do it –" ("You're always wondering," said the Tiger-lily), "but she's more bushy than you are."

"Is she like me?" Alice asked eagerly, for the thought crossed her mind, "There's another little girl in the garden, somewhere!"

*"I've been in many gardens before,
but none of the flowers could talk."*

"Well, she has the same awkward shape as you," the Rose said, "but she's redder – and her petals are shorter, I think."

"They're done up close, almost like a dahlia," said the Tiger-lily: "not tumbled about, like yours."

"But that's not *your* fault," the Rose added kindly. "You're beginning to fade, you know – and then one can't help one's petals getting a little untidy."

Alice didn't like this idea at all: so, to change the subject, she asked, "Does she ever come out here?"

"I daresay you'll see her soon," said the Rose. "She's one of the kind that has nine spikes, you know."

"Where does she wear them?" Alice asked with some curiosity.

"Why, all round her head, of course," the Rose replied. "I was wondering *you* hadn't got some too. I thought it was the regular rule."

"She's coming!" cried the Larkspur. "I hear her footstep, thump, thump, along the gravel-walk!"

Alice looked round eagerly, and found that it was the Red Queen. "She's grown a good deal!" was her first remark. She had indeed: when Alice first found her in the ashes, she had been only three inches high – and here she was, half a head taller than Alice herself!

"It's the fresh air that does it," said the Rose: "wonderfully fine air it is, out here."

"I think I'll go and meet her," said Alice, for, though the flowers were interesting enough, she felt that it would be far grander to have a talk with a real Queen.

"You can't possibly do that," said the Rose: "*I* should advise you to walk the other way."

This sounded nonsense to Alice, so she said nothing, but set off at once towards the Red Queen. To her surprise, she lost sight of her in a moment, and found herself walking in at the front-door again.

A little provoked, she drew back, and after looking everywhere for the Queen (whom she spied out at last, a long way off), she thought she would try the plan, this time, of walking in the opposite direction.

It succeeded beautifully. She had not been walking a minute before she found herself face to face with the Red Queen, and full in sight of the hill she had been so long aiming at.

"Where do you come from?" said the Red Queen. "And where are you going? Look up, speak nicely, and don't twiddle your fingers all the time."

Alice attended to all these directions, and explained, as well as she could, that she had lost her way.

"I don't know what you mean by *your* way," said the Queen: "all the ways about here belong to *me* – but why did you come out here at all?" she added in a kinder tone. "Curtsey while you're thinking what to say. It saves time."

Alice wondered a little at this, but she was too much in awe of the Queen to disbelieve it. "I'll try it when I go home," she thought to herself, "the next time I'm a little late for dinner."

"It's time for you to answer now," the Queen said, looking at her watch: "open your mouth a little wider when you speak, and always say 'your Majesty'."

"I only wanted to see what the garden was like, your Majesty –"

"That's right," said the Queen, patting her on the head,

which Alice didn't like at all: "though, when you say 'garden', – *I've* seen gardens, compared with which this would be a wilderness."

Alice didn't dare to argue the point, but went on: "– and I thought I'd try and find my way to the top of that hill –"

"When you say 'hill'," the Queen interrupted, "*I* could show you hills, in comparison with which you'd call that a valley."

"No, I shouldn't," said Alice, surprised into contradicting her at last: "a hill *can't* be a valley, you know. That would be nonsense –"

The Red Queen shook her head. "You may call it 'nonsense' if you like," she said, "but *I've* heard nonsense, compared with which that would be as sensible as a dictionary!"

Alice curtseyed again, as she was afraid from the Queen's tone that she was a *little* offended: and they walked on in silence till they got to the top of the little hill.

For some minutes Alice stood without speaking, looking out in all directions over the country – and a most curious country it was. There were a number of tiny little brooks running straight across it from side to side, and the ground between was divided up into squares by a number of little green hedges, that reached from brook to brook.

"I declare it's marked out just like a large chess-board!" Alice said at last. "There ought to be some men moving about somewhere – and so there are!" she added in a tone of delight, and her heart began to beat quick with excitement as she went on. "It's a great huge game of chess that's being played – all over the world – if this is the world at all, you know. Oh, what fun it is! How I wish I was one of them! I wouldn't mind being a Pawn, if only I might join – though of course I should like to be a Queen, best."

She glanced rather shyly at the real Queen as she said this, but her companion only smiled pleasantly, and said, "That's easily managed. You can be the White Queen's Pawn, if you like, as Lily's too young to play; and you're in the Second Square to begin with: when you get to the Eighth Square you'll be a Queen –" Just at this moment, somehow or other, they began to run.

Alice never could quite make out, in thinking it over afterwards, how it was that they began: all she remembers is, that they were running hand in hand, and the Queen went so fast that it was all she could do to keep up with her: and still the Queen kept crying, "Faster! Faster!" but Alice felt she *could not* go faster, though she had no breath left to say so.

The most curious part of the thing was, that the trees and the other things round them never changed their places at all: however fast they went, they never seemed to pass anything. "I wonder if all the things move along with us?" thought poor puzzled Alice. And the Queen seemed to guess her thoughts, for she cried, "Faster! Don't try to talk!"

Not that Alice had any idea of doing *that*. She felt as if she would never be able to talk again, she was getting so much out of breath: and still the Queen cried "Faster! Faster!" and dragged her along. "Are we nearly there?" Alice managed to pant out at last.

"Nearly there!" the Queen repeated. "Why, we passed it ten minutes ago! Faster!" And they ran on for a time in silence, with the wind whistling in Alice's ears, and almost blowing her hair off her head, she fancied.

"Now! Now!" cried the Queen. "Faster! Faster!" And they went so fast that at last they seemed to skim through the air, hardly touching the ground with their feet, till suddenly, just as Alice was getting quite exhausted, they stopped, and she found herself sitting on the ground, breathless and giddy.

The Queen propped her up against a tree, and said kindly, "You may rest a little now."

Alice looked round her in great surprise. "Why, I do believe we've been under this tree the whole time! Everything's just as it was!"

"Of course it is," said the Queen. "What would you have it?"

"Well, in *our* country," said Alice, still panting a little, "you'd generally get to somewhere else – if you ran very fast for a long time, as we've been doing."

"A slow sort of country!" said the Queen. "Now, *here*, you see, it takes all the running *you* can do, to keep in the same place. If you want to get somewhere else, you must run at least twice as fast as that!"

"I'd rather not try, please!" said Alice. "I'm quite content to stay here – only I *am* so hot and thirsty!"

"I know what *you'd* like!" the Queen said good-naturedly,

taking a little box out of her pocket. "Have a biscuit?"

Alice thought it would not be civil to say "No", though it wasn't at all what she wanted. So she took it, and ate it as well as she could: and it was *very* dry; and she thought she had never been so nearly choked in all her life.

"While you're refreshing yourself," said the Queen, "I'll just take the measurements." And she took a ribbon out of her pocket, marked in inches, and began measuring the ground, and sticking little pegs in here and there.

"At the end of two yards," she said, putting in a peg to mark the distance, "I shall give you your directions – have another biscuit?"

"No, thank you," said Alice, "one's *quite* enough!"

"Thirst quenched, I hope?" said the Queen.

Alice did not know what to say to this, but luckily the Queen did not wait for an answer, but went on. "At the end of *three* yards I shall repeat them – for fear of your forgetting them. At the end of *four*, I shall say good-bye. And at the end of *five*, I shall go!"

She had got all the pegs put in by this time, and Alice looked on with great interest as she returned to the tree, and then began slowly walking down the row.

At the two-yard peg she faced round, and said, "A pawn goes two squares in its first move, you know. So you'll go *very* quickly through the Third Square – by railway, I should think – and you'll find yourself in the Fourth Square in no time. Well, *that* square belongs to Tweedledum and Tweedledee – the Fifth is mostly water – the Sixth belongs to Humpty Dumpty – But you make no remark?"

"I – I didn't know I had to make one – just then," Alice faltered out.

"You *should* have said," the Queen went on in a tone of grave reproof, "'It's extremely kind of you to tell me all this'– however, we'll suppose it said – the Seventh Square is all forest – however, one of the Knights will show you the way – and in the Eighth Square we shall be Queens together, and it's all feasting and fun!" Alice got up and curtseyed, and sat down again.

At the next peg the Queen turned again, and this time she said, "Speak in French when you can't think of the English for a thing – turn out your toes as you walk – and remember who you are!" She did not wait for Alice to curtsey, this time, but walked on quickly to the next peg, where she turned for a moment to say "Good-bye", and then hurried on to the last.

How it happened, Alice never knew, but exactly as she came to the last peg, she was gone. Whether she vanished into the air, or whether she ran quickly into the wood ("and she *can* run very fast!" thought Alice), there was no way of guessing, but she was gone, and Alice began to remember that she was a Pawn, and that it would soon be time for her to move.

CHAPTER THREE

♥ Looking-Glass Insects ♥

Of course the first thing to do was to make a grand survey of the country she was going to travel through. "It's something very like learning geography," thought Alice, as she stood on tiptoe in hopes of being able to see a little further. "Principal rivers – there *are* none. Principal mountains – I'm on the only one, but I don't think it's got any name. Principal towns – why, what *are* those creatures, making honey down there? They can't be bees – nobody ever saw bees a mile off, you know –" and for some time she stood silent, watching one of them that was bustling about among the flowers, poking its proboscis into them, "just as if it was a regular bee," thought Alice.

However, this was anything but a regular bee: in fact, it was an elephant – as Alice soon found out, though the idea quite took her breath away at first. "And what enormous flowers they must be!" was her next idea. "Something like cottages with the roofs taken off, and stalks put to them – and what quantities of honey they must make! I think I'll go down and – no, I won't go *just* yet," she went on, checking herself just as she was beginning to run down the hill, and trying to find some excuse for turning shy so suddenly. "It'll never do to go down among them without a good long branch to brush them away – and what fun it'll be when they ask me how I liked my walk. I shall say – 'Oh, I liked it well enough –'" (here came the favourite little toss of the head), "'only it *was* so dusty and hot, and the elephants *did* tease so!'"

"I think I'll go down the other way," she said after a pause: "and perhaps I may visit the elephants later on. Besides, I *do* so want to get into the Third Square!"

So, with this excuse, she ran down the hill, and jumped over the first of the six little brooks.

"Tickets, please!" said the Guard, putting his head in at the window. In a moment everybody was holding a ticket: they were about the same size as the people, and quite seemed to fill the carriage.

"Now then! Show your ticket, child!" the Guard went on, looking angrily at Alice. And a great many voices all said together ("like the chorus of a song," thought Alice), "Don't keep him waiting, child! Why, his time is worth a thousand pounds a minute!"

"I'm afraid I haven't got one," Alice said in a frightened tone: "there wasn't a ticket-office where I came from." And again the chorus of voices went on. "There wasn't room for one where she came from. The land there is worth a thousand pounds an inch!"

"Don't make excuses," said the Guard: "you should have bought one from the engine-driver." And once more the chorus of voices went on with "The man that drives the engine. Why, the smoke alone is worth a thousand pounds a puff!"

Alice thought to herself, "Then there's no use in speaking." The voices didn't join in *this* time, as she hadn't spoken, but to her great surprise, they all *thought* in chorus (I hope you understand what *thinking in chorus* means – for I must confess that *I* don't), "Better say nothing at all. Language is worth a thousand pounds a word!"

"I shall dream about a thousand pounds to-night, I know I shall!" thought Alice.

All this time the Guard was looking at her, first through a telescope, then through a microscope, and then through an opera-glass. At last he said, "You're travelling the wrong way," and shut up the window, and went away.

"So young a child," said the gentleman sitting opposite to her (he was dressed in white paper), "ought to know which way she's going, even if she doesn't know her own name!"

A Goat, that was sitting next to the gentleman in white, shut his eyes and said in a loud voice, "She ought to know her way to the ticket-office, even if she doesn't know her alphabet!"

There was a Beetle sitting next the Goat (it was a very queer carriage-full of passengers altogether), and, as the rule seemed to be that they should all speak in turn, *he* went on with "She'll have to go back from here as luggage!"

Alice couldn't see who was sitting beyond the Beetle, but a hoarse voice spoke next. "Change engines –" it said, and there it choked and was obliged to leave off.

"It sounds like a horse," Alice thought to herself. And an extremely small voice, close to her ear, said,

"You might make a joke on that – something about 'horse' and 'hoarse', you know."

Then a very gentle voice in the distance said, "She must be labelled 'Lass, with care,' you know –"

And after that other voices went on ("What a number of people there are in the carriage!" thought Alice), saying, "She must go by post, as she's got a head on her –" "She must be sent as a message by the telegraph –" "She must draw the train herself the rest of the way –", and so on.

But the gentleman dressed in white paper leaned forwards and whispered in her ear, "Never mind what they all say, my dear, but take a return-ticket every time the train stops."

"Indeed I shan't!" Alice said rather impatiently. "I don't belong to this railway journey at all – I was in a wood just now – and I wish I could get back there."

"You might make a joke on *that*," said the little voice close to her ear: "something about 'you *would* if you could', you know."

"Don't tease so," said Alice, looking about in vain to see where the voice came from; "if you're so anxious to have a joke made, why don't you make one yourself?"

The little voice sighed deeply: it was *very* unhappy, evidently, and Alice would have said something pitying to comfort it, "if it would only sigh like other people!" she thought. But this was such a wonderfully small sigh, that she wouldn't have heard it at all, if it hadn't come *quite* close to her ear. The consequence of this was that it tickled her ear very much, and quite took off her thoughts from the unhappiness of the poor little creature.

*"Now then! Show your ticket, child!" the Guard
went on, looking angrily at Alice.*

"I know you are a friend," the little voice went on; "a dear friend, and an old friend. And you won't hurt me, though I *am* an insect."

"What kind of insect?" Alice inquired a little anxiously. What she really wanted to know was, whether it could sting or not, but she thought this wouldn't be quite a civil question to ask.

"What, then you don't –" the little voice began, when it was drowned by a shrill scream of the engine, and everybody jumped up in alarm, Alice among the rest.

The Horse, who had put his head out of the window, quietly drew it in and said, "It's only a brook we have to jump over." Everybody seemed satisfied with this, though Alice felt a little nervous at the idea of trains jumping at all. "However, it'll take us into the Fourth Square, that's some comfort!" she said to herself. In another moment she felt the carriage rise straight up into the air, and in her fright she caught at the thing nearest to her hand, which happened to be the Goat's beard.

But the beard seemed to melt away as she touched it, and she found herself sitting quietly under a tree – while the Gnat (for that was the insect she had been talking to) was balancing itself on a twig just over her head, and fanning her with its wings.

It certainly was a *very* large Gnat: "about the size of a chicken," Alice thought. Still, she couldn't feel nervous with it, after they had been talking together so long.

"– then you don't like *all* insects?" the Gnat went on, as quietly as if nothing had happened.

"I like them when they can talk," Alice said. "None of them ever talk, where *I* come from."

"What sort of insects do you rejoice in, where *you* come from?" the Gnat inquired.

"I don't *rejoice* in insects at all," Alice explained, "because I'm rather afraid of them – at least the large kinds. But I can tell you the names of some of them."

"Of course they answer to their names?" the Gnat remarked carelessly.

"I never knew them do it."

"What's the use of their having names," the Gnat said, "if they won't answer to them?"

"No use to *them*," said Alice; "but it's useful to the people that name them, I suppose. If not, why do things have names at all?"

"I can't say," the Gnat replied. "Further on, in the wood down there, they've got no names – however, go on with your list of insects: you're wasting time."

"Well, there's the Horse-fly," Alice began, counting off the names on her fingers.

"All right," said the Gnat: "half way up that bush, you'll see a Rocking-horse-fly, if you look. It's made entirely of wood, and gets about by swinging itself from branch to branch."

"What does it live on?" Alice asked, with great curiosity.

"Sap and sawdust," said the Gnat. "Go on with the list."

Alice looked up at the Rocking-horse-fly with great interest, and made up her mind that it must have been just repainted, it looked so bright and sticky; and then she went on.

"And there's the Dragon-fly."

"Look on the branch above your head," said the Gnat, "and there you'll find a Snap-dragon-fly. Its body is made of plum-pudding, its wings of holly-leaves, and its head is a raisin burning in brandy."

"And what does it live on?" Alice asked, as before.

"Frumenty and mince-pie," the Gnat replied; "and it makes its nest in a Christmas-box."

"And then there's the Butterfly," Alice went on, after she had taken a good look at the insect with its head on fire, and had thought to herself, "I wonder if that's the reason insects are so fond of flying into candles – because they want to turn into Snap-dragon-flies!"

"Crawling at your feet," said the Gnat (Alice drew her feet back in some alarm), "you may observe a Bread-and-butter-fly. Its wings are thin slices of bread-and-butter, its body is a crust, and its head is a lump of sugar."

"And what does *it* live on?"

"Weak tea with cream in it."

A new difficulty came into Alice's head. "Supposing it couldn't find any?" she suggested.

"Then it would die, of course."

"But that must happen very often," Alice remarked thoughtfully.

"It always happens," said the Gnat.

After this, Alice was silent for a minute or two, pondering. The Gnat amused itself meanwhile by humming round and round her head: at last it settled again and remarked, "I suppose you don't want to lose your name?"

"No, indeed," Alice said, a little anxiously.

"And yet I don't know," the Gnat went on in a careless tone: "only think how convenient it would be if you could manage to go home without it! For instance, if the governess wanted to call you to your lessons, she would call out "Come here – ," and there she would have to leave off, because there wouldn't be any name for her to call, and of course you wouldn't have to go, you know."

"That would never do, I'm sure," said Alice: "the governess would never think of excusing me lessons for that. If she couldn't remember my name, she'd call me 'Miss', as the servants do."

"Well, if she said 'Miss', and didn't say anything more,' the Gnat remarked, "of course you'd miss your lessons. That's a joke. I wish *you* had made it."

"Why do you wish *I* had made it?" Alice asked. "It's a very bad one."

But the Gnat only sighed deeply, while two large tears came rolling down its cheeks.

"You shouldn't make jokes," Alice said, "if it makes you so unhappy."

Then came another of those melancholy little sighs, and this time the poor Gnat really seemed to have sighed itself away, for, when Alice looked up, there was nothing whatever to be seen on the twig, and, as she was getting quite chilly with sitting still so long, she got up and walked on.

She very soon came to an open field, with a wood on the other side of it: it looked much darker than the last wood, and Alice felt a *little* timid about going into it. However, on second thoughts, she made up her mind to go on: "for I certainly won't go *back*," she thought to herself, and this was the only way to the Eighth Square.

"This must be the wood," she said thoughtfully to herself, "where things have no names. I wonder what'll become of *my* name when I go in? I shouldn't like to lose it at all – because they'd have to give me another, and it would be almost certain to be an ugly one. But then the fun would be, trying to find the creature that had got my old name! That's just like the advertisements, you know, when people lose dogs – '*answers to the name of "Dash": had on a brass collar*' – just fancy calling everything you met 'Alice', till one of them answered! Only they wouldn't answer at all, if they were wise."

She was rambling on in this way when she reached the wood: it looked very cool and shady. "Well, at any rate it's a great comfort," she said as she stepped under the trees, "after being so hot, to get into the – into the – into *what*?" she went on, rather surprised at not being able to think of the word. "I mean to get under the – under the – under *this*, you know!" putting her hand on the trunk of the tree. "What *does* it call itself, I wonder? I do believe it's got no name – why, to be sure it hasn't!"

She stood silent for a minute, thinking: then she suddenly began again. "Then it really *has* happened, after all! And now, who am I? I *will* remember, if I can! I'm determined to do it!"

But being determined didn't help her much, and all she could say, after a great deal of puzzling, was, "L, I *know* it begins with L!"

Just then a Fawn came wandering by: it looked at Alice with its large gentle eyes, but didn't seem at all frightened. "Here then! Here then!" Alice said, as he held out her hand and tried to stroke it; but it only started back a little, and then stood looking at her again.

"What do you call yourself?" the Fawn said at last. Such a soft sweet voice it had!

"I wish I knew!" thought poor Alice. She answered, rather sadly, "Nothing, just now."

"Think again," it said: "that won't do."

Alice thought, but nothing came of it. "Please, would you tell me what *you* call yourself?" she said timidly. "I think that might help a little."

"I'll tell you, if you'll come a little further on," the Fawn said. "I can't remember *here*."

So they walked on together though the wood, Alice with her arms clasped lovingly round the soft neck of the Fawn, till they came out into another open field, and here the Fawn gave a sudden bound into the air, and shook itself free from Alice's arms. "I'm a Fawn," it cried out in a voice of delight. "And, dear me! you're a human child!" A sudden look of alarm came into its beautiful brown eyes, and in another moment it had darted away at full speed.

Alice stood looking after it, almost ready to cry with vexation at having lost her dear little fellow-traveller so suddenly. "However, I know my name now," she said, "that's *some* comfort. Alice – Alice – I won't forget it again. And now, which of these finger-posts ought I to follow, I wonder?"

It was not a very difficult question to answer, as there was only one road through the wood, and the two finger-posts both pointed along it. "I'll settle it," Alice said to herself, "when the road divides and they point different ways."

But this did not seem likely to happen. She went on and on, a long way, but wherever the road divided there were sure to be two finger-posts pointing the same way, one marked "TO TWEEDLEDUM'S HOUSE", and the other "TO THE HOUSE OF TWEEDLEDEE".

"I do believe," said Alice at last, "that they live in the *same* house! I wonder I never thought of that before – But I can't stay there long. I'll just call and say "How d'ye do?" and ask them the way out of the wood. If I could only get to the Eighth Square before it gets dark!" So she wandered on, talking to herself as she went, till, on turning a sharp corner, she came upon two fat little men, so suddenly that she could not help starting back, but in another moment she recovered herself, feeling sure that they must be

CHAPTER FOUR

♥ Tweedledum and Tweedledee ♥

They were standing under a tree, each with an arm around the other's neck, and Alice knew which was which in a moment, because one of them had "DUM" embroidered on his collar, and the other "DEE". "I suppose they've each got "TWEEDLE" round at the back of the collar," she said to herself.

They stood so still that she quite forgot they were alive, and she was just looking round to see if the word "TWEEDLE" was written at the back of each collar, when she was startled by a voice coming from the one marked "DUM".

"If you think we're wax-works," he said, "you ought to pay, you know. Wax-works weren't made to be looked at for nothing. Nohow!"

"Contrariwise," added the one marked "DEE", "if you think we're alive, you ought to speak."

"I'm sure I'm very sorry," was all Alice could say; for the

words of the old song kept ringing through her head like the ticking of a clock, and she could hardly help saying them out loud:

> *"Tweedledum and Tweedledee*
> *Agreed to have a battle;*
> *For Tweedledum said Tweedledee*
> *Had spoiled his nice new rattle.*
>
> *Just then flew down a monstrous crow,*
> *As black as a tar-barrel;*
> *Which frightened both the heroes so,*
> *They quite forgot their quarrel."*

"I know what you're thinking about," said Tweedledum: "but it isn't so, nohow."

"Contrariwise," continued Tweedledee, "if it was so, it might be; and if it were so, it would be; but as it isn't, it ain't. That's logic."

"I was thinking," Alice said very politely, "which is the best way out of this wood: it's getting so dark. Would you tell me, please?"

But the fat little men only looked at each other and grinned.

They looked so exactly like a couple of great schoolboys, that Alice couldn't help pointing her finger at Tweedledum, and saying, "First Boy!"

"Nohow!" Tweedledum cried out briskly, and shut his mouth up again with a snap.

"Next Boy!" said Alice, passing on to Tweedledee, though

she felt quite certain he would only shout out "Contrariwise!" and so he did.

"You've begun wrong!" cried Tweedledum. "The first thing in a visit is to say 'How d'ye do?' and shake hands!" And here the two brothers gave each other a hug, and then they held out the two hands that were free, to shake hands with her.

Alice did not like shaking hands with either of them first, for fear of hurting the other one's feelings; so, as the best way out of the difficulty, she took hold of both hands at once: the next moment they were dancing round in a ring. This seemed quite natural (she remembered afterwards), and she was not even surprised to hear music playing: it seemed to come from the tree under which they were dancing, and it was done (as well as she could make it out) by the branches rubbing one across the other, like fiddles and fiddle-sticks.

"But it certainly *was* funny," (Alice said afterwards, when she was telling her sister the history of all this) "to find myself singing '*Here we go round the mulberry bush*'. I don't know when I began it, but somehow I felt as if I'd been singing it a long long time!"

The other two dancers were fat, and very soon out of breath. "Four times round is enough for one dance,"

Tweedledum panted out, and they left off dancing as suddenly as they had begun: the music stopped at the same moment.

Then they let go of Alice's hands, and stood looking at her for a minute: there was a rather awkward pause, as Alice didn't know how to begin a conversation with people she had just been dancing with. "It would never do to say 'How d'ye do?' *now*," she said to herself: "we seem to have got beyond that, somehow!"

"I hope you're not much tired?" she said at last.

"Nohow. And thank you *very* much for asking," said Tweedledum.

"So *much* obliged!" added Tweedledee. "You like poetry?"

"Ye-es, pretty well – *some* poetry," Alice said doubtfully. "Would you tell me which road leads out of the wood?"

"What shall I repeat to her?" said Tweedledee, looking round at Tweedledum with great solemn eyes, and not noticing Alice's question.

"'*The Walrus and the Carpenter*' is the longest," Tweedledum replied, giving his brother an affectionate hug.

Tweedledee began instantly:

"The sun was shining –"

Here Alice ventured to interrupt him. "If it's *very* long," she said, as politely as she could, "would you please tell me first which road –"

Tweedledee smiled gently, and began again:

Then they let go of Alice's hands, and stood looking at her for a minute: there was a rather awkward pause ...

"The sun was shining on the sea,
  Shining with all his might:
He did his very best to make
  The billows smooth and bright –
And this was odd, because it was
  The middle of the night.

The moon was shining sulkily,
  Because she thought the sun
Had got no business to be there
  After the day was done –
'It's very rude of him,' she said,
  'To come and spoil the fun!'

The sea was wet as wet could be,
  The sands were dry as dry.
You could not see a cloud, because
  No cloud was in the sky:
No birds were flying overhead –
  There were no birds to fly.

The Walrus and the Carpenter
  Were walking close at hand:
They wept like anything to see
  Such quantities of sand:
'If this were only cleared away,'
  They said, 'it would be grand!'

'If seven maids with seven mops
   Swept it for half a year,
Do you suppose,' the Walrus said,
   'That they could get it clear?'
'I doubt it,' said the Carpenter,
   And shed a bitter tear.

'O Oysters, come and walk with us!'
   The Walrus did beseech.
'A pleasant walk, a pleasant talk,
   Along the briny beach:
We cannot do with more than four,
   To give a hand to each.'

The eldest Oyster looked at him,
   But never a word he said:
The eldest Oyster winked his eye,
   And shook his heavy head –
Meaning to say he did not choose
   To leave the oyster-bed.

But four young Oysters hurried up,
   All eager for the treat:
Their coats were brushed, their faces washed,
   Their shoes were clean and neat –
And this was odd, because, you know,
   They hadn't any feet.

Four other Oysters followed them,
*   And yet another four;*
And thick and fast they came at last,
*   And more, and more, and more –*
All hopping through the frothy waves,
*   And scrambling to the shore.*

The Walrus and the Carpenter
*   Walked on a mile or so,*
And then they rested on a rock
*   Conveniently low:*
And all the little Oysters stood
*   And waited in a row.*

'The time has come,' the Walrus said,
*   'To talk of many things:*
Of shoes – and ships – and sealing-wax –
*   Of cabbages – and kings –*
And why the sea is boiling hot –
*   And whether pigs have wings.'*

'But wait a bit,' the Oysters cried,
*   'Before we have our chat;*
For some of us are out of breath,
*   And all of us are fat!'*
'No hurry!' said the Carpenter.
*   They thanked him much for that.*

'A loaf of bread,' the Walrus said,
   'Is what we chiefly need:
Pepper and vinegar besides
   Are very good indeed –
Now if you're ready, Oysters dear,
   We can begin to feed.'

'But not on us!' the Oysters cried,
   Turning a little blue,
'After such kindness, that would be
   A dismal thing to do!'
'The night is fine,' the Walrus said.
   'Do you admire the view?

'It was so kind of you to come!
   And you are very nice!'
The Carpenter said nothing but
   'Cut us another slice:
I wish you were not quite so deaf –
   I've had to ask you twice!'

'It seems a shame,' the Walrus said,
  'To play them such a trick,
After we've brought them out so far,
  And made them trot so quick!'
The Carpenter said nothing but
  'The butter's spread too thick!'

'I weep for you,' the Walrus said.
  'I deeply sympathize.'
With sobs and tears he sorted out
  Those of the largest size,
Holding his pocket-handkerchief
  Before his streaming eyes.

'O Oysters,' said the Carpenter.
  'You've had a pleasant run!
Shall we be trotting home again?'
  But answer came there none —
And that was scarcely odd, because
  They'd eaten every one."

"I like the Walrus best," said Alice: "because you see he was a *little* sorry for the poor oysters."

"He ate more than the Carpenter, though," said Tweedledee. "You see he held his handkerchief in front, so that the Carpenter couldn't count how many he took: contrariwise."

"That was mean!" Alice said indignantly. "Then I like the Carpenter best – if he didn't eat so many as the Walrus."

"But he ate as many as he could get," said Tweedledum.

This was a puzzler. After a pause, Alice began, "Well!

They were *both* very unpleasant characters –" Here she checked herself in some alarm, at hearing something that sounded to her like the puffing of a large steam-engine in the wood near them, though she feared it was more likely to be a wild beast. "Are there any lions or tigers about here?" she asked timidly.

"It's only the Red King snoring," said Tweedledee.

"Come and look at him!" the brothers cried, and they each took one of Alice's hands, and led her up to where the King was sleeping.

"Isn't he a *lovely* sight?" said Tweedledum.

Alice couldn't say honestly that he was. He had a tall red night-cap on, with a tassel, and he was lying crumpled up into a sort of untidy heap, and snoring loud – "fit to snore his head off!" as Tweedledum remarked.

"I'm afraid he'll catch cold lying on the damp grass," said Alice, who was a very thoughtful little girl.

"He's dreaming now," said Tweedledee: "and what do you think he's dreaming about?"

Alice said, "Nobody can guess that."

"Why, about *you*!" Tweedledee exclaimed, clapping his hands triumphantly. "And if he left off dreaming about you, where do you suppose you'd be?"

"Where I am now, of course," said Alice.

"Not you!" Tweedledee retorted contemptuously. "You'd be nowhere. Why, you're only a sort of thing in his dream!"

"If that there King was to wake," added Tweedledum, "you'd go out – bang! – just like a candle!"

"I shouldn't!" Alice exclaimed indignantly. "Besides, if *I'm* only a sort of thing in his dream, what are *you*,

I should like to know?"

"Ditto," said Tweedledum.

"Ditto, ditto!" cried Tweedledee.

He shouted this so loud that Alice couldn't help saying, "Hush! You'll be waking him, I'm afraid, if you make so much noise."

"Well, it no use *your* talking about waking him," said Tweedledum, "when you're only one of the things in his dream. You know very well you're not real."

"I *am* real!" said Alice, and began to cry.

"You won't make yourself a bit realler by crying," Tweedledee remarked: "there's nothing to cry about."

"If I wasn't real," Alice said – half-laughing though her tears, it all seemed so ridiculous – "I shouldn't be able to cry."

"I hope you don't suppose those are *real* tears?" Tweedledum interrupted in a tone of great contempt.

"I know they're talking nonsense," Alice thought to herself: "and it's foolish to cry about it." So she brushed away her tears, and went on as cheerfully as she could, "At any rate I'd better be getting out of the wood, for really it's coming on very dark. Do you think it's going to rain?"

Tweedledum spread a large umbrella over himself and his brother, and looked up into it. "No, I don't think it is," he said: "at least – not under *here*. Nohow."

"But it may rain *outside*?"

"It may – if it chooses," said Tweedledee: "we've no objection. Contrariwise."

"Selfish things!" thought Alice, and she was just going to say "Good-night" and leave them, when Tweedledum sprang out from under the umbrella and seized her by the wrist.

"Do you see *that*?" he said, in a voice choking with passion, and his eyes grew large and yellow all in a moment, as he pointed with a trembling finger at a small white thing lying under the tree.

"It's only a rattle," Alice said, after a careful examination of the little white thing. "Not a rattle-*snake*, you know," she added hastily, thinking that he was frightened: "only an old rattle – quite old and broken."

"I knew it was!" cried Tweedledum, beginning to stamp about wildly and tear his hair. "It's spoilt, of course!" Here he looked at Tweedledee who immediately sat down on the ground, and tried to hide himself under the umbrella.

Alice laid her hand upon his arm, and said in a soothing tone, "You needn't be so angry about an old rattle."

"But it *isn't* old!" Tweedledum cried, in a greater fury than ever. "It's *new*, I tell you – I bought it yesterday –

my nice NEW RATTLE!" and his voice rose to a perfect scream.

All this time Tweedledee was trying his best to fold up the umbrella, with himself in it: which was such an extraordinary thing to do, that it quite took off Alice's attention from the angry brother. But he couldn't quite succeed, and it ended in his rolling over, bundled up in the umbrella, with only his head out: and there he lay, opening and shutting his mouth and his large eyes – "looking more like a fish than anything else," Alice thought.

"Of course you agree to have a battle?" Tweedledum said in a calmer tone.

"I suppose so," the other sulkily replied, as he crawled out of the umbrella: "only *she* must help us to dress up, you know."

So the two brothers went off hand-in-hand into the wood, and returned in a minute with their arms full of things – such as bolsters, blankets, hearth-rugs, table-cloths, dish-covers and coal-scuttles. "I hope you're a good hand at pinning and tying strings?" Tweedledum remarked. "Every one of these things has got to go on, somehow or other."

Alice said afterwards she had never seen such a fuss made about anything in all her life – the way those two bustled about – and the quantity of things they put on – and the trouble they gave her in tying strings and fastening buttons – "Really they'll be more like bundles of old clothes than anything else, by the time they're ready!" she said to herself, as she arranged a bolster round the neck of Tweedledee, "to keep his head from being cut off," as he said.

"You know," he added very gravely, "it's one of the most serious things that can possibly happen to one in a battle – to get one's head cut off."

*So the two brothers went off hand-in-hand ... and returned
in a minute with their arms full of things ...*

Alice laughed loud: but she managed to turn it into a cough, for fear of hurting his feelings.

"Do I look very pale?" said Tweedledum, coming up to have his helmet tied on. (He *called* it a helmet, though it certainly looked much more like a saucepan.)

"Well – yes – a *little*," Alice replied gently.

"I'm very brave generally," he went on in a low voice: "only to-day I happen to have a headache."

"And *I've* got a toothache!" said Tweedledee, who had overheard the remark. "I'm far worse than you!"

"Then you'd better not fight to-day," said Alice, thinking it a good opportunity to make peace.

"We *must* have a bit of a fight, but I don't care about going on long," said Tweedledum. "What's the time now?"

Tweedledee looked at his watch, and said "Half-past four."

"Let's fight till six, and then have dinner," said Tweedledum.

"Very well," the other said, rather sadly: "and *she* can watch us – only you'd better not come *very* close," he added: "I generally hit everything I can see – when I get really excited."

"And *I* hit everything within reach," cried Tweedledum, "whether I can see it or not!"

Alice laughed. "You must hit the *trees* pretty often, I should think," she said.

Tweedledum looked round him with a satisfied smile. "I don't suppose," he said, "there'll be a tree left standing, for ever so far round, by the time we've finished!"

"And all about a rattle!" said Alice, still hoping to make

them a *little* ashamed of fighting for such a trifle.

"I shouldn't have minded it so much," said Tweedledum, "if it hadn't been a new one."

"I wish the monstrous crow would come!" thought Alice.

"There's only one sword, you know," Tweedledum said to his brother: "but you can have the umbrella – it's quite as sharp. Only we must begin quick. It's getting as dark as it can."

"And darker," said Tweedledee.

It was getting dark so suddenly that Alice thought there must be a thunderstorm coming on. "What a thick black cloud that is!" she said. "And how fast it comes! Why, I do believe it's got wings!"

"It's the crow!" Tweedledum cried out in a shrill voice of alarm: and the two brothers took to their heels and were out of sight in a moment.

Alice ran a little way into the wood, and stopped under a large tree. "It can never get at me *here*," she thought, "it's far too large to squeeze itself in among the trees. But I wish it wouldn't flap its wings so – it makes quite a hurricane in the wood – here's somebody's shawl being blown away!"

CHAPTER FIVE

♥ Wool and Water ♥

She caught the shawl as she spoke, and looked about for the owner: in another moment the White Queen came running wildly through the wood, with both arms stretched out wide, as if she were flying, and Alice very civilly went to meet her with the shawl.

"I'm very glad I happened to be in the way," Alice said, as she helped her to put on the shawl again.

The White Queen only looked at her in a helpless, frightened sort of way, and kept repeating something in a whisper to herself that sounded like "Bread-and-butter, bread-and-butter," and Alice felt that if there was to be any conversation at all, she must manage it herself. So she began rather timidly: "Am I addressing the White Queen?"

"Well, yes, if you call that a-dressing," the Queen said. "It isn't *my* notion of the thing, at all."

Alice thought it would never do to have an argument at

the very beginning of their conversation, so she smiled and
said, "If your Majesty will only tell me the right way to begin,
I'll do it as well as I can."

"But I don't want it done at all!" groaned the poor Queen.
"I've been a-dressing myself for the last two hours."

It would have been all the better, as it seemed to Alice, if
she had got some one else to dress her, she was so dreadfully
untidy. "Every single thing's crooked," Alice thought to herself,
"and she's all over pins! – May I put your shawl straight for
you?" she added aloud.

"I don't know what's the matter with it!" the Queen said,
in a melancholy voice. "It's out of temper, I think. I've pinned
it here, and I've pinned it there, but there's no pleasing it!"

"It *can't* go straight, you know, if you pin it all on one side,"
Alice said, as she gently put it right for her; "and, dear me,
what a state your hair is in!"

"The brush has got entangled in it!" the Queen said with
a sigh. "And I lost the comb yesterday."

Alice carefully released the brush and did her best to get
the hair into order. "Come, you look rather better now!" she
said, after altering most of the pins. "But really you should
have a lady's maid!"

"I'm sure I'll take *you* with pleasure!" the Queen said.
"Twopence a week, and jam every other day."

Alice couldn't help laughing, as she said, "I don't want you
to hire *me* – and I don't care for jam."

"It's very good jam," said the Queen.

"Well, I don't want any *to-day*, at any rate."

"You couldn't have it if you *did* want it," the Queen
said. "The rule is, jam to-morrow and jam yesterday –

but never jam *to-day*."

"It *must* come sometimes to 'jam to-day'," Alice objected.

"No, it can't," said the Queen. "It's jam every *other* day: to-day isn't any *other* day, you know."

"I don't understand you," said Alice. "It's dreadfully confusing!"

"That's the effect of living backwards," the Queen said kindly: "it always makes one a little giddy at first –"

"Living backwards!" Alice repeated in great astonishment. "I never heard of such a thing!"

"– but there's one great advantage in it, that one's memory works both ways."

"I'm sure *mine* only works one way," Alice remarked. "I can't remember things before they happen."

"It's a poor sort of memory that only works backwards," the Queen remarked.

"What sort of things do *you* remember best?" Alice ventured to ask.

"Oh, things that happened the week after next," the Queen replied in a careless tone. "For instance, now," she went on, sticking a large piece of plaster on her finger as she spoke, "there's the King's Messenger. He's in prison now, being punished: and the trial doesn't even begin till next Wednesday: and of course the crime comes last of all."

"Suppose he never commits the crime?" said Alice.

"That would be all the better, wouldn't it?" the Queen said, as she bound the plaster round her finger with a bit of ribbon.

Alice felt there was no denying *that*. "Of course it would be all the better," she said: "but it wouldn't be all the better his being punished."

"You're wrong *there*, at any rate," said the Queen: "were *you* ever punished?"

"Only for faults," said Alice.

"And you were all the better for it, I know!" the Queen said triumphantly.

"Yes, but then I *had* done the things I was punished for," said Alice: "that makes all the difference."

"But if you *hadn't* done them," the Queen said, "that would have been better still; better, and better, and better!" Her voice went higher with each "better", till it got quite to a squeak at last.

Alice was just beginning to say "There's a mistake somewhere –," when the Queen began screaming, so loud that she had to leave the sentence unfinished. "Oh, oh, oh!" shouted the Queen, shaking her hand about as if she wanted to shake it off. "My finger's bleeding! Oh, oh, oh, oh!"

Her screams were so exactly like the whistle of a steam-engine, that Alice had to hold both her hands over her ears.

"What *is* the matter?" she said, as soon as there was a chance of making herself heard. "Have you pricked your finger?"

"I haven't pricked it *yet*," the Queen said, "but I soon shall

– oh, oh, oh!"

"When do you expect to do it?" Alice asked, feeling very much inclined to laugh.

"When I fasten my shawl again," the poor Queen groaned out: "the brooch will come undone directly. Oh, oh!" As she said the words the brooch flew open, and the Queen clutched wildly at it, and tried to clasp it again.

"Take care!" cried Alice. "You're holding it all crooked!" And she caught at the brooch; but it was too late: the pin had slipped, and the Queen had pricked her finger.

"That accounts for the bleeding, you see," she said to Alice with a smile. "Now you understand the way things happen here."

"But why don't you scream *now*?" Alice asked, holding her hands ready to put over her ears again.

"Why, I've done all the screaming already," said the Queen. "What would be the good of having it all over again?"

By this time it was getting light. "The crow must have flown away, I think," said Alice: "I'm so glad it's gone. I thought it was the night coming on."

"I wish *I* could manage to be glad!" the Queen said. "Only I never can remember the rule. You must be very happy, living in this wood, and being glad whenever you like!"

"Only it is so *very* lonely here!" Alice said in a melancholy voice; and at the thought of her loneliness two large tears came rolling down her cheeks.

"Oh, don't go on like that!" cried the poor Queen, wringing her hands in despair. "Consider what a great girl you are. Consider what a long way you've come to-day. Consider what o'clock it is. Consider anything, only don't cry!"

... she caught at the brooch; but it was too late: the pin had slipped, and the Queen had pricked her finger.

Alice could not help laughing at this, even in the midst of her tears. "Can *you* keep from crying by considering things?" she asked.

"That's the way it's done," the Queen said with great decision: "nobody can do two things at once, you know. Let's consider your age to begin with – how old are you?"

"I'm seven and a half, exactly."

"You needn't say 'exactually'," the Queen remarked: "I can believe it without that. Now I'll give *you* something to believe. I'm just one hundred and one, five months and a day."

"I can't believe *that*!" said Alice.

"Can't you?" the Queen said in a pitying tone. "Try again: draw a long breath, and shut your eyes."

Alice laughed. "There's no use trying," she said: "one *can't* believe impossible things."

"I daresay you haven't had much practice," said the Queen. "When I was your age, I always did it for half-an-hour a day. Why, sometimes I've believed as many as six impossible things before breakfast. There goes the shawl again!"

The brooch had come undone as she spoke, and a sudden gust of wind blew the Queen's shawl across a little brook. The Queen spread out her arms again, and went flying after it, and this time she succeeded in catching it for herself. "I've got it!" she cried in a triumphant tone. "Now you shall see me pin it on again, all by myself!"

"Then I hope your finger is better now?" Alice said very politely, as she crossed the little brook after the Queen.

"Oh, much better!" cried the Queen, her voice rising to a squeak as she went on. "Much be-etter! Be-etter! Be-e-e-etter!

Be-e-ehh!" The last word ended
in a long bleat, so like a sheep
that Alice quite started.

She looked at the
Queen, who seemed to have
suddenly wrapped herself up
in wool. Alice rubbed her
eyes, and looked again. She
couldn't make out what
had happened at all. Was
she in a shop? And was
that really – was it really a
sheep that was sitting on the
other side of the counter?
Rub as she would, she could
make nothing more of it: she
was in a little dark shop,
leaning with her elbows on
the counter, and opposite to
her was an old Sheep, sitting
in an arm-chair, knitting, and
every now and then leaving off to
look at her through a great pair of spectacles.

"What is it you want to buy?" the Sheep said at last,
looking up for a moment from her knitting.

"I don't *quite* know yet," Alice said very gently. I should
like to look all round me first, if I might."

"You may look in front of you, and on both sides, if you
like," said the Sheep; "but you can't look *all* round you – unless
you've got eyes at the back of your head."

But these, as it happened, Alice had *not* got: so she contented herself with turning round, looking at the shelves as she came to them.

The shop seemed to be full of all manner of curious things – but the oddest part of it all was that, whenever she looked hard at any shelf, to make out exactly what it had on it, that particular shelf was always quite empty: though the others round it were crowded as full as they could hold.

"Things flow about so here!" she said at last in a plaintive tone, after she had spent a minute or so in vainly pursuing a large bright thing, that looked sometimes like a doll and sometimes like a work-box, and was always in the shelf next above the one she was looking at. "And this one is the most provoking of all – but I'll tell you what –" she added, as a sudden thought struck her, "I'll follow it up to the very top shelf of all. It'll puzzle it to go through the ceiling, I expect!"

But even this plan failed: the "thing" went through the ceiling as quietly as possible, as if it were quite used to it.

"Are you a child or a teetotum?" the Sheep said, as she took up another pair of needles. "You'll make me giddy soon, if you go on turning round like that." She was now working with fourteen pairs at once, and Alice couldn't help looking at her in great astonishment.

"How *can* she knit with so many?" the puzzled child thought to herself. "She gets more and more like a porcupine every minute!"

"Can you row?" the Sheep asked, handing her a pair of knitting-needles as she spoke.

"Yes, a little – but not on land – and not with needles –" Alice was beginning to say, when suddenly the needles turned into oars in her hands, and she found they were in a little boat, gliding along between banks: so there was nothing for it but to do her best.

"Feather!" cried the Sheep, as she took up another pair of needles.

This didn't sound like a remark that needed any answer: so Alice said nothing, but pulled away. There was something very queer about the water, she thought, as every now and then the oars got fast in it, and would hardly come out again.

"Feather! Feather!" the Sheep cried again, taking more needles. "You'll be catching a crab directly."

"A dear little crab!" thought Alice. "I should like that."

"Didn't you hear me say 'Feather'?" the Sheep cried angrily, taking up quite a bunch of needles.

"Indeed I did," said Alice: "you've said it very often – and very loud. Please, where *are* the crabs?"

"In the water, of course!" said the Sheep, sticking some of the needles into her hair, as her hands were full. "Feather, I say!"

"*Why* do you say 'feather' so often?" Alice asked at last, rather vexed. "I'm not a bird!"

"You are," said the Sheep: "you're a little goose."

This offended Alice a little, so there was no more conversation for a minute or two, while the boat glided gently on, sometimes among beds of weeds (which made the oars stick fast in the water, worse then ever), and sometimes under trees, but always with the same tall river-banks frowning over their heads.

"Oh, please! There are some scented rushes!" Alice cried in a sudden transport of delight. "There really are – and *such* beauties!"

"You needn't say 'please' to *me* about 'em," the Sheep said, without looking up from her knitting: "I didn't put 'em there, and I'm not going to take 'em away."

"No, but I meant – please, may we wait and pick some?" Alice pleaded. "If you don't mind stopping the boat for a minute."

"How am *I* to stop it?" said the Sheep. "If you leave off rowing, it'll stop of itself."

So the boat was left to drift down the stream as it would, till it glided gently in among the waving rushes. And then the little sleeves were carefully rolled up, and the little arms were plunged in elbow-deep, to get hold of the rushes a good long way down before breaking them off – and for a while Alice forgot all about the Sheep and the knitting, as she bent over the side of the boat, with just the ends of her tangled hair dipping into the water – while with bright eager eyes she caught at one bunch after another of the darling scented rushes.

"I only hope the boat won't tipple over!" she said to herself. "Oh, *what* a lovely one! Only I couldn't quite reach it." And it certainly *did* seem a little provoking ("almost as if it happened on purpose," she thought) that, though she managed to pick plenty of beautiful rushes as the boat glided by, there was always a more lovely one that she couldn't reach.

"The prettiest are always further!" she said at last, with a sigh at the obstinacy of the rushes in growing so far off, as, with flushed cheeks and dripping hair and hands, she scrambled back into her place, and began to arrange her new-found treasures.

What mattered it to her just then that the rushes had begun to fade, and to lose all their scent and beauty, from the

... for a while Alice forgot all about the Sheep and the knitting, as she bent over the side of the boat ...

very moment that she picked them? Even real scented rushes, you know, last only a very little while – and these, being dream-rushes, melted away almost like snow, as they lay in heaps at her feet – but Alice hardly noticed this, there were so many other curious things to think about.

They hadn't gone much farther before the blade of one of the oars got fast in the water and *wouldn't* come out again (so Alice explained it afterwards), and the consequence was that the handle of it caught her under the chin, and, in spite of a series of little shrieks of "Oh, oh, oh!" from poor Alice, it swept her straight off the seat, and down among the heap of rushes.

However, she wasn't a bit hurt, and was soon up again: the Sheep went on with her knitting all the while, just as if nothing had happened. "That was a nice crab you caught!" she remarked, as Alice got back into her place, very much relieved to find herself still in the boat.

"Was it? I didn't see it," said Alice, peeping cautiously over the side of the boat into the dark water. "I wish it hadn't let go – I should so like to see a little crab to take home with me!" But the Sheep only laughed scornfully, and went on with her knitting.

"Are there many crabs here?" said Alice.

"Crabs, and all sorts of things," said the Sheep: "plenty of choice, only make up your mind. Now, what *do* you want to buy?"

"To buy!" Alice echoed in a tone that was half astonished and half frightened – for the oars, and the boat, and the river, had vanished all in a moment, and she was back again in the little dark shop.

"I should like to buy an egg, please," she said timidly. "How do you sell them?"

"Fivepence farthing for one – twopence for two," the Sheep replied.

"Then two are cheaper than one?" Alice said in a surprised tone, taking out her purse.

"Only you *must* eat them both, if you buy two," said the Sheep.

"Then I'll have *one*, please," said Alice, as she put the money down on the counter. For she thought to herself, "They mightn't be at all nice, you know."

The Sheep took the money, and put it away in a box: then she said, "I never put things into people's hands – that would never do – you must get it for yourself." And so saying, she went off to the other end of the shop, and set the egg upright on a shelf.

"I wonder *why* it wouldn't do?" thought Alice, as she groped her way among the tables and chairs, for the shop was very dark towards the end. "The egg seems to get further away the more I walk towards it. Let me see, is this a chair? Why, it's got branches, I declare! How very odd to find trees growing here! And actually here's a little brook! Well, this is the very queerest shop I ever saw!"

So she went on, wondering more and more at every step, as everything turned into a tree the moment she came up to it, and she quite expected the egg to do the same.

Chapter Six

♥ Humpty Dumpty ♥

However, the egg only got larger and larger, and more and more human: when she had come within a few yards of it, she saw that it had eyes and a nose and mouth; and when she had come close to it, she saw clearly that it was HUMPTY DUMPTY himself. "It can't be anybody else!" she said to herself. "I'm as certain of it, as if his name were written all over his face."

It might have been written a hundred times, easily, on that enormous face. Humpty Dumpty was sitting, with his legs crossed like a Turk, on the top of a high wall – such a narrow one that Alice quite wondered how he could keep his balance – and, as his eyes were steadily fixed in the opposite direction, and he didn't take the least notice of her, she thought he must be a stuffed figure after all.

"And how exactly like an egg he is!" she said aloud, standing with her hands ready to catch him, for she was every moment expecting him to fall.

"It's *very* provoking," Humpty Dumpty said after a long silence, looking away from Alice as he spoke, "to be called an egg – *very*!"

"I said you *looked* like an egg, Sir," Alice gently explained. "And some eggs are very pretty, you know," she added, hoping to turn her remark into a sort of compliment.

"Some people," said Humpty Dumpty, looking away from her as usual, "have no more sense than a baby!"

Alice didn't know what to say to this: it wasn't at all like conversation, she thought, as he never said anything to *her*; in fact, his last remark was evidently addressed to a tree – so she stood and softly repeated to herself:

> "*Humpty Dumpty sat on a wall:*
> *Humpty Dumpty had a great fall.*
> *All the King's horses and all the King's men*
> *Couldn't put Humpty Dumpty in*
>   *his place again.*"

"That last line is much too long for the poetry," she added, almost out loud, forgetting that Humpty Dumpty would hear her.

"Don't stand chattering to yourself like that," Humpty Dumpty said, looking at her for the first time, "but tell me your name and your business."

"My *name* is Alice, but –"

"It's a stupid name enough!" Humpty Dumpty interrupted impatiently. "What does it mean?"

"*Must* a name mean something?" Alice asked doubtfully.

"Of course it must," Humpty Dumpty said with a short

laugh: "*my* name means the shape I am – and a good handsome shape it is, too. With a name like yours, you might be any shape, almost."

"Why do you sit out here all alone?" said Alice, not wishing to begin an argument.

"Why, because there's nobody with me!" cried Humpty Dumpty. "Did you think I didn't know the answer to *that*? Ask another."

"Don't you think you'd be safer down on the ground?" Alice went on, not with any idea of making another riddle, but simply in her good-natured anxiety for the queer creature. "That wall is so *very* narrow!"

"What tremendously easy riddles you ask!" Humpty Dumpty growled out. "Of course I don't think so! Why, if ever I *did* fall off – which there's no chance of – but *if* I did –" Here he pursed his lips and looked so solemn and grand that Alice could hardly help laughing. "*If* I *did* fall," he went on, "*the King has promised me* – ah, you may turn pale, if you like! You didn't think I was going to say that, did you? *The King has promised me – with his very own mouth – to – to –*"

"To send all his horses and all his men," Alice interrupted, rather unwisely.

"Now I declare that's too bad!" Humpty Dumpty cried, breaking into a sudden passion. "You've been listening at doors – and behind trees – and down chimneys – or you couldn't have known it!"

"I haven't, indeed!" Alice said very gently. "It's in a book."

"Ah, well! They may write such things in a *book*," Humpty Dumpty said in a calmer tone. "That's what you call a History of England, that is. Now, take a good look at me! I'm one that

"Don't you think you'd be safer down on the ground?"
Alice went on ... "That wall is so very narrow!"

has spoken to a King, *I* am: mayhap you'll never see such another: and to show you I'm not proud, you may shake hands with me!" And he grinned almost from ear to ear, as he leant forwards (and as nearly as possible fell off the wall in doing so) and offered Alice his hand. She watched him a little anxiously as she took it. "If he smiled much more, the ends of his mouth might meet behind," she thought: "and then I don't know what would happen to his head! I'm afraid it would come off!"

"Yes, all his horses and all his men," Humpty Dumpty went on. "They'd pick me up again in a minute, *they* would! However, this conversation is going on a little too fast: let's go back to the last remark but one."

"I'm afraid I can't quite remember it," Alice said, very politely.

"In that case we start afresh," said Humpty Dumpty, "and it's my turn to choose a subject –" ("He talks about it just as if it was a game!" thought Alice.) "So here's a question for you. How old did you say you were?"

Alice made a short calculation, and said, "Seven years and six months."

"Wrong!" Humpty Dumpty exclaimed triumphantly. "You never said a word like it!"

"I thought you meant 'How old *are* you?'" Alice explained.

"If I'd meant that, I'd have said it," said Humpty Dumpty.

Alice didn't want to begin another argument, so she said nothing.

"Seven years and six months!" Humpty Dumpty repeated thoughtfully. "An uncomfortable sort of age. Now if you'd asked *my* advice, I'd have said 'Leave off at seven' – but it's too late now."

"I never ask advice about growing," Alice said indignantly.

"Too proud?" the other inquired.

Alice felt even more indignant at this suggestion. "I mean," she said, "that one can't help growing older."

"*One* can't, perhaps," said Humpty Dumpty, "but *two* can. With proper assistance, you might have left off at seven."

"What a beautiful belt you've got on!" Alice suddenly remarked. (They had had quite enough of the subject of age, she thought: and if they really were to take turns in choosing subjects, it was her turn now.) "At least," she corrected herself on second thoughts, "a beautiful cravat, I should have said – no, a belt, I mean – I beg your pardon!" she added in dismay, for Humpty Dumpty looked thoroughly offended, and she began to wish she hadn't chosen that subject. "If I only knew," she thought to herself, "which was neck and which was waist!"

Evidently Humpty Dumpty was very angry, though he said nothing for a minute or two. When he *did* speak again, it was in a deep growl.

"It is a – *most* – *provoking* – thing," he said at last, "when a person doesn't know a cravat from a belt!"

"I know it's very ignorant of me," Alice said, in so humble a tone that Humpty Dumpty relented.

"It's a cravat, child, and a beautiful one, as you say. It's a present from the White King and Queen. There now!"

"Is it really?" said Alice, quite pleased to find that she *had* chosen a good subject, after all.

"They gave it me," Humpty Dumpty continued thoughtfully, as he crossed one knee over the other and clasped his hands round it, "they gave it me – for an un-birthday present."

"I beg your pardon?" Alice said with a puzzled air.

"I'm not offended," said Humpty Dumpty.

"I mean, what *is* an un-birthday present?"

"A present given when it isn't your birthday, of course."

Alice considered a little. "I like birthday presents best," she said at last.

"You don't know what you're talking about!" cried Humpty Dumpty. "How many days are there in a year?"

"Three hundred and sixty-five," said Alice.

"And how many birthdays have you?"

"One."

"And if you take one from three hundred and sixty-five, what remains?"

"Three hundred and sixty-four, of course."

Humpty Dumpty looked doubtful. "I'd rather see that done on paper," he said.

Alice couldn't help smiling as she took out her memorandum-book, and worked the sum for him:

$$365$$
$$\underline{1}$$
$$\underline{364}$$

Humpty Dumpty took the book, and looked at it carefully. "That seems to be done right –" he began.

"You're holding it upside down!" Alice interrupted.

"To be sure I was!" Humpty Dumpty said gaily, as she turned it round for him. "I thought it looked a little queer. As I was saying, that *seems* to be done right – though I haven't time to look it over thoroughly just now – and that shows that there are three hundred and sixty-four days when you might get un-birthday presents –"

"Certainly," said Alice.

"And only *one* for birthday presents, you know. There's glory for you!"

"I don't know what you mean by 'glory'," Alice said.

Humpty Dumpty smiled contemptuously. "Of course you don't – till I tell you. I meant 'there's a nice knock-down argument for you!'"

"But 'glory' doesn't mean 'a nice knock-down argument'," Alice objected.

"When *I* use a word," Humpty Dumpty said in rather a scornful tone, "it means just what I choose it to mean – neither more nor less."

"The question is," said Alice, "whether you *can* make words mean so many different things."

"The question is," said Humpty Dumpty, "which is to be master – that's all."

Alice was too much puzzled to say anything, so after a minute Humpty Dumpty began again. "They've a temper, some of them – particularly verbs, they're the proudest – adjectives you can do anything with, but not verbs – however, *I* can manage the whole lot of them! Impenetrability! That's what *I* say!"

"Would you tell me, please," said Alice, "what that means?"

"Now you talk like a reasonable child," said Humpty Dumpty, looking very much pleased. "I meant by 'impenetrability' that we've had enough of that subject, and it would be just as well if you'd mention what you mean to do next, as I suppose you don't mean to stop here all the rest of your life."

"That's a great deal to make one word mean," Alice said in a thoughtful tone.

"When I make a word do a lot of work like that," said Humpty Dumpty, "I always pay it extra."

"Oh!" said Alice. She was too much puzzled to make any other remark.

"Ah, you should see 'em come round me of a Saturday night," Humpty Dumpty went on, wagging his head gravely from side to side: "for to get their wages, you know."

(Alice didn't venture to ask what he paid them with; and so you see I can't tell *you*.)

"You seem very clever at explaining words, Sir," said Alice. "Would you kindly tell me the meaning of the poem called 'Jabberwocky'?"

"Let's hear it," said Humpty Dumpty. "I can explain all the poems that were ever invented – and a good many that haven't been invented just yet."

This sounded very hopeful, so Alice repeated the first verse:

> "*'Twas brillig, and the slithy toves*
> *Did gyre and gimble in the wabe;*
> *All mimsy were the borogoves,*
> *And the mome raths outgrabe.*"

"That's enough to begin with," Humpty Dumpty interrupted: "there are plenty of hard words there. '*Brillig*' means four o'clock in the afternoon – the time when you begin *broiling* things for dinner."

"That'll do very well," said Alice: and '*slithy*'?"

"Well, '*slithy*' means 'lithe and slimy'. 'Lithe' is the same as 'active'. You see it's like a portmanteau – there are two meanings packed up into one word."

"I see it now," Alice remarked thoughtfully: "and what are '*toves*'?"

"Well, '*toves*' are something like badgers – they're something like lizards – and they're something like corkscrews."

"They must be very curious looking creatures."

"They are that," said Humpty Dumpty: "also they make their nests under sundials – also they live on cheese."

"And what's to '*gyre*' and to '*gimble*'?"

"To '*gyre*' is to go round and round like a gyroscope. To '*gimble*' is to make holes like a gimblet."

"And '*the wabe*' is the grass-plot round a sundial, I suppose?" said Alice, surprised at her own ingenuity.

"Of course it is. It's called '*wabe*', you know, because it goes a long way before it, and a long way behind it –"

"And a long way beyond it on each side," Alice added.

"Exactly so. Well, then, '*mimsy*' is 'flimsy and miserable' (there's another portmanteau for you). And a '*borogove*' is a thin shabby-looking bird with its feathers sticking out all round – something like a live mop."

"And then '*mome raths*'?" said Alice. "I'm afraid I'm giving you a great deal of trouble."

"Well, a '*rath*' is a sort of green pig: but '*mome*' I'm not certain about. I think it's short for 'from home' – meaning that they'd lost their way, you know."

"And what does '*outgrabe*' mean?"

"Well, '*outgribing*' is something between bellowing and whistling, with a kind of sneeze in the middle: however, you'll hear it done, maybe – down in the wood yonder – and when you've once heard it you'll be *quite* content. Who's been repeating all that hard stuff to you?"

"I read it in a book," said Alice. "But I *had* some poetry repeated to me, much easier than that, by – Tweedledee, I think it was."

"As to poetry, you know," said Humpty Dumpty, stretching out one of his great hands, "*I* can repeat poetry as well as other folk, if it comes to that –"

"Oh, it needn't come to that!" Alice hastily said, hoping to keep him from beginning.

"The piece I'm going to repeat," he went on without noticing her remark, "was written entirely for your amusement."

Alice felt that in that case she really *ought* to listen to it, so she sat down, and said "Thank you" rather sadly.

> "*In winter, when the fields are white,*
> *I sing this song for your delight –*

only I don't sing it," he added, as an explanation.

"I see you don't," said Alice.

"If you can *see* whether I'm singing or not, you've sharper eyes than most," Humpty Dumpty remarked severely. Alice was silent.

> *"In spring, when woods are getting green,*
> *I'll try and tell you what I mean:"*

"Thank you very much," said Alice.

> *"In summer, when the days are long,*
> *Perhaps you'll understand the song:*
>
> *In autumn, when the leaves are brown,*
> *Take pen and ink, and write it down."*

"I will, if I can remember it so long," said Alice.
"You needn't go on making remarks like that," Humpty
Dumpty said: "they're not sensible, and they put me out."

> *"I sent a message to the fish:*
> *I told them, 'This is what I wish.'*

"The little fishes of the sea,
 They sent an answer back to me.

"The little fishes' answer was
 'We cannot do it, Sir, because –'"

"I'm afraid I don't quite understand," said Alice.
"It gets easier further on," Humpty Dumpty replied.

"I sent to them again to say
 'It will be better to obey.'

"The fishes answered with a grin,
 'Why, what a temper you are in!'

"I told them once, I told them twice:
 They would not listen to advice.

"I took a kettle large and new,
 Fit for the deed I had to do.

"My heart went hop, my heart went thump:
 I filled the kettle at the pump.

"Then some one came to me and said,
 'The little fishes are in bed.'

"I said to him, I said it plain,
 'Then you must wake them up again.'

"I said it very loud and clear:
I went and shouted in his ear."

Humpty Dumpty raised his voice almost to a scream as he repeated this verse, and Alice thought with a shudder, "I wouldn't have been the messenger for *anything*!"

"But he was very stiff and proud:
He said 'You needn't shout so loud!'

"And he was very proud and stiff:
He said 'I'd go and wake them, if –'

"I took a corkscrew from the shelf:
I went to wake them up myself.

"And when I found the door was locked,
I pulled and pushed and kicked and knocked.

"And when I found the door was shut,
I tried to turn the handle, but –"

There was a long pause.

"Is that all?" Alice timidly asked.

"That's all," said Humpty Dumpty. "Good-bye."

This was rather sudden, Alice thought: but, after such a *very* strong hint that she ought to be going, she felt that it would hardly be civil to stay. So she got up, and held out her hand. "Good-bye, till we meet again!" she said as cheerfully as she could.

"I shouldn't know you again if we *did* meet," Humpty Dumpty replied in a discontented tone, giving her one of his fingers to shake; "you're so exactly like other people."

"The face is what one goes by, generally," Alice remarked in a thoughtful tone.

"That's just what I complain of," said Humpty Dumpty. "Your face is the same as everybody has – the two eyes, so –" (marking their places in the air with this thumb) "nose in the middle, mouth under. It's always the same. Now if you had the two eyes on the same side of the nose, for instance – or the mouth at the top – that would be *some* help."

"It wouldn't look nice," Alice objected. But Humpty Dumpty only shut his eyes and said "Wait till you've tried."

Alice waited a minute to see if he would speak again, but, as he never opened his eyes or took any further notice of her, she said "Good-bye!" once more, and, getting no answer to this, she quietly walked away: but she couldn't help saying to herself as she went, "Of all the unsatisfactory –" (she repeated this aloud, as it was a great comfort to have such a long word to say) "of all the unsatisfactory people I *ever* met –" She never finished the sentence, for at this moment a heavy crash shook the forest from end to end.

CHAPTER SEVEN

♥ The Lion and the Unicorn ♥

The next moment soldiers came running through the wood, at first in twos and threes, then ten or twenty together, and at last in such crowds that they seemed to fill the whole forest. Alice got behind a tree, for fear of being run over, and watched them go by.

She thought that in all her life she had never seen soldiers so uncertain on their feet: they were always tripping over something or other, and whenever one went down, several more always fell over him, so that the ground was soon covered with little heaps of men.

Then came the horses. Having four feet, these managed rather better than the foot-soldiers; but even *they* stumbled now and then; and it seemed to be a regular rule that, whenever a horse stumbled, the rider fell off instantly. The confusion got worse every moment, and Alice was very glad to get out of the wood into an open place, where she found the

White King seated on the ground, busily writing in his memorandum-book.

"I've sent them all!" the King cried in a tone of delight, on seeing Alice. "Did you happen to meet any soldiers, my dear, as you came through the wood?"

"Yes, I did," said Alice: "several thousand, I should think."

"Four thousand two hundred and seven, that's the exact number," the King said, referring to his book. "I couldn't send all the horses, you know, because two of them are wanted in the game. And I haven't sent the two Messengers, either. They're both gone to the town. Just look along the road, and tell me if you can see either of them."

"I see nobody on the road," said Alice.

"I only wish I had such eyes," the King remarked in a fretful tone. "To be able to see Nobody! And at that distance too! Why, it's as much as I can do to see real people, by this light!"

All this was lost on Alice, who was still looking intently along the road, shading her eyes with one hand. "I see somebody now!" she exclaimed at last. "But he's coming very slowly – and what curious attitudes he goes into!"(For the Messenger kept skipping up and down, and wriggling like an eel, as he came along, with his great hands spread out like fans on each side.)

"Not at all," said the King. "He's an Anglo-Saxon Messenger – and those are Anglo-Saxon attitudes. He only does them when he's happy. His name is Haigha." (He pronounced it so as to rhyme with 'mayor'.)

"I love my love with an H," Alice couldn't help beginning, "because he is Happy. I hate him with an H, because he is

Hideous. I fed him with – with – with Ham-sandwiches and Hay. His name is Haigha, and he lives –"

"He lives on the Hill," the King remarked simply, without the least idea that he was joining in the game, while Alice was still hesitating for the name of a town beginning with H. "The other Messenger's called Hatta. I must have *two*, you know – to come and go. One to come, and one to go."

"I beg your pardon?" said Alice.

"It isn't respectable to beg," said the King.

"I only meant that I didn't understand," said Alice. "Why one to come and one to go?"

"Don't I tell you?" the King repeated impatiently. "I must have *two* – to fetch and carry. One to fetch, and one to carry."

At this moment the Messenger arrived: he was far too much out of breath to say a word and could only wave his hands about, and make the most fearful faces at the poor King.

"This young lady loves you with an H," the King said, introducing Alice in the hope of turning off the Messenger's attention from himself – but it was of no use – the Anglo-Saxon attitudes only got more extraordinary every moment, while the great eyes rolled wildly from side to side.

"You alarm me!" said the King. "I feel faint – Give me a ham sandwich!"

On which the Messenger, to Alice's great amusement, opened a bag that hung round his neck, and handed a sandwich to the King, who devoured it greedily.

"Another sandwich!" said the King.

"There's nothing but hay left now," the Messenger said, peeping into the bag.

"Hay, then," the King murmured in a faint whisper.

Alice was glad to see that it revived him a good deal. "There's nothing like eating hay when you're faint," he remarked to her, as he munched away.

"I should think throwing cold water over you would be better," Alice suggested: "or some sal-volatile."

"I didn't say there was nothing *better*," the King replied. "I said there was nothing *like* it." Which Alice did not venture to deny.

"Who did *you* pass on the road?" the King went on, holding out his hand to the Messenger for some more hay.

"Nobody," said the Messenger.

"Quite right," said the King: "this young lady saw him too. So of course Nobody walks slower than you."

"I do my best," the Messenger said in a sulky tone. "I'm sure nobody walks much faster than I do!"

"He can't do that," said the King, "or else he'd have been

"There's nothing like eating hay when you're faint,"
he remarked to her, as he munched away.

here first. However, now you've got your breath, you may tell us what's happened in the town."

"I'll whisper it," said the Messenger, putting his hands to his mouth in the shape of a trumpet, and stooping so as to get close to the King's ear. Alice was sorry for this, as she wanted to hear the news too. However, instead of whispering, he simply shouted at the top of his voice, "They're at it again!"

"Do you call *that* a whisper?" cried the poor King, jumping up and shaking himself. "If you do such a thing again, I'll have you buttered! It went through and through my head like an earthquake!"

"It would have to be a very tiny earthquake!" thought Alice. "Who are at it again?" she ventured to ask.

"Why the Lion and the Unicorn, of course," said the King.

"Fighting for the crown?"

"Yes, to be sure," said the King: "and the best of the joke is, that it's *my* crown all the while! Let's run and see them." And they trotted off, Alice repeating to herself, as she ran, the words of the old song:

"The Lion and the Unicorn were fighting for the crown:
The Lion beat the Unicorn all round the town.
Some gave them white bread, some gave them brown;
Some gave them plum-cake and drummed them
  out of town."

"Does – the one – that wins – get the crown?" she asked, as well as she could, for the run was putting her quite out of breath.

"Dear me, no!" said the King. "What an idea!"

"Would you – be good enough," Alice panted out, after running a little further, "to stop a minute – just to get – one's breath again?"

"I'm *good* enough," the King said, "only I'm not *strong* enough. You see, a minute goes by so fearfully quick. You might as well try to stop a Bandersnatch!"

Alice had no more breath for talking; so they trotted on in silence, till they came in sight of a great crowd, in the middle of which the Lion and the Unicorn were fighting. They were in such a cloud of dust, that at first Alice could not make out which was which; but she soon managed to distinguish the Unicorn by his horn.

They placed themselves close to where Hatta, the other Messenger, was standing watching the fight, with a cup of tea in one hand and a piece of bread-and-butter in the other.

"He's only just out of prison, and he hadn't finished his tea when he was sent in," Haigha whispered to Alice: "and they only give them oyster-shells in there – so you see he's very hungry and thirsty. How are you, dear child?" he went on, putting his arm affectionately round Hatta's neck.

Hatta looked round and nodded, and went on with his bread-and-butter.

"Were you happy in prison, dear child?" said Haigha.

Hatta looked round once more, and this time a tear or two trickled down his cheek: but not a word would he say.

"Speak, can't you!" Haigha cried impatiently. But Hatta only munched away, and drank some more tea.

"Speak, won't you!" cried the King. "How are they getting on with the fight?"

Hatta made a desperate effort, and swallowed a large piece of bread-and-butter. "They're getting on very well," he said in a choking voice: "each of them has been down about eighty-seven times."

"Then I suppose they'll soon bring the white bread and the brown?" Alice ventured to remark.

"It's waiting for 'em now," said Hatta: "this is a bit of it as I'm eating."

There was a pause in the fight just then, and the Lion and the Unicorn sat down, panting, while the King called out, "Ten minutes allowed for refreshments!" Haigha and Hatta set to work at once, carrying round trays of white and brown bread. Alice took a piece to taste, but it was *very* dry.

"I don't think they'll fight any more to-day," the King said to Hatta: "go and order the drums to begin." And Hatta went bounding away like a grasshopper.

For a minute or two Alice stood silent, watching him. Suddenly she brightened up. "Look, look!" she cried, pointing eagerly. "There's the White Queen running across the country! She came flying out of the wood over yonder – How fast those Queens *can* run!"

"There's some enemy after her, no doubt," the King said, without even looking round. "That wood's full of them."

"But aren't you going to run and help her?" Alice asked, very much surprised at his taking it so quietly.

"No use, no use!" said the King. "She runs so fearfully quick. You might as well try to catch a Bandersnatch! But I'll make a memorandum about her, if you like – She's a dear good creature," he repeated softly to himself, as he opened his memorandum-book. "Do you spell 'creature' with a double 'e'?"

At this moment the Unicorn sauntered by them, with his hands in his pockets. "I had the best of it this time?" he said to the King, just glancing at him as he passed.

"A little – a little," the King replied, rather nervously. "You shouldn't have run him through with your horn, you know."

"It didn't hurt him," the Unicorn said carelessly, and he was going on, when his eye happened to fall upon Alice: he turned round instantly, and stood for some time looking at her with an air of the deepest disgust.

"What – is – this?" he said at last.

"This is a child!" Haigha replied eagerly, coming in front of Alice to introduce her, and spreading out both his hands towards her in an Anglo-Saxon attitude. "We only found it to-day. It's as large as life, and twice as natural!"

"I always thought they were fabulous monsters!" said the Unicorn. "Is it alive?"

"It can talk," said Haigha, solemnly.

The Unicorn looked dreamily at Alice, and said "Talk, child."

Alice could not help her lips curling up into a smile as she began: "Do you know, I always thought Unicorns were fabulous monsters, too? I never saw one alive before!"

"Well, now that we *have* seen each other," said the Unicorn, "if you'll believe in me, I'll believe in you. Is that a bargain?"

"Yes, if you like," said Alice.

"Come, fetch out the plum-cake, old man!" the Unicorn went on, turning from her to the King. "None of your brown bread for me!"

"Certainly – certainly!" the King muttered, and beckoned to Haigha. "Open the bag!" he whispered. "Quick! Not that one – that's full of hay!"

Haigha took a large cake out of the bag, and gave it to Alice to hold, while he got out a dish and carving-knife. How they all came out of it Alice couldn't guess. It was just like a conjuring-trick, she thought.

The Lion had joined them while this was going on: he looked very tired and sleepy, and his eyes were half shut. "What's this!" he said, blinking lazily at Alice, and speaking in a deep hollow tone that sounded like the tolling of a great bell.

"Ah, what *is* it, now?" the Unicorn cried eagerly. "You'll never guess! *I* couldn't."

The Lion looked at Alice wearily. "Are you an animal or vegetable – or mineral?" he said, yawning at every other word.

"It's a fabulous monster!" the Unicorn cried out, before Alice could reply.

"Then hand round the plum-cake, Monster," the Lion said, lying down and putting his chin on his paws. "And sit down, both of you," (to the King and the Unicorn): "fair play with the cake, you know!"

The King was evidently very uncomfortable at having to sit down between the two great creatures; but there was no other place for him.

"What a fight we might have for the crown, *now*!" the Unicorn said, looking slyly up at the crown, which the poor King was nearly shaking off his head, he trembled so much.

"I should win easy," said the Lion.

"I'm not so sure of that," said the Unicorn.

"Why, I beat you all round the town, you chicken!" the Lion replied angrily, half getting up as he spoke.

Here the King interrupted, to prevent the quarrel going on: he was very nervous, and his voice quite quivered. "All round the town?" he said. "That's a good long way. Did you go by the old bridge, or the market-place? You get the best view by the old bridge."

"I'm sure I don't know," the Lion growled out as he lay down again. "There was too much dust to see anything. What a time the Monster is, cutting up that cake!"

Alice had seated herself on the bank of a little brook, with the great dish on her knees, and was sawing away diligently with the knife. "It's very provoking!" she said, in reply to the Lion (she was getting quite used to being called "the Monster"). "I've cut several slices already, but they always join on again!"

"You don't know how to manage Looking-glass cakes,"

the Unicorn remarked. "Hand it round first, and cut it afterwards."

This sounded nonsense, but Alice very obediently got up, and carried the dish round, and the cake divided itself into three pieces as she did so. "*Now* cut it up,"said the Lion, as she returned to her place with the empty dish.

"I say, this isn't fair!" cried the Unicorn, as Alice sat with the knife in her hand, very much puzzled how to begin. "The Monster has given the Lion twice as much as me!"

"She's kept none for herself, anyhow," said the Lion. "Do you like plum-cake, Monster?"

But before Alice could answer him, the drums began.

Where the noise came from, she couldn't make out: the air seemed full of it, and it rang through and through her head till she felt quite deafened. She started to her feet and sprang across the little brook in her terror,

and had just time to see the Lion and the Unicorn rise to their feet, with angry looks at being interrupted in their feast, before she dropped to her knees, and put her hands over her ears, vainly trying to shut out the dreadful uproar.

"If *that* doesn't 'drum them out of town'," she thought to herself, "nothing ever will!"

CHAPTER EIGHT

♥ "It's My Own Invention." ♥

After a while the noise seemed gradually to die away, till all was dead silence, and Alice lifted up her head in some alarm. There was no one to be seen, and her first thought was that she must have been dreaming about the Lion and the Unicorn and those queer Anglo-Saxon Messengers. However, there was the great dish still lying at her feet, on which she had tried to cut the plum-cake, "So I wasn't dreaming, after all," she said to herself, "unless – unless we're all part of the same dream. Only I do hope it's *my* dream, and not the Red King's! I don't like belonging to another person's dream," she went on in a rather complaining tone: "I've a great mind to go and wake him, and see what happens!"

At this moment her thoughts were interrupted by a loud shouting of "Ahoy! Ahoy! Check!" and a Knight, dressed in crimson armour, came galloping down upon her, brandishing a great club. Just as he reached her, the horse stopped suddenly:

"You're my prisoner!" the Knight cried, as he tumbled off his horse.

Startled as she was, Alice was more frightened for him than for herself at the moment, and watched him with some anxiety as he mounted again. As soon as he was comfortably in the saddle, he began once more "You're my –" but here another voice broke in "Ahoy! Ahoy! Check!" and Alice looked round in some surprise for the new enemy.

This time it was a White Knight. He drew up at Alice's side, and tumbled off his horse just as the Red Knight had done: and then he got on again, and the two Knights sat and looked at each other for some time without speaking. Alice looked from one to the other in some bewilderment.

"She's *my* prisoner, you know!" the Red Knight said at last.

"Yes, but then *I* came and rescued her!" the White Knight replied.

"Well, we must fight for her, then," said the Red Knight, as he took up his helmet (which hung from the saddle, and was something the shape of a horse's head), and put it on.

"You will observe the Rules of Battle, of course?" the White Knight remarked, putting on his helmet too.

"I always do," said the Red Knight, and they began banging away at each other with such fury that Alice got behind a tree to be out of the way of the blows.

"I wonder, now, what the Rules of Battle are," she said to herself, as she watched the fight, timidly peeping out from her hiding-place. "One Rule seems to be, that if one Knight hits the other, he knocks him off his horse; and if he misses, he tumbles off himself – and another Rule seems to be that they hold their clubs with their arms, as if they were Punch and Judy – What a noise they make when they tumble! Just like a whole set of

... they began banging away at each other with such fury that Alice got behind a tree to be out of the way of the blows.

fire-irons falling into the fender! And how quiet the horses are! They let them get on and off them just as if they were tables!"

Another Rule of Battle, that Alice had not noticed, seemed to be that they always fell on their heads; and the battle ended with their both falling off in this way, side by side: when they got up again, they shook hands, and then the Red Knight mounted and galloped off.

"It was a glorious victory, wasn't it?" said the White Knight, as he came up panting.

"I don't know," Alice said doubtfully. "I don't want to be anybody's prisoner. I want to be a Queen."

"So you will, when you've crossed the next brook," said the White Knight. "I'll see you safe to the end of the wood – and then I must go back, you know. That's the end of my move."

"Thank you very much," said Alice. "May I help you off with your helmet?" It was evidently more than he could manage by himself: however, she managed to shake him out of it at last.

"Now one can breathe more easily," said the Knight, putting back his shaggy hair with both hands, and turning his gentle face and large mild eyes to Alice. She thought she had never seen such a strange-looking soldier in all her life.

He was dressed in tin armour, which seemed to fit him very badly, and he had a queer-shaped little deal box fastened across his shoulder, upside-down, and with the lid hanging open. Alice looked at it with great curiosity.

"I see you're admiring my little box," the Knight said in a friendly tone. "It's my own invention – to keep clothes and sandwiches in. You see I carry it upside-down, so that the rain can't get in."

"But the things can get *out*," Alice gently remarked. "Do you know the lid's open?"

"I didn't know it," the Knight said, a shade of vexation passing over his face. "Then all the things must have fallen out! And the box is no use without them." He unfastened it as he spoke, and was just going to throw it into the bushes when a sudden thought seemed to strike him, and he hung it carefully on a tree. "Can you guess why I did that?" he said to Alice.

Alice shook her head.

"In hopes some bees may make a nest in it – then I should get the honey."

"But you've got a bee-hive – or something like one – fastened to the saddle," said Alice.

"Yes, it's a very good bee-hive," the Knight said in a discontented tone, "one of the best kind. But not a single bee has come near it yet. And the other thing is a mouse-trap. I suppose the mice keep the bees out – or the bees keep the mice out, I don't know which."

"I was wondering what the mouse-trap was for," said Alice. "It isn't very likely there would be any mice on the horse's back."

"Not very likely, perhaps," said the Knight: "but if they *do* come, I don't choose to have them running all about."

"You see," he went on after a pause, "it's as well to be provided for *everything*. That's the reason the horse has all those anklets round his feet."

"But what are they for?" Alice asked in a tone of great curiosity.

"To guard against the bites of sharks," the Knight replied. "It's an invention of my own. And now help me on. I'll go with you to the end of the wood – What's that dish for?"

"It's meant for plum-cake," said Alice.

"We'd better take it with us," the Knight said. "It'll come in handy if we find any plum-cake. Help me to get it into this bag."

This took a very long time to manage, though Alice held the bag open very carefully, because the Knight was so *very* awkward in putting in the dish: the first two or three times that he tried he fell in himself instead. "It's rather a tight fit, you see," he said, as they got it in at last; "there are so many candlesticks in the bag." And he hung it to the saddle, which was already loaded with bunches of carrots, and fire-irons, and many other things.

"I hope you've got your hair well fastened on?" he continued, as they set off.

"Only in the usual way," Alice said, smiling.

"That's hardly enough," he said, anxiously. "You see the wind is so *very* strong here. It's as strong as soup."

"Have you invented a plan for keeping the hair from being blown off?" Alice enquired.

"Not yet," said the Knight. "But I've got a plan for keeping it from *falling* off."

"I should like to hear it, very much."

"First you take an upright stick," said the Knight. "Then you make your hair creep up it, like a fruit-tree. Now the reason hair falls off is because it hangs *down* – things never fall *upwards*, you know. It's a plan of my own invention. You may try it if you like."

It didn't sound a comfortable plan, Alice thought, and for a few minutes she walked on in silence, puzzling over the idea, and every now and then stopping to help the poor Knight, who certainly was *not* a good rider.

Whenever the horse stopped (which it did very often), he fell off in front; and, whenever it went on again (which it generally did rather suddenly), he fell off behind. Otherwise he kept on pretty well, except that he had a habit of now and then falling off sideways; and as he generally did this on the side on which Alice was walking, she soon found that it was the best plan not to walk *quite* close to the horse.

"I'm afraid you've not had much practice in riding," she ventured to say, as she was helping him up from his fifth tumble.

The Knight looked very much surprised, and a little offended at the remark. "What makes you say that?" he asked, as he scrambled back into the saddle, keeping hold of Alice's hair with one hand, to save himself from falling over on the other side.

"Because people don't fall off quite so often, when they've had much practice."

"I've had plenty of practice," the Knight said very gravely: "plenty of practice!"

Alice could think of nothing better to say than "Indeed?" but she said it as heartily as she could. They went on a little way in silence after this, the Knight with his eyes shut, muttering to himself, and Alice watching anxiously for the next tumble.

"The great art of riding," the Knight suddenly began in a loud voice, waving his right arm as he spoke, "is to keep –" Here the sentence ended as suddenly as it had begun, as the Knight fell heavily on the top of his head exactly in the path where Alice was walking. She was quite frightened this time, and said in an anxious tone, as she picked him up, "I hope no bones are broken?"

"None to speak of," the Knight said, as if he didn't mind breaking two or three of them. "The great art of riding, as I was saying, is – to keep your balance properly. Like this, you know –"

He let go the bridle, and stretched out both his arms to show Alice what he meant, and this time he fell flat on his back, right under the horse's feet.

"Plenty of practice!" he went on repeating, all the time that Alice was getting him on his feet again. "Plenty of practice!"

"It's too ridiculous!" cried Alice, losing all her patience this time. "You ought to have a wooden horse on wheels, that you ought!"

"Does that kind go smoothly?" the Knight asked in a tone of great interest, clasping his arms round the horse's neck as he spoke, just in time to save himself from tumbling off again.

"Much more smoothly than a live horse," Alice said, with a little scream of laughter, in spite of all she could do to prevent it.

"I'll get one," the Knight said thoughtfully to himself. "One or two – several."

There was a short silence after this, and then the Knight went on again. "I'm a great hand at inventing things. Now, I daresay you noticed, the last time you picked me up, that I was looking rather thoughtful?"

"You *were* a little grave," said Alice.

"Well, just then I was inventing a new way of getting over a gate – would you like to hear it?"

"Very much indeed," Alice said politely.

"I'll tell you how I came to think of it," said the Knight. "You see, I said to myself, 'The only difficulty is with the feet: the *head* is high enough already.' Now, first I put my head on the top of the gate – then the head's high enough – then I stand on my head – then the feet are high enough, you see – then I'm over, you see."

"Yes, I suppose you'd be over when that was done," Alice said thoughtfully: "but don't you think it would be rather hard?"

"I haven't tried it yet," the Knight said, gravely: "so I can't tell for certain – but I'm afraid it *would* be a little hard."

He looked so vexed at the idea, that Alice changed the subject hastily. "What a curious helmet you've got!" she said cheerfully. "Is that your invention too?"

The Knight looked down proudly at his helmet, which hung from the saddle. "Yes," he said; "but I've invented a better one than that – like a sugar loaf. When I used to wear it, if I fell off the horse, it always touched the ground directly. So I had a *very* little way to fall, you see – But there *was* the danger of falling *into* it, to be sure. That happened to me once – and the worst of it was, before I could get out again, the other White Knight came and put it on. He thought it was his own helmet."

The Knight looked so solemn about it that Alice did not dare to laugh. "I'm afraid you must have hurt him," she said in a trembling voice, "being on the top of his head."

"I had to kick him, of course," the Knight said, very

seriously. "And then he took the helmet off again – but it took hours and hours to get me out. I was as fast as – as lightning, you know."

"But that's a different kind of fastness," Alice objected.

The Knight shook his head. "It was all kinds of fastness with me, I can assure you!" he said. He raised his hands in some excitement as he said this, and instantly rolled out of the saddle, and fell headlong into a deep ditch.

Alice ran to the side of the ditch to look for him. She was rather startled by the fall, as for some time he had kept on very well, and she was afraid that he really *was* hurt this time. However, though she could see nothing but the soles of his feet, she was much relieved to hear that he was talking on in his usual tone. "All kinds of fastness," he repeated: "but it was careless of him to put another man's helmet on – with the man in it, too."

"How *can* you go on talking so quietly, head downwards?" Alice asked, as she dragged him out by the feet, and laid him in a heap on the bank.

The Knight looked surprised at the question. "What does it matter where my body happens to be?" he said. "My mind goes on working all the same. In fact, the more head-downwards I am, the more I keep inventing new things."

"Now the cleverest thing of the sort that I ever did," he went on after a pause, "was inventing a new pudding during the meat-course."

"In time to have it cooked for the next course?" said Alice. "Well, that *was* quick work, certainly!"

"Well, not the *next* course," the Knight said in a slow thoughtful tone: "no, certainly not the next *course*."

*He raised his hands ... and instantly rolled out of the
saddle, and fell headlong into a deep ditch.*

"Then it would have to be the next day. I suppose you wouldn't have two pudding-courses in one dinner?"

"Well, not the *next* day," the Knight repeated as before: "not the next *day*. In fact," he went on, holding his head down, and his voice getting lower and lower, "I don't believe that pudding ever *was* cooked! In fact, I don't believe that pudding ever *will* be cooked! And yet it was a very clever pudding to invent."

"What did you mean it to be made of?" Alice asked, hoping to cheer him up, for the poor Knight seemed quite low-spirited about it.

"It began with blotting paper," the Knight answered with a groan.

"That wouldn't be very nice, I'm afraid —"

"Not very nice *alone*," he interrupted, quite eagerly: "but you've no idea what a difference it makes mixing it with other things — such as gun-powder and sealing-wax. And here I must leave you." They had just come to the end of the wood.

Alice could only look puzzled: she was thinking of the pudding.

"You are sad," the Knight said in an anxious tone: "let me sing you a song to comfort you."

"Is it very long?" Alice asked, for she had heard a good deal of poetry that day.

"It's long," said the Knight, "but it's very, *very* beautiful. Everybody that hears me sing it — either it brings the *tears* into their eyes, or else —"

"Or else what?" said Alice, for the Knight had made a sudden pause.

"Or else it doesn't, you know. The name of the song is called '*Haddocks' Eyes*'."

"Oh, that's the name of the song, is it?" Alice said, trying to feel interested.

"No, you don't understand," the Knight said, looking a little vexed. "That's what the name is *called*. The name really is '*The Aged Aged Man*'."

"Then I ought to have said, 'That's what the *song* is called'?" Alice corrected herself.

"No, you oughtn't: that's quite another thing! The *song* is called '*Ways and Means*': but that's only what it's *called*, you know!"

"Well, what *is* the song, then?" said Alice, who was by this time completely bewildered.

"I was coming to that," the Knight said. "The song really is '*A-sitting On a Gate*': and the tune's my own invention."

So saying, he stopped his horse and let the reins fall on its neck: then, slowly beating time with one hand, and with a faint smile lighting up his gentle foolish face, as if he enjoyed the music of his song, he began.

Of all the strange things that Alice saw in her journey Through The Looking-Glass, this was the one that she always remembered most clearly. Years afterwards she could bring the whole scene back again, as if it had been only yesterday – the mild blue eyes and kindly smile of the Knight – the setting sun gleaming through his hair, and shining on his armour in a blaze of light that quite dazzled her – the horse quietly moving about, with the reins hanging loose on his neck, cropping the grass at her feet – and the black shadows of the forest behind – all this she took in like a picture, as, with one hand shading her eyes, she leant against a tree, watching the strange pair, and listening, in a half dream, to the melancholy music of the song.

"But the tune *isn't* his own invention," she said to herself: "it's 'I give thee all, I can no more'." She stood and listened very attentively, but no tears came into her eyes.

"I'll tell thee everything I can:
  There's little to relate.
I saw an aged aged man,
  A-sitting on a gate.
'Who are you, aged man?' I said.
  'And how is it you live?'
And his answer trickled through my head,
  Like water through a sieve.

"He said, 'I look for butterflies
  That sleep among the wheat:
I make them into mutton-pies,
  And sell them in the street.
I sell them unto men,' he said,
  'Who sail on stormy seas;
And that's the way I get my bread –
  A trifle, if you please.'

"But I was thinking of a plan
  To dye one's whiskers green,
And always use so large a fan
  That they could not be seen.
So, having no reply to give
  To what the old man said,
I cried, 'Come, tell me how you live!'
  And thumped him on the head.

"It's My Own Invention."

"His accents mild took up the tale:
  He said 'I go my ways,
And when I find a mountain-rill,
  I set it in a blaze;
And thence they make a stuff they call
  Rowland's Macassar Oil –
Yet twopence-halfpenny is all
  They give me for my toil.'

"But I was thinking of a way
  To feed oneself on batter,
And so go on from day to day
  Getting a little fatter.
I shook him well from side to side,
  Until his face was blue:
'Come, tell me how you live,' I cried,
  'And what it is you do!'

"He said 'I hunt for haddocks' eyes
  Among the heather bright,
And work them into
    waistcoat-buttons
  In the silent night.

And these I do not sell for gold
  Or coin of silvery shine,
But for a copper halfpenny,
  And that will purchase nine.

"'I sometimes dig for buttered rolls,
  Or set limed twigs for crabs:
I sometimes search the grassy knolls
  For wheels of Hansom-cabs.
And that's the way' (he gave a wink)
  'By which I get my wealth –
And very gladly will I drink
  Your Honour's noble health.'

"I heard him then, for I had just
  Completed my design
To keep the Menai bridge from rust
  By boiling it in wine.
I thanked him much for telling me
  The way he got his wealth,
But chiefly for his wish that he
  Might drink my noble health.

"And now, if e'er by chance I put
  My fingers into glue,
Or madly squeeze a right-hand foot
  Into a left-hand shoe,
Or if I drop upon my toe
  A very heavy weight,
I weep, for it reminds me so

> *Of that old man I used to know –*
> *Whose look was mild, whose speech was slow,*
> *Whose hair was whiter than the snow,*
> *Whose face was very like a crow,*
> *With eyes, like cinders, all aglow,*
> *Who seemed distracted with his woe,*
> *Who rocked his body to and fro,*
> *And muttered mumblingly and low,*
> *As if his mouth were full of dough,*
> *Who snorted like a buffalo –*
> *That summer evening, long ago,*
> *A-sitting on a gate."*

As the Knight sang the last words of the ballad, he gathered up the reins, and turned his horse's head along the road by which they had come. "You've only a few yards to go," he said, "down the hill and over that little brook, and then you'll be a Queen – But you'll stay and see me off first?" he added as Alice turned with an eager look in the direction to which he pointed. "I shan't be long. You'll wait and wave your handkerchief when I get to that turn in the road? I think it'll encourage me, you see."

"Of course I'll wait," said Alice: "and thank you very much for coming so far – and for the song – I liked it very much."

"I hope so," the Knight said doubtfully: "but you didn't cry so much as I thought you would."

So they shook hands, and then the Knight rode slowly away into the forest. "It won't take long to see him *off*, I expect," Alice said to herself, as she stood watching him.

"There he goes! Right on his head as usual! However, he gets on again pretty easily – that comes of having so many things hung round the horse –" So she went on talking to herself, as she watched the horse walking leisurely along the road, and the Knight tumbling off, first on one side and then on the other. After the fourth or fifth tumble he reached the turn, and then she waved her handkerchief to him, and waited till he was out of sight.

"I hope it encouraged him," she said, as she turned to run down the hill: "and now for the last brook, and to be a Queen! How grand it sounds!" A very few steps brought her to the edge of the brook. "The Eighth Square at last!" she cried as she bounded across,

and threw herself down to rest on a lawn as soft as moss, with little flower-beds dotted about it here and there. "Oh, how glad I am to get here! And what *is* this on my head?" she exclaimed in a tone of dismay, as she put her hands up to something very heavy, and fitted tight all round her head.

"But how *can* it have got there without my knowing it?" she said to herself, as she lifted it off, and set it on her lap to make out what it could possibly be.

It was a golden crown.

CHAPTER NINE

♥ Queen Alice ♥

"Well, this *is* grand!" said Alice. "I never expected I should be a Queen so soon – and I'll tell you what it is, your majesty," she went on in a severe tone (she was always rather fond of scolding herself), "it'll never do for you to be lolling about on the grass like that! Queens have to be dignified, you know!"

So she got up and walked about – rather stiffly just at first, as she was afraid that the crown might come off: but she comforted herself with the thought that there was nobody to see her, "and if I really am a Queen," she said as she sat down again, "I shall be able to manage it quite well in time."

Everything was happening so oddly that she didn't feel a bit surprised at finding the Red Queen and the White Queen sitting close to her, one on each side: she would have liked very much to ask them how they came there, but she feared it would not be quite civil. However, there would be no harm, she thought, in asking if the game was over. "Please, would you tell me –" she began, looking timidly at the Red Queen.

"Speak when you're spoken to!" the Queen sharply interrupted her.

"But if everybody obeyed that rule," said Alice, who was always ready for a little argument, "and if you only spoke when you were spoken to, and the other person always waited for *you* to begin, you see nobody would ever say anything, so that –"

"Ridiculous!" cried the Queen. "Why, don't you see, child –" here she broke off with a frown, and, after thinking for a minute, suddenly changed the subject of the conversation. "What do you mean by 'If you really are a Queen'? What right have you to call yourself so? You can't be a Queen, you know, till you've passed the proper examination. And the sooner we begin it, the better."

"I only said 'if'!" poor Alice pleaded in a piteous tone.

The two Queens looked at each other, and the Red Queen remarked, with a little shudder, "She *says* she only said 'if' –"

"But she said a great deal more than that!" the White Queen moaned, wringing her hands. "Oh, ever so much more than that!"

"So you did, you know," the Red Queen said to Alice. "Always speak the truth – think before you speak – and write it down afterwards."

"I'm sure I didn't mean –" Alice was beginning, but the Red Queen interrupted her impatiently.

"That's just what I complain of! You *should* have meant! What do you suppose is the use of a child without any meaning? Even a joke should have some meaning – and a child's more important than a joke, I hope. You couldn't deny that, even if you tried with both hands."

"I don't deny things with my *hands*," Alice objected.

"Nobody said you did," said the Red Queen. "I said you couldn't if you tried."

"She's in that state of mind," said the White Queen, "that she wants to deny *something* – only she doesn't know what to deny!"

"A nasty, vicious temper," the Red Queen remarked; and then there was an uncomfortable silence for a minute or two.

The Red Queen broke the silence by saying, to the White Queen, "I invite you to Alice's dinner-party this afternoon."

The White Queen smiled feebly, and said "And I invite *you*."

"I didn't know I was to have a party at all," said Alice; "but if there *is* to be one, I think *I* ought to invite the guests."

"We gave you the opportunity of doing it," the Red Queen remarked: "but I daresay you've not had many lessons in manners yet?"

"Manners are not taught in lessons," said Alice. "Lessons teach you to do sums, and things of that sort."

"Can you do Addition?" the White Queen asked. "What's one and one and one and one and one and one and one and one and one and one?"

"I don't know," said Alice. "I lost count."

"She can't do Addition," the Red Queen interrupted. "Can you do Subtraction? Take nine from eight."

"Nine from eight I can't, you know," Alice replied very readily: "but –"

"She can't do Subtraction," said the White Queen. "Can

you do Division? Divide a loaf by a knife – what's the answer to *that*?"

"I suppose –" Alice was beginning, but the Red Queen answered for her. "Bread-and-butter, of course. Try another Subtraction sum. Take a bone from a dog: what remains?"

Alice considered. "The bone wouldn't remain, of course, if I took it – and the dog wouldn't remain; it would come to bite me – and I'm sure *I* shouldn't remain!"

"Then you think nothing would remain?" said the Red Queen.

"I think that's the answer."

"Wrong, as usual," said the Red Queen: "the dog's temper would remain."

"But I don't see how –"

"Why, look here!" the Red Queen cried. "The dog would lose its temper, wouldn't it?"

"Perhaps it would," Alice replied cautiously.

"Then if the dog went away, its temper would remain!" the Queen exclaimed triumphantly.

Alice said, as gravely as she could, "They might go different ways." But she couldn't help thinking to herself, "What dreadful nonsense we *are* talking!"

"She can't do sums a *bit*!" the Queens said together, with great emphasis.

"Can *you* do sums?" Alice said, turning suddenly on the White Queen, for she didn't like being found fault with so much.

The Queen gasped and shut her eyes. "I can do Addition," she said, "if you give me time – but I can't do Subtraction, under *any* circumstances!"

*"Can you do sums?" Alice said, turning suddenly on the
White Queen, for she didn't like being found fault with so much.*

"Of course you know your A B C?" said the Red Queen.

"To be sure I do," said Alice.

"So do I," the White Queen whispered: "we'll often say it over together, dear. And I'll tell you a secret – I can read words of one letter! Isn't *that* grand! However, don't be discouraged. You'll come to it in time."

Here the Red Queen began again. "Can you answer useful questions?" she said. "How is bread made?"

"I know *that*!" Alice cried eagerly. "You take some flour –"

"Where do you pick the flower?" the White Queen asked. "In a garden, or in the hedges?"

"Well, it isn't *picked* at all," Alice explained: "it's ground –"

"How many acres of ground?" said the White Queen. "You mustn't leave out so many things."

"Fan her head!" the Red Queen anxiously interrupted. "She'll be feverish after so much thinking." So they set to work and fanned her with bunches of leaves, till she had to beg them to leave off, it blew her hair about so.

"She's all right again now," said the Red Queen. "Do you know Languages? What's the French for fiddle-de-dee?"

"Fiddle-de-dee's not English," Alice replied gravely.

"Who ever said it was?" said the Red Queen.

Alice thought she saw a way out of the difficulty this time. "If you'll tell me what language 'fiddle-de-dee' is, I'll tell you the French for it!" she exclaimed triumphantly.

But the Red Queen drew herself up rather stiffly, and said, "Queens never make bargains."

"I wish Queens never asked questions," Alice thought to herself.

"Don't let us quarrel," the White Queen said in an

anxious tone. "What is the cause of lightning?"

"The cause of lightning," Alice said very decidedly, for she felt quite certain about this, "is the thunder – no, no!" she hastily corrected herself. "I meant the other way."

"It's too late to correct it," said the Red Queen: "when you've once said a thing, that fixes it, and you must take the consequences."

"Which reminds me –" the White Queen said, looking down and nervously clasping and unclasping her hands, "we had *such* a thunderstorm last Tuesday – I mean one of the last set of Tuesdays, you know."

Alice was puzzled. "In *our* country," she remarked, "there's only one day at a time."

The Red Queen said, "That's a poor thin way of doing things. Now *here*, we mostly have days and nights two or three at a time, and sometimes in the winter we take as many as five nights together – for warmth, you know."

"Are five nights warmer than one night, then?" Alice ventured to ask.

"Five times as warm, of course."

"But they should be five times as *cold*, by the same rule –"

"Just so!" cried the Red Queen. "Five times as warm,

and five times as cold – just as I'm five times as rich as you are, *and* five times as clever!"

Alice sighed and gave it up. "It's exactly like a riddle with no answer!" she thought.

"Humpty Dumpty saw it too," the White Queen went on in a low voice, more as if she were talking to herself. "He came to the door with a corkscrew in his hand –"

"What did he want?" said the Red Queen.

"He said he *would* come in," the White Queen went on, "because he was looking for a hippopotamus. Now, as it happened, there wasn't such a thing in the house, that morning."

"Is there generally?" Alice asked in an astonished tone.

"Well, only on Thursdays," said the Queen.

"I know what he came for," said Alice: "he wanted to punish the fish, because –"

Here the White Queen began again. "It was *such* a thunderstorm, you can't think!" (She *never* could, you know," said the Red Queen.) "And part of the roof came off, and ever so much thunder got in – and it went rolling round the room in great lumps – and knocking over the tables and things – till I was so frightened, I couldn't remember my own name!"

Alice thought to herself, "I never should *try* to remember my name in the middle of an accident! Where would be the use of it?" but she did not say this aloud, for fear of hurting the poor Queen's feelings.

"Your Majesty must excuse her," the Red Queen said to Alice, taking one of the White Queen's hands in her own, and gently stroking it: "she means well, but she can't help saying foolish things, as a general rule."

The White Queen looked timidly at Alice, who felt she *ought* to say something kind, but really couldn't think of anything at the moment.

"She never was really well brought up," the Red Queen went on: "but it's amazing how good-tempered she is! Pat her on the head, and see how pleased she'll be!" But this was more than Alice had courage to do.

"A little kindness – and putting her hair in papers – would do wonders with her –"

The White Queen gave a deep sigh, and laid her head on Alice's shoulder. "I *am* so sleepy!" she moaned.

"She's tired, poor thing!" said the Red Queen. "Smooth her hair – lend her your night-cap and sing her a soothing lullaby."

"I haven't got a night-cap with me," said Alice, as she tried to obey the first direction: "and I don't know any soothing lullabies."

"I must do it myself, then," said the Red Queen, and she began:

> *"Hush-a-by lady, in Alice's lap!*
> *Till the feast's ready, we've time for a nap.*
> *When the feast's over, we'll go to the ball –*
> *Red Queen, and White Queen, and*
> *   Alice, and all!"*

"And now you know the words," she added, as she put her head down on Alice's other shoulder, "just sing it through to *me*. I'm getting sleepy, too." In another moment both Queens were fast asleep, and snoring loud.

"What *am* I to do?" exclaimed Alice, looking about in great perplexity, as first one round head, and then the other, rolled down from her shoulder, and lay like a heavy lump in her lap. "I don't think it *ever* happened before, that any one had to take care of two Queens asleep at once! No, not in all the History of England – it couldn't, you know, because there never was more than one Queen at a time. Do wake up, you heavy things!" she went on in an impatient tone; but there was no answer but a gentle snoring.

The snoring got more distinct every minute, and sounded more like a tune: at last she could even make out the words, and she listened so eagerly that, when the two great heads suddenly vanished from her lap, she hardly missed them.

She was standing before an arched doorway over which were the words "QUEEN ALICE" in large letters, and on each side of the arch there was a bell-handle; one was marked "Visitors' Bell," and the other "Servants' Bell".

"I'll wait till the song's over," thought Alice, "and then I'll ring the – the – *which* bell must I ring?" she went on, very much puzzled by the names. "I'm not a visitor, and I'm not a servant. There *ought* to be one marked 'Queen', you know –"

Just then the door opened a little way, and a creature with a long beak put its head out for a moment and said, "No admittance till the week after next!" and shut the door again with a bang.

Alice knocked and rang in vain for a long time; but at last

a very old Frog, who was sitting under a tree, got up and hobbled slowly towards her: he was dressed in bright yellow, and had enormous boots on.

"What is it, now?" the Frog said in a deep hoarse whisper.

Alice turned round, ready to find fault with anybody. "Where's the servant whose business it is to answer the door?" she began angrily.

"Which door?" said the Frog.

Alice almost stamped with irritation at the slow drawl in which he spoke. "*This* door, of course!"

The Frog looked at the door with his large dull eyes for a minute: then he went nearer and rubbed it with his thumb, as if he were trying whether the paint would come off; then he looked at Alice.

"To answer the door?" he said. "What's it been asking of?" He was so hoarse that Alice could scarcely hear him.

"I don't know what you mean," she said.

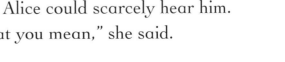

"I speaks English, doesn't I?" the Frog went on. "Or are you deaf? What did it ask you?"

"Nothing!" Alice said impatiently. "I've been knocking at it!"

"Shouldn't do that – shouldn't do that –" the Frog muttered. "Wexes it, you know." Then he went up and gave the door a kick with one of his great feet. "You let *it* alone," he panted, as he hobbled back to his tree, "and it'll let *you* alone, you know."

At this moment the door was flung open, and a shrill voice was heard singing:

> *"To the Looking-Glass world it was Alice that said,*
> *'I've a sceptre in hand, I've a crown on my head.*
> *Let the Looking-Glass creatures, whatever they be,*
> *Come and dine with the Red Queen,*
>   *the White Queen, and me.'"*

And hundreds of voices joined in the chorus:

> *"Then fill up the glasses as quick as you can,*
> *And sprinkle the table with buttons and bran:*
> *Put cats in the coffee, and mice in the tea –*
> *And welcome Queen Alice with thirty-times-three!"*

Then followed a confused noise of cheering, and Alice thought to herself, "Thirty times three makes ninety. I wonder if any one's counting?" In a minute there was silence again, and the same shrill voice sang another verse:

"'O Looking-Glass creatures,' quoth Alice, 'draw near!
'Tis an honour to see me, a favour to hear:
'Tis a privilege high to have dinner and tea
Along with the Red Queen, the White Queen,
*   and me!'"*

Then came the chorus again:

"Then fill up the glasses with treacle and ink,
Or anything else that is pleasant to drink:
Mix sand with the cider, and wool with the wine –
And welcome Queen Alice with
*   ninety-times-nine!"*

"Ninety times nine!" Alice repeated in despair, "Oh, that'll never be done! I'd better go in at once –" and in she went, and there was a dead silence the moment she appeared.

Alice glanced nervously along the table, as she walked up the large hall, and noticed that there were about fifty guests, of all kinds: some were animals, some birds, and there were even a few flowers among them. "I'm glad they've come without waiting to be asked," she thought: "I should never have known who were the right people to invite!"

There were three chairs at the head of the table: the Red and White Queens had already taken two of them, but the middle one was empty. Alice sat down in it, rather uncomfortable at the silence, and longing for someone to speak.

At last the Red Queen began. "You've missed the soup and fish," she said. "Put on the joint!" And the waiters set a leg

of mutton before Alice, who looked at it rather anxiously, as she had never had to carve a joint before.

"You look a little shy: let me introduce you to that leg of mutton," said the Red Queen. "Alice – Mutton: Mutton – Alice." The leg of mutton got up in the dish and made a little bow to Alice; and Alice returned the bow, not knowing whether to be frightened or amused.

"May I give you a slice?" she said, taking up the knife and fork, and looking from one Queen to the other.

"Certainly not," the Red Queen said, very decidedly: "it isn't etiquette to cut any one you've been introduced to. Remove the joint!" And the waiters carried it off, and brought a large plum-pudding in its place.

"I won't be introduced to the pudding, please," Alice said rather hastily, "or we shall get no dinner at all. May I give you some?"

But the Red Queen looked sulky, and growled, "Pudding – Alice: Alice – Pudding. Remove the pudding!", and the waiters took it away so quickly that Alice couldn't return its bow.

However, she didn't see why the Red Queen should be the

only one to give orders; so, as an experiment, she called out "Waiter! Bring back the pudding!", and there it was again in a moment, like a conjuring-trick. It was so large that she couldn't help feeling a *little* shy with it, as she had been with the mutton; however, she conquered her shyness by a great effort, and cut a slice and handed it to the Red Queen.

"What impertinence!" said the Pudding. "I wonder how you'd like it, if I were to cut a slice out of *you*, you creature!"

It spoke in a thick, suety sort of voice, and Alice hadn't a word to say in reply: she could only sit and look at it and gasp.

"Make a remark," said the Red Queen: "it's ridiculous to leave all the conversation to the pudding!"

"Do you know, I've had such a quantity of poetry repeated to me to-day," Alice began, a little frightened at finding that, the moment she opened her lips, there was dead silence, and all eyes were fixed upon her; "and it's a very curious thing, I think – every poem was about fishes in some way. Do you know why they're so fond of fishes, all about here?"

She spoke to the Red Queen, whose answer was a little wide of the mark. "As to fishes," she said, very slowly and solemnly, putting her mouth close to Alice's ear, "her White Majesty knows a lovely riddle – all in poetry – all about fishes. Shall she repeat it?"

"Her Red Majesty's very kind to mention it," the White Queen murmured into Alice's other ear, in a voice like the cooing of a pigeon. "It would be *such* a treat! May I?"

"Please do," Alice said very politely.

The White Queen laughed with delight, and stroked Alice's cheek. She began:

"'First, the fish must be caught.'
That is easy: a baby, I think, could have caught it.
'Next, the fish must be bought.'
That is easy: a penny, I think, would have bought it.

'Now cook me the fish!'
That is easy, and will not take more than a minute.
'Let it lie in a dish!'
That is easy, because it already is in it.
'Bring it here! Let me sup!'
It is easy to set such a dish on the table.
'Take the dish-cover up!'
Ah, that is so hard that I fear I'm unable!

For it holds it like glue —
Holds the lid to the dish, while it lies in the middle:
Which is easiest to do,
Un-dish-cover the fish, or dishcover the riddle?"

"Take a minute to think about it, and then guess," said the Red Queen. "Meanwhile, we'll drink your health – Queen Alice's health!" she screamed at the top of her voice, and all the guests began drinking it directly, and very queerly they managed it: some of them put their glasses upon their heads like extinguishers, and drank all that trickled down their faces – others upset the decanters, and drank the wine as it ran off the edges of the table – and three of them (who looked like kangaroos) scrambled into the dish of roast mutton, and began eagerly lapping up the gravy, "just like pigs in a trough!" thought Alice.

"Meanwhile, we'll drink your health – Queen Alice's health!" she screamed at the top of her voice ...

"You ought to return thanks in a neat speech," the Red Queen said, frowning at Alice as she spoke.

"We must support you, you know," the White Queen whispered, as Alice got up to do it, very obediently, but a little frightened.

"Thank you very much," she whispered in reply, "but I can do quite well without."

"That wouldn't be at all the thing," the Red Queen said very decidedly: so Alice tried to submit to it with good grace.

("And they *did* push so!" she said afterwards, when she was telling her sister the history of the feast. "You would have thought they wanted to squeeze me flat!")

In fact it was difficult for her to keep in her place while she made her speech: the two Queens pushed her so, one on each side, that they nearly lifted her up into the air. "I rise to return thanks —" Alice began: and she really *did* rise as she spoke, several inches; but she got hold of the edge of the table, and managed to pull herself down again.

"Take care of yourself!" screamed the White Queen, seizing Alice's hair with both her hands. "Something's going to happen!"

And then (as Alice afterwards described it) all sorts of thing happened in a moment. The candles all grew up to the ceiling, looking something like a bed of rushes with fireworks at the top. As to the bottles, they each took a pair of plates, which they hastily fitted on as wings, and so, with forks for legs, went fluttering about in all directions: "and very like birds they look," Alice thought to herself, as well as she could in the dreadful confusion that was beginning.

At this moment she heard a hoarse laugh at her side, and turned to see what was the matter with the White Queen; but, instead of the Queen, there was the leg of mutton sitting in the chair. "Here I am!" cried a voice from the soup-tureen, and Alice turned again, just in time to see the Queen's broad good-natured face grinning at her for a moment over the edge of the tureen, before she disappeared into the soup.

There was not a moment to be lost. Already several of the guests were lying down in the dishes, and the soup-ladle was walking up the table towards Alice's chair, and beckoning to her impatiently to get out of its way.

"I can't stand this any longer!" she cried as she jumped up and seized the table-cloth with both hands: one good pull, and plates, dishes, guests, and candles came crashing down together in a heap on the floor.

"And as for *you*," she went on, turning fiercely upon the Red Queen, whom she considered as the cause of all the mischief – but the Queen was no longer at her side – she had suddenly dwindled down to the size of a little doll, and was now on the table, merrily running round and round after her own shawl, which was trailing behind her.

At any other time, Alice would have felt surprised at this, but she was far too much excited to be surprised at anything *now*. "As for *you*," she repeated, catching hold of the little creature in the very act of jumping over a bottle which had just lighted upon the table, "I'll shake you into a kitten, that I will!"

CHAPTER TEN

♥ Shaking ♥

She took her off the table as she spoke, and shook her backwards and forwards with all her might.

The Red Queen made no resistance whatever; only her face grew very small, and her eyes got large and green: and still, as Alice went on shaking her, she kept on growing shorter – and fatter – and softer – and rounder – and –

CHAPTER ELEVEN

♥ Waking ♥

– and it really *was* a kitten, after all.

Chapter Twelve

♥ Which Dreamed It? ♥

"Your Red Majesty shouldn't purr so loud," Alice said, rubbing her eyes, and addressing the kitten, respectfully, yet with some severity. "You woke me out of oh! such a nice dream! And you've been with me, Kitty – all through the Looking-Glass world. Did you know it, dear?"

It is a very inconvenient habit of kittens (Alice had once made the remark) that, whatever you say to them, they *always* purr. "If they would only purr for 'yes', and mew for 'no', or any rule of that sort," she had said, "so that one could keep up a conversation! But how *can* you talk with a person if they *always* say the same thing?"

On this occasion the kitten only purred: and it was impossible to guess whether it meant "yes" or "no".

So Alice hunted among the chessmen on the table till she had found the Red Queen: then she went down on her knees on the hearth-rug, and put the kitten and the Queen to look at each other. "Now, Kitty!" she cried, clapping her hands triumphantly. "Confess that was what you turned into!"

("But it wouldn't look at it," she said, when she was explaining the thing afterwards to her sister: "it turned away its head, and pretended not to see it: but it looked a *little* ashamed of itself, so I think it *must* have been the Red Queen.")

"Sit up a little more stiffly, dear!" Alice cried with a merry laugh. "And curtsey while you're thinking what to – what to purr. It saves time, remember!" And she caught it up and gave it one little kiss, "just in honour of having been a Red Queen."

"Snowdrop, my pet!" she went on, looking over her shoulder at the White Kitten, which was still patiently undergoing its toilet, "when *will* Dinah have finished with your White Majesty, I wonder? That must be the reason you were so untidy in my dream – Dinah! Do you know that you're scrubbing a White Queen? Really, it's most disrespectful of you!

"And what did *Dinah* turn to, I wonder?" she prattled on, as she settled comfortably down, with one elbow on the rug, and her chin in her hand, to watch the kittens. "Tell me, Dinah, did you turn to Humpty Dumpty? I *think* you did – however, you'd better not mention it to your friends just yet, for I'm not sure.

"By the way, Kitty, if only you'd been really with me in my dream, there was one thing you *would* have enjoyed – I had such a quantity of poetry said to me, all about fishes! Tomorrow morning you shall have a real treat. All the time you're eating your breakfast, I'll repeat 'The Walrus and the Carpenter' to you; and then you can make believe it's oysters, dear!

*... she settled comfortably down, with one elbow on the rug,
and her chin in her hand, to watch the kittens.*

"Now, Kitty, let's consider who it was that dreamed it all. This is a serious question, my dear, and you should *not* go on licking your paw like that – as if Dinah hadn't washed you this morning! You see, Kitty, it *must* have been either me or the Red King. He was part of my dream, of course – but then I was part of his dream, too! *Was* it the Red King, Kitty? You were his wife, my dear, so you ought to know – Oh, Kitty, *do* help to settle it! I'm sure your paw can wait!" But the provoking kitten only began on the other paw, and pretended it hadn't heard the question.

Which do *you* think it was?

A boat, beneath a sunny sky,
Lingering onward dreamily
In an evening of July —

Children three that nestle near,
Eager eye and willing ear,
Pleased a simple tale to hear —

Long has paled that sunny sky:
Echoes fade and memories die:
Autumn frosts have slain July.

Still she haunts me, phantomwise,
Alice moving under skies
Never seen by waking eyes.

Children yet, the tale to hear,
Eager eye and willing ear,
Lovingly shall nestle near.

In a Wonderland they lie,
Dreaming as the days go by,
Dreaming as the summers die:

Ever drifting down the stream —
Lingering in the golden gleam —
Life, what is it but a dream?

MY DEAR CHILD,

Please to fancy, if you can, that you are reading a letter, from a real friend whom you have seen, and whose voice you can seem to yourself to hear, wishing you, as I do now with all my heart, a happy Easter.

Do you know that delicious dreamy feeling, when one first wakes on a summer morning, with the twitter of birds in the air and the fresh breeze coming in at the open window – when, lying lazily with eyes half shut, one sees as in a dream green boughs waving, or waters rippling in a golden light? It is a pleasure very near to sadness, bringing tears to one's eyes like a beautiful picture or poem. And is not that a Mother's gentle hand that undraws your curtains, and a Mother's sweet voice that summons you to rise? To rise and forget, in the bright sunlight, the ugly dreams that frightened you when all was so dark – to rise and enjoy another day, first kneeling to thank that unseen Friend who sends you the beautiful sun?

Are these strange words from a writer of such tales as "Alice"? And is this a strange letter to find in a book of nonsense? It may be so. Some perhaps may blame me for thus mixing together things grave and gay; others may smile and think it odd that any one should speak of solemn things at all, except in Church and on a Sunday: but I think – nay, I am sure – that some children will read this gently and lovingly, and in the spirit in which I have written it.

For I do not believe that God means us thus to divide life into two halves – to wear a grave face on Sunday, and to think it out-of-place to even so much as mention Him on a week-day. Do you think he cares to see only kneeling figures and to hear only tones of prayer – and that He does not also love to see the lambs leaping in the sunlight, and to hear the merry voices of the children, as they roll among the hay? Surely their innocent laughter is as sweet in His ears as the grandest anthem that ever rolled up from the "dim religious light" of some solemn cathedral?

And if I have written anything to add to those stores of innocent and healthy amusement that are laid up in books for the children I love so well, it is surely something I may hope to look back upon without shame and sorrow (as how much life must then be recalled!) when my turn comes to walk through the valley of shadows.

This Easter sun will rise on you, dear child, "feeling your life in every limb", and eager to rush out into the fresh morning air – and many an Easter-day will come and go, before it finds you feeble and grey-headed, creeping wearily out to bask once more in the sunlight – but it is good, even now, to think sometimes of that great morning when
"the Sun of righteousness" shall "arise with healing in his wings".

Surely your gladness need not be the less for the thought that you will one day see a brighter dawn than this – when lovelier sights will meet your eyes than any waving trees or rippling waters – when angel-hands shall undraw your curtains, and sweeter tones than ever loving Mother breathed shall wake you to a new and glorious day – and when all the sadness, and the sin, that darkened life on this little earth, shall be forgotten like the dreams of a night that is past!

Your affectionate Friend,
LEWIS CARROLL

Easter, 1876

THE EXTRA VIRGIN KITCHEN

Recipes for Wheat-free, Sugar-free and Dairy-free Eating

by Susan Jane White

Gill & Macmillan

Gill and Macmillan
Hume Avenue
Park West
Dublin 12
with associated companies throughout the world
www.gillmacmillanbooks.ie

© Susan Jane White, 2014

978 07171 5933 8

Design by www.grahamthew.com
Photography © Joanne Murphy
Styling by Orla Neligan
Assistants to photographer and stylist: Liosa MacNamara and Kerrie Mitchell
Food preparation by Susan Jane White
Edited by Kristin Jensen
Indexed by Adam Pozner
Printed by Printer Trento Srl, Italy

This book is typeset in 9 on 12pt Botanika Mono.

PROPS

Avoca: HQ Kilmacanogue, Bray, Co. Wicklow.
T: (01) 2746939; E: info@avoca.ie; www.avoca.ie

Meadows & Byrne: Dublin, Cork, Galway, Clare, Tipperary.
T: (01) 2804554/(021) 4344100; E: info@meadowsandbyrne.ie; www.meadowsandbyrne.com

Eden Home & Garden: 1-4 Temple Grove, Temple Road, Blackrock, Co. Dublin.
T: (01) 7642004; E: edenhomeandgarden@hotmail.com; www.edenhomeandgarden.ie

Article: Powerscourt Townhouse, South William Street, Dublin 2.
T: (01) 6799268; E: items@articledublin.com; www.articledublin.com

House of Fraser: Dundrum Town Centre, Dublin 16.
T: (01) 2991400; E: dundrum@hof.co.uk; www.houseoffraser.co.uk

Harold's Bazaar: 208 Harold's Cross Road, Dublin 6W.
T: 087 7228789.

Historic Interiors: Oberstown, Lusk, Co. Dublin.
T: (01) 8437174; E: killian@historicinteriors.net

Helen Turkington: 47 Dunville Avenue, Ranelagh, Dublin 6.
T: (01) 4125138; E: info@helenturkington.com; www.helenturkington.com

The Third Policeman: 121 Lower Rathmines Road, Dublin 6.
T: 085 8487763; www.facebook.com/t3rdpoliceman

CONTENTS

+ + + + + + + +

SNACKS AND OTHER NUTRITIONAL HITS

SOUPS

SALADS

SUPPERS

EXTRA VIRGIN TREATS

THANK YOUS

A big high five to my suave publisher Nicki Howard, whose wisdom and dynamism whipped this book into shape. You're one hell of a lady.

To Catherine, Teresa, Paul and everyone at Gill & Macmillan. Thank you for making this book everything I had hoped, and so much more. I am eternally grateful for your hard work and support.

Design guru Graham Thew — I blush at your brilliance.

A thunderous thank you to photographer Jo Murphy, stylist Orla Neligan and assistants Kerrie and Liosa. I never expected to have so much fun or to make new friends in the process. Working with you all was beyond inspiring.

Mary O'Sullivan, Brendan O'Connor and Anne Harris at *The Sunday Independent* — all brilliant people at the top of their game. Thank you for taking a chance on me.

To lovely Kristin Jensen and Maggie Armstrong for your patience and meticulous proofreading.

Tom Dunne and producer Joe Donnelly — radio was never so much fun. A heartfelt thank you.

My agent Rebecca Morgan for her tenacity, loyalty and tireless enthusiasm. Thank you for putting up with me these past 14 years.

I'm grateful to Oliver and his team at Wall & Keogh in Portobello, where I spend hours sipping gorgeous teas, tapping toes and writing.

To my beloved, the most nourishing superfood my body has ever known. You electrify me. Mostly.

Our adorable boys Benjamin and Marty, whose laughter rings through our home.

To mum. What a marvel.

Many impressive commentators and activists continue to inspire and inform me. My sincere gratitude to you all: Joanna Blythman, Felicity Lawrence, Bee Wilson, Mark Bittman, Michael Pollan, Marion Nestle, Robyn O'Brien, Dr David A. Kessler, Michael Moss, Gary Taubes, Dr Marilyn Glenville, Eric Schlosser, Robert Lustig, Hugh Fearnley-Whittingstall, Dr John Briffa, Dr John McKenna, Colin Tudge, Claudia Hammond and George Monbiot.

And lastly, YOU. I have the best readers in the world. You give flight to my imagination and make it all possible for me. I wrote this book for you.

Introduction:

FALLING DOWN THE RABBIT HOLE

My name is Susan Jane. Picture MacGyver in an apron with a grumpy husband who thinks he's a restaurant critic and two ravenous little punks to feed six times a day. Food is my thing, it keeps me happy. People say my energy levels would rival Graham Norton on acid. But I wasn't always so bionic.

Thirteen years ago I was a model student. Literally. Modelling became a valuable source of income at college in Dublin, and later, at Oxford. It's supposed to be a glamorous job, but when you see what models live on - cigarettes and diet cola - you have to wonder.

Back then, I never saw myself as someone who needed to change. I was hyper, stubborn and deluded - what could possibly go wrong? After all, there was nothing out of the ordinary about my diet: jam-filled scones, toast, pasta, breakfast cereals, toast, take-out sambos and more toast. Standard Irish fare. No wonder I tried to regulate my moods with criminal amounts of caffeine.

Let's be honest: consumers are highly submissive. I hardly thought to ask any questions about the ingredients in my energy drink or the Monster Munch I devoured with the giddy determination of a clamper kneecapping a Bentley in the bus lane. I blindly trusted the 'food authorities', whoever they were, and I never imagined that beef burgers, for example, might contain horsemeat, that chicken products could test positive for pork or that our modern diet would lead millions into diabesity. Like Alice in Wonderland, I was jumping feet first into a deep, dark rabbit hole. Except this was no tea party.

First we form habits - and then they form us. It wasn't alcohol or cigarettes that ruined my health, though I experimented as much as any student. It was food. To be more specific: junk food. I convinced myself that only boring people had time to cook. Turns out smarter people *make* time to cook.

One day in the summer of 2005 my body said no, enough. First came the shakes. Horrid urinary infections. Constipation. Mouth ulcers. Exhaustion. But nobody suggested that maybe I was contributing to my ill health. My digestive system wheezed like an asthmatic snail, yet diet apparently had nothing to do with it. Ten years ago the medical community dismissed the idea of food sensitivities like industry tycoons scoffing at global warming. Contemplating such an idea was daft. After all, test results had shown I was not coeliac or diabetic. Case closed.

The chronic conditions started to make themselves at home. Thrush. Earaches. Dizziness. Psoriasis. Headaches. Cold sores. But I didn't have time to respect the symptoms and turned to self-medication. I had papers to submit and was hell bent on a place on Oxford Uni's modern pentathlon team. There was literally no time to be sick.

I ended up in hospital, with tubes coming out of … well, everywhere. They sent in doctor after doctor. As the consultants handed me their cards, I noticed they had more and more letters after their names. Yet no one could figure out why my body was as limp as a wet lettuce. I was numb, physically and emotionally.

After twelve courses of antibiotics, several hospitalisations, a course of steroids, anti-fungal colon treatments and many futile vaccinations, I felt unlucky but in no way responsible. Then my white blood cells packed up.

One afternoon in hospital I got chatting to an elderly lady
called Lucy in the cubicle next to me. I wasn't certain why
Lucy had been admitted. She was frail but so sweet in her
papery mint gown, smiling back over the sheets. We talked
for hours. I cried inside when she asked to hold my hand
to give her strength. Lucy cooed about her love of bread
making, yet she was coeliac (so her body could not handle

gluten). I remember thinking how strange that was: ignoring the signals her system was sending.

Across the room, another patient was tucking into jelly and ice cream from the hospital canteen. She was being treated for 'complications' arising from diabetes and obesity. It was like death on a plate, and horribly ironic that the hospital staff were her accomplices. The sight sent a chill up my arms. Both women knew their poison but chose to ignore it. They were digging the way to their graves with their teeth.

A little later, I heard a loud flat bell. Doctors and nurses ran in and sectioned me off from Lucy. I never saw her adorable face again. No one did.

The following morning I looked in the mirror, and what I saw made me cry. I turned away from the mirror, and in that instant - a wrenching minute of pure self-knowledge, accompanied by a sort of grief for the person I was now saying goodbye to - I made the most important decision of my life: to take control of my health. Raising my head, I looked into that mirror once again. And I nodded.

Deal.

My nutritional pilgrimage started with a journey to Dr Joe Fitzgibbon, a doctor who specialises in food sensitivities and fatigue. I travelled six hours by train for every visit. Together we tackled the elimination diet, stripping my meals to very basic foods like meat, fish, pulses, beans and vegetables. Every couple of weeks I reintroduced specific foods to my diet to monitor symptoms, like a food detective. **It felt like someone was sucking the illness out of my body.**

That austere diet made me see the intimate connection between energy levels and the food we eat. Good food keeps you on your tippy toes. Poor food will have you on your knees. Wheat and sugar were lethal in my system, so I waved goodbye to bread, pasta, sugar and all manner of processed food. That was nine years ago.

The first three weeks off wheat, sugar and dairy were horrific. I don't want you thinking I was running barefoot through fields of cornflowers, throwing my arms around trees in a state of orgasmic self-enlightenment. Nor did I ever choose to give up junk food. I had to. My body was falling apart. There was no other choice.

So I tramped around health food stores with a mixture
of confusion and nervous elation, like an ornithologist
sighting a new species of bird. All the time I was busy
mourning for Diet Cola Girl. 'Jaysus, I could buy a bottle
of wine for the price of those berries.' 'I can't afford
that strange flour, it's three times the price of normal
white stuff!'

Eventually I realised there is nothing restrictive about
this way of eating. It's the opposite. Food intolerances
are an opportunity to escape the shackles of processed
food and the excesses of the Wheat-Sugar-Dairy merry-go-
round. There are legions of grains, flours and funky beans
to experiment with in place of boring pasta and bread, and
healthy fats like walnut, coconut, sesame and hemp seed
oils. Discovering this wealth of options was my second
light bulb moment. **My 'restrictive' diet was nothing of the
sort. It was incredibly liberating.**

By continuing to feed our bodies with one-dimensional foods
made from white sugar, white flour and industrially produced
chemicals, we condition our brains to accept crap. Breaking
the habit is challenging, but once you experience the
benefits of eating whole, unprocessed foods, you will never
look back. Make no mistake, it's a love affair like no other.
But don't just take my word for it. See for yourself.

**Here are my favourite recipes. Don't worry - I won't
threaten you with cabbage soup or Lycra tights.** These
recipes are less about denial and more about pleasure:
banana malt ice cream, raw chocolate tortes, chestnut
crêpes, and chia seed fishcakes with curried coconut. If you
approach this book with a sense of adventure, I bet your
palate will be tickled and your mojo will return. In time
your weight will stabilise, you will sleep more soundly and
hum louder. But there's more! We now know that a healthy
diet significantly reduces your risk of developing heart
disease, many cancers and type 2 diabetes. If there was
a pill promising the same, wouldn't you want to take it?
Whole food cooking isn't a pill. It's a ticket.

Of course, you don't have to give up wheat, sugar and
dairy to eat well, and slip-ups are a natural (and
necessary) part of the journey. **Everyone has different needs
and different poisons. That's what makes humans so damn
charming.** But whatever your reasons for exploring new and
nourishing foods away from the circus of convenience, you
are very welcome to the Extra Virgin Kitchen.

Let's do this together.

NIFTY Q&As
==========

Do I need any special equipment before I start?

Definitely - get yourself some tenacity and a sense of adventure. Fleetwood Mac's Greatest Hits is also useful. Or Billie Holiday. Whatever tickles your serotonin.

Where do I buy all these weird things?

In good health food stores and specialist grocers. Most large supermarkets stock 80% of the ingredients listed, such as millet, quinoa, seaweed, tamari and even coconut water. Check out my sources at the back of the book for online ordering.

How come you use cups instead of grams?

Cups are friendlier and make it easier to visualise quantities. I think the metric system alienates people in the kitchen. It has a disempowering effect. Do you know what 65g of dates looks like? Or 325g of flour? The only time I use the weighing scales is when every tiny bit of ingredient is imperative (e.g. the Delinquent Brownies recipe on page 212).

You can pick up measuring cups in the baking aisle of most supermarkets or on Amazon for less than a fiver. Dean & DeLuca probably do frilly ones.

Why don't you use gluten-free flour?

I struggle to see the point of swapping white flour for a 'gluten-free' version. It reminds me of when I used to drink decaf coffee, thinking I was being healthy. Gluten-free white flour is just as processed as its first cousin, the all-purpose white flour.

Admittedly, wholegrain flours are a little trickier to tame into happy biscuits and breads, but their nutritional profile makes them much more desirable. If you've met my husband, you'll understand why I'm attracted to stubborn and contrary ingredients. I find them indecently exciting once you finally conquer them.

Are all your recipes gluten free as well as wheat free?

Not all, but most. Gluten is found in wheat, rye, barley and some oats.

Why don't you use spelt?

Spelt is wheat.

If this cookbook is wheat free, why does it feature lots of buckwheat recipes?

Despite its name, buckwheat is no relation to the cereal wheat. There's no gluten in buckwheat either. How awesome is that?

Any pasta recipes?

No. But plenty of quinoa, which is far tastier. It's like a new friend with super-human powers. Pasta would blush in quinoa's presence.

I live in the US. Ground almonds are the same as almond flour, right?

Almost. Both are healthy and come from almonds, but ground almonds give a heavier finish in baked goodies. Almond flour is much finer and easier to find in the US, but not so much in Europe.

Feel free to try almond flour in place of ground almonds whenever you see a recipe bound for the oven. However, almond flour will not work in any raw recipe, such as the Chia Bonbons, Hazelnut and Raisin Freezer Cookies or Fancy Pants Lúcuma Fudge.

Is margarine okay instead of butter?

Not in my opinion. Be sceptical of pseudo foods tailored to 'reduce cholesterol'. Investigative journalist Felicity Lawrence warns that many manufac-turers use the cheapest possible oils to make margarine and hide under the pretence of

being 'healthy'. Most of these oils must be processed or hydro-genated to extend their shelf life, but not your life. 'Cholesterol free' is a similarly deceptive marketing device among companies that use hydrogenated fats. So an ostensibly healthy product can do more harm to your cholesterol than good. Professor Walter Willet of Harvard Medical School slammed this as 'the biggest food-processing disaster in US history'.

How about regular sunflower oil?

For taste reasons, you're welcome to use whatever oil you fancy. However, as a cautious mummy of two growing boys I only use extra virgin, cold-pressed oils that have not been brutalised by processors or adulterated by manufacturers. When in doubt, leave it out.

Isn't coconut oil fattening?

It is a fat, yes. But it's a good fat. Our relationship with fat is perverse. We need it in order to manufacture brain cells and hormones (without which everyone would be suffering from depression). However, choose judiciously.

There are good fats and bad fats. Extra virgin, cold-pressed coconut oil is a good fat.

The saturated fat in coconut is made up of medium chain triglyc-erides (MCTs), the mere mention of which makes triathletes indecently excitable. These MCTs are metabolised quickly by the body and can be used as an alternative source of energy to carbohydrates. MCTs are also easier to break down than the longer chain triglycerides in olive, sunflower or canola oil. More impor-tantly, coconut's MCTs are composed of lauric and capric acids. These heroic anti-viral, anti-fungal and anti-bacterial agents are also present in mother's milk to give her baba the best start in life.

Can I fry with olive oil?

Frying at a high temper-ature will denature almost any oil. It doesn't matter if you use the best cold-pressed extra virgin oil money can buy. Heating, as opposed to warming, chemically disfigures oil and spoils many health benefits. Basically, you are creating unhealthy free radicals that are liable to fraternise with your arteries.

If you suffer from cholesterol or weight problems, it might be worth writing this on the inside of your kitchen cupboard to remind you!

We use coconut oil because of its high smoke point. This means it's a more sturdy oil to cook with than, say, linseed or sunflower oil. When I'm gently sweating veg, I'm happy to use olive oil, as the heat never reaches a perilous point.

Ghee is clarified butter, which many lactose-intolerant cooks find they can eat without side effects. Just like butter, ghee is solid at room temperature and holds a higher smoke point than most oils. We always have some in our fridge.

I love agave and use it all the time. Is it good for me?

Let's be clear - no sugar is healthy. Agave is touted as a low glycemic fructose syrup that does not require insulin to break it down. A health boon, right? But science is rarely that simple. Eating this page wouldn't require insulin either. Hardly a reason to include it in our diet. It's fair

to say that agave is not a health food, but a useful food. This is an important differenti-ation. Evidence suggests that a diet rich in *liquid* fructose has a deleterious effect on the body. The addition of high fructose corn syrup (HFCS), for example, has caused much controversy between health scien-tists and food manufac-turers. While agave does not fall within the same category as HFCS, it is still classified as fructose.

Agave wouldn't be my first choice of sweetener unless I was diabetic (and even still, moder-ation is critical). Try raw, unadulterated organic agave if possible. Other issues to consider include processing methods and added ingredients. Agave piracy dates back to 2008, when several super-market brands of agave were found to be highly processed and contami-nated with other forms of syrups. It's hardly surprising that manufac-turers want a slice of success when a new food enjoys such attention. This applies to all newfangled foods. Keep your antennae finely tuned and your gut on speaking terms with you! As with all sweeteners, no matter what you choose, moderation is key.

What's so terrific about maple syrup anyway? Isn't it just as bad for you as sugar?

No. Unless you plan to neck a pint of it. Maple syrup is a wonderfully wholesome natural sugar. But if you're diabetic, it's off limits.

Maple syrup is harvested naturally from maple trees and contains surprising amounts of iron and calcium. It's one of the only sweeteners that helps alkalise the body - other sugars can be highly acidic to the system. Acidic systems have been shown to leach calcium from our bones, while alkaline systems actually enhance calcium absorption. This is useful information for those who suffer from arthritic or osteo conditions.

A pal in Québec, Canada, is strug-gling to find local maple syrup. Rumour has it the middle-class Chinese are buying up all of Canada's stocks. This has conse-quences for us too, one of which is a rise in the price of this deliciously sticky nectar. Another is the surge of imposters on the market. To avoid being duped by 'maple-flavoured' syrup, always interrogate the labelling. It should have one ingredient: 100% pure Canadian maple syrup.Grade B is preferable.

What's the story with brown rice syrup? Healthy or not?

Okay, so, no sugar is healthy. The key is to find one that works for you and use it moderately or sparingly.

Despite brown rice syrup being a fairly processed product, it has low levels of glucose (about 5%) and high levels of the more complex carbohydrate maltose (around 55%). This gives brown rice syrup an attractive glycemic load. Alicia Silverstone, author of *The Kind Diet*, totally digs it. As a result, Hollywood does too.

It's made by fermenting the cooked grain with cultured enzymes to break down the carbohydrates. The liquid by-product is boiled to make a sweet, sticky syrup. Like all trendy products, there are good versions and seriously processed versions. It's worth doing your own research. Sticking to organic seems sensible given the volume of

agrichemicals used in rice production. There were issues with arsenic in the soil a few years back too.

What on earth is coconut sugar?

Coconut blossom sugar is a relatively new unrefined sugar on the Western market. Stunning stuff. Not as sweet as regular cane sugar, it offers a burnt toffee kick. It's not heavily processed either. The sap of the coconut flower is dehydrated to form honeyed crystals. While coconut sugar can be classified as a palm sugar, it is not to be confused with regular palm sugar, which is produced differently and is no friend to the diabetic. Coconut sugar is thought to have a low glycemic value. Good news for hyperactive children, diabetics and bored sedentary workers.

But watch out! My cynical side predicts that adulterated forms will begin to appear on our shelves. Look for trusted brands and ask your local health food stockist for advice if you're suspicious. Coconut sugar is pricey and will attract piracy. Them is the facts of life. Rapadura

sugar is much more difficult to adulterate and is a very good sub for coconut sugar if glycemic load does not concern you.

If rapadura is a sugar, what's it doing in this book?

You'll notice that rapadura sugar features in just three recipes. I wanted to introduce readers to a range of healthier sugars in place of the nutritionally void white variety.

Rapadura is a unique extra-fine sugar made from dehydrating sugarcane juice. It is caramel in colour with a deep mineral taste to it. Find it online and in all good food stores. Pricey, but worth experiencing.

However, if your diet obliges you to stay off sugar, this would mean quarantining all forms of good and bad sugars, including rapadura, honey, maple syrup, brown rice syrup and even fruit. My cookbook only manages to evict nasty white sugar from our kitchens.

I'm type 2 diabetic. Is this book for me?

Absolutely! However, it's important to stick to your low GL principles. Wherever you see maple syrup, use raw agave. Coconut sugar is apparently low GL, but at the time of going to print, there was insufficient independent research to corroborate this for me. I urge you to do your own research. Remember that date syrup, maple syrup and honey are all high GL and therefore unsuitable. Stevia leaves are an interesting and popular source of sweetness, but I don't like the taste. Perhaps you will have better luck than me.

Can I use barley malt extract in place of maple syrup? It's so much cheaper.

Sure. Although I haven't tried barley malt in all my recipes, I can assure you it gives tremendous results in baking. Even raw chocolates work with barley malt. Just remember that it's only half as sweet as honey and maple syrup. This syrup is made from fermenting and boiling barley, in a similar way to brown rice syrup. Some of the original nutrients found in barley are transferred to the nectar. While barley malt is not as sweet as maple syrup, it's unusually malty and licky-sticky.

Barley malt is a complex sugar, meaning that it takes quite some time for it to be broken down by the body. Simple sugars, like white sugar or corn syrup, are absorbed immediately, resulting in blood sugar spikes and yo-yo moods. For evidence of this, spend 30 minutes at a children's birthday party. It's pretty mental.

Cutting out convenience food is difficult. How can I cope with cooking all the time?

With great music, the sort that makes your blood pelt around your body and electrifies your fingertips. Nothing is a chore when your favourite tunes massage your neurotransmitters. It's key to cooking.

I also throw lots of suppers and treats into my freezer, ready to plunder on lazy days. Be selfish with your time – conquer many meals in one session, rather than cooking three times a day. With practice, you'll motor through these recipes.

How do I know if I have a food intolerance?

If you've already bought this book, chances are something's not agreeing with you. Find a registered dietician or doctor to do an elimination diet with you. I'm not a huge fan of allergy testing, simply because it didn't bring any relief to me. For best results, become your own food detective (with the encouragement of and direction from a professional).

Why are soya and tofu controversial? I'm confused. Are they the same thing?

Tofu is made from the soya bean. You're probably familiar with other soya bean products, such as soya milk, miso soup, soya sauce and tempeh. Milk is extracted from the soya bean and used to make soya curd, referred to as tofu. It's not unlike cheese making. Made this way, tofu is supposedly replete with isoflavones, a big pal of calcium. Isoflavones have been found to assist in bone density as well as hormonal imbalances. So far, so good.

Once soya's health benefits became clear outside of Japan, consumer demand rocketed. I think its explosive rise here in the West encouraged food companies to find cheaper ways of producing it. Consequently, soya's reputation has been muddied with chemical isolation techniques, synthetic adulteration and genetic modification, all of which raise serious questions about the beneficial effects of the end product. That's why soya is so contro-versial. The chemi-cally altered soya is a whole different creature to the whole-bean soya associated with the Asian diet. Frustrating, isn't it?

The only way you can tell the difference is to read the manufacturer's label on food before you buy. I've been advised to avoid soya protein isolates. Up to 60% of packaged supermarket foods use this syntheti-cally debased soya as a cheap bulking agent. So don't be fooled into thinking soya is synon-ymous with health.

To tap into soya beans' bone fide health benefits, my advice is to stick with organic, non-GM tofu and eat it no more than once a week. Even the Japanese don't eat as much soya as we do. There are also ethical issues to consider. Animal feed is largely composed of soya, which drives demand for soya plantations. We are witnessing the destruction of hundreds of thousands of wildlife acres to satiate demand for soya production. In short, the world has gone bonkers for the stuff. If you can live without it, all the better.

Do you eat Quorn?

Nope, never. Cutting down on meat seems to be a much more sensible approach. Swapping one bad habit for another makes little sense.

Are these recipes suitable for children?

Definitely. Just leave out the salt, black pepper, garlic or tamari – and add these to your own plate. Good nutrition is the best health insurance you can offer your family.

YOUR KITCHEN'S ARTILLERY
****

HERE ARE YOUR NEW ALLIES IN THE KITCHEN, IN ORDER OF IMPORTANCE.

Measuring cups

You'll notice I measure in cups, handfuls and drizzles, which makes it easier to visualise quantities as you read the recipe and write your shopping list. I've always found grams and ounces alienating. It may as well be trigonometry to me. Like most tactile people, I function on a sort of visual mathematics.

Tenacity

Available deep down, often in the same aisle as drive and desperation.

Pestle and mortar

If you don't have a pestle and mortar, find an Asian food store. You'll pick up an excellent deal, save yourself a small fortune and instantly acquire bragging rights in the pub. A pestle and mortar propels you into an underground club of serious cooks. Think Jamie Oliver meets Thomas Keller. No good meal can be made without a bit of muscle action in the kitchen. I guess the bottom of a heavy saucepan would also work, but it might scare the bejaysus out of the neighbours.

Food processor

Mine's a Magimix from my mother-in-law. The lady's got style. I use it every day.

Hand-held or personal blender

Also referred to as a soup gun or whizzy thing, hand-held blenders give a much smoother finish than a food processor (unless you have a swanky Vitamix). Particularly important for hummus (page 114). Pick one up for a tenner.

Heavy-based saucepan or large sauté pan

Heavy-based saucepans spread heat evenly, which helps prevent burning or ingredients 'catching' on the bottom of the pan and driving your patience batty. Le Creuset are the Bentleys of the kitchen. Look out for them during sale season or in discount stores like TK Maxx. The bigger, the better.

Oven thermometer

This is like a lie detector for ovens. Available online on Amazon and in kitchen stores.

Spiraliser

Mine is a Lurch, and it's definitely love. Not essential to your kitchen, it's more of a nerdy toy. Expect one to set you back about €40 or €50.

Tefal 8-in-1 Rice Cooker

To make perfectly fluffy quinoa, measure 2 cups of quinoa to level 2 in the basin. Season with a few turns of the sea salt and peppercorn mill. Press the 'grains' programme. The rice cooker will steam the grain and produce the most perfect quinoa you're ever likely to taste.

For details on how to cook almost every brown rice on the market using this rice cooker, visit my blog at www.susanjanewhite.com.

Empty jam jars

To transport food into work with you.

Ideas for Breakfast

'Keep your face to the sunshine,
and you will never see the shadows.'
Helen Keller

The breakfast roll is dead. Who wants to hoover up
chemically enhanced meat, bleached rolls and puddles
of cholesterol?

We've designed this chapter for anyone who dreads the
shrill of their alarm clock. Some recipes involve a little
forward planning, but will ultimately gift you with more
snoozage and go-go juice (the High-octane Banana Nutmeg
Flapjacks on page 34 last all week in the fridge,
for example).

Only 6 seconds to fuel up? No problem. Stick your hand
in the freezer to loot your store of ready-made goodies
from this book: Lemon and Pistachio Pie (page 224), Office
Bombs (page 62), Your New Wheat-free Bread (page 51), Goji
Berry Smudge (page 207), Strawberry Shortbread (page 231),
Hazelnut and Raisin Freezer Cookies (page 228), Blackberry
Tart (page 235), Black Bread with Sun-dried Tomatoes (page
54), Barley Grass Balls (page 66) or Chia Bonbons (page 64).

I swear you won't miss your breakfast cereal and milk.
In fact, I bet you'll look back on your favourite cereal
packet like a bad ex and wonder what on earth you ever saw
in it. It was a love affair controlled by a sugar rush, and
little else. Good riddance.

THE ONLY GRANOLA RECIPE YOU'LL EVER NEED

****

A bowl of DIY granola and nut milk is a great way to start the day. It takes just 20 minutes to make and the benefits last all week. The beauty of making your own granola is the satisfaction of knowing exactly what went into it - none of the cheap fats, preservatives, sugar or gunk regularly found in commercial ones.

For your inner Mary Poppins, tie a ribbon around a jar of granola and give it as Christmas pressies. Parachute some blue cornflower petals in there too, available online and from Fallon & Byrne in Dublin.

2 cups nuts (pecans, walnuts, Brazil nuts, hazelnuts)
2 1/2 cups jumbo oats
1 cup quinoa flakes
1 cup combination of sunflower and pumpkin seeds
5 tablespoons ground linseeds or ground almonds
1 teaspoon sea salt flakes
3/4 cup raw honey or maple syrup
3/4 cup extra virgin coconut oil
grated zest of 1 orange
2 cups dried fruit (cranberries, dates, raisins, unsulphured apricots)
1 rough cup dried banana, chopped

Makes 20 servings

Preheat the oven to 170°C/150°C fan/340°F. Line 2 baking trays with parchment paper.

Roughly chop any big nuts (pecans are fine left whole). Toss the nuts in a large bowl with the oats, quinoa flakes, seeds, ground linseeds and salt. Feeling adventurous? A tablespoon of cinnamon or dried ginger will add another flavour layer.

Gently warm the honey, oil and orange zest together. Pour over the bowl of oats and coat well. You won't be adding the dried fruit until after baking.

Spread thinly on the baking trays and transfer to the middle shelf of the oven. Bake for 17-20 minutes. Shake the trays after 8 minutes to prevent burning. You're aiming for a light golden colour. Oats and nuts taste bitter if you let them turn brown.

Remove from the oven and allow to cool and solidify completely before tossing through the dried fruit. Store in an airtight container for 2-3 weeks. Great with the Brazil nut milk on page 75 or cultured coconut yoghurt. Makes enough to last all week for a large family.

MANGO, BLACKBERRY AND BUCKWHEAT PORRIDGE

****

This is no ordinary porridge. But then again, this is no ordinary cookbook. Every recipe is designed to feed your battery and have you high-jumping those afternoon slumps.

Despite its name, buckwheat is not related to wheat and it does not contain gluten. That's a high five and a back flip for coeliacs.

1/2 cup buckwheat grain, soaked overnight
squeeze of lemon juice
1 small apple, grated
a bite-sized chunk of coconut cream*
1/2 mango, sliced (or soak some dried mango overnight)
handful of blackberries (optional)
maple or apple syrup, to serve

Serves 1

* You can use coconut milk in place of water, but it works out to be a lot more expensive. Coconut cream comes in a block and you can chip off bits as you need it. Just store it in the fridge.

Soak the buckwheat overnight in water and a squeeze of lemon juice. In the morning, pour off the excess water (and debris), then rinse in a sieve to separate the grains once more. This process breaks down the phytic acid in the cereal and makes it more digestible as well as quicker to cook.

Bring 1 cup of water to the boil. Add the soaked buckwheat, grated apple and the shavings or chunks of coconut cream. Cook for 15–20 minutes at a put-putter rather than a ferocious boil. It will thicken and become creamy with time.

Best adorned with juicy mango slivers, messy blackberries and DIY apple syrup (see page 25). While mangos can be pricey, you can sniff out massive boxes of them in Asian stores every June, July and August for buttons. Soaked dried mango works for the rest of the year.

METRO MUESLI WITH CHIA JAM

****

Rushed for breakfast? Time for muesli-making, darling. Not that fancy expensive stuff you pass wistfully in trendy delis. I mean your very own creations, transported in a snazzy jar with a spoon, appetite and sleepy smile. It makes the M50 actually enjoyable.

Oats don't always have to be eaten as molten-hot porridge. Soaking oat flakes overnight in a liquid (water, milk, apple juice) makes them delectably sweet and more digestible. Prepping this breakfast is an easy habit to acquire, sparing those brain cells first thing in the morning. But don't take my word for it. Try it and see.

Gastroenterologists - the specialists who look after your pipes - recommend getting between 25-35g of dietary fibre every day. A bowl of Metro Muesli with Chia Jam will give you an almighty 22g of fibre before the day even dawns. Add grated apple for an extra 5g or banana for 3g. Want to know the average daily intake in Ireland? A measly 10g. Highly processed diets are devoid of fibre. Given that colon cancer and heart disease are this country's top killers, it's probably time to make friends with a new breakfast regime.

This is just a variation on Bircher muesli. Stir all the ingredients together except the cinnamon. Use whatever ingredients to hand that you feel really work for you - a tablespoon of buckwheat? Blueberries? Grated apple? Cacao nibs? Banana? Hazelnuts? The following morning, scoop into a jar and crown with cinnamon before you dash out the door. Don't forget a spoon.

If you have the time, try making some chia jam. It's a quirky variation to the sugar-laden stuff. Soak the listed ingredients for 30 minutes or overnight. Store in a jam jar for up to 3 days. Ta-da!

For the muesli:
2/3 cup jumbo oats
1/3 cup raisins
1 cup water, apple juice,
  soya or nut milk
2 tablespoons linseeds
squeeze of lemon juice
sprinkle of pumpkin seeds
sprinkle of sunflower seeds
sprinkle of ground cinnamon

Serves 1

For the chia jam:
1/2 cup apple juice
dash of lime juice
2 tablespoons chia
1 tablespoon raw honey
1 tablespoon acai or
  beetroot powder

Makes 6-8 servings

DECENT MILLET PORRIDGE AND APPLE SYRUP

****

Millet is not a fabulously tasty grain. My nostrils balked and my palate winced the first time I made porridge with it. But by teaming millet with strong flavours, you'll bring out this grain's best quality - its texture.

Millet's nutritional kudos and affordability are good enough reasons to introduce it to your breakfast table. Sprinkle with coconut blossom sugar for the food nerd in you, but living in Ireland means I'm able to get my hands on Highbank Orchard Syrup. This is our answer to maple syrup, made from 100% local organic apples and love.

Cook the millet and water on a medium heat for 3-5 minutes before adding the creamed corn and salt. That's it!

To make your own apple syrup, press the apples and boil the juice for 25 minutes until it resembles a viscous syrup. Store in an airtight jar and summon when required. Ideally, you'll need to use fresh apple syrup within 4-5 days.

This delicious sticky nectar is rich in potassium, the mineral that helps evacuate hangovers.

For the porridge:
1/3 cup millet flakes
2/3 cup water
1/3 cup puréed sweetcorn
pinch of salt flakes

Serves 1

For the apple syrup:
12 apples

Makes 6-8 servings

DOUBLE DECKER AMARANTH AND BANANA PUD

****

Amaranth is another one of those supergrains that have the Hollywood glitterati genuflecting. It has serious nutritional gravitas, rivalling quinoa as the number one seed. Amaranth's got more muscle than wheat, clocking in four times the amount of calcium and twice as much iron. And with generous stores of lysine, you can kiss cold sores toodle-loo. Not bad for half a cent per gram.

A caveat for the cook: bananas used in this recipe need to be over-ripe. Any green areas on the banana skin means they have not ripened fully and will make the pudding bitter. Look for older bananas with blackened sweet spots.

Please don't try this recipe with coconut milk or almond milk. Something offensive happens.

1 cup amaranth grain
1 1/2 cups water
1/4 teaspoon sea salt
3 tablespoons maple syrup
3 tablespoons tahini or
  almond butter
2 large eggs, beaten
500ml soya, hemp or oat milk
2 very ripe bananas, chopped
1/2 cup raisins
1 teaspoon vanilla extract
1 tablespoon rapadura or
  coconut sugar
1 tablespoon ground cinnamon

Serves 6-8

Preheat the oven to 160°C/140°C fan/325°F.

In a small saucepan with a tight-fitting lid, bring the amaranth, water and salt to a soft boil. This means a gentle putter rather than a violent bubble that will blow the lid off and scare the bejaysus out of your budgie. Cook for 15 minutes, until the water is fully absorbed. Amaranth is not a dry, fluffy grain when cooked. Expect something that looks like a gluey couscous.

While the amaranth is doing its thing, prep the rest of the gear. Blend the maple syrup and nut butter together until smooth, then add the eggs. Pour this mixture into the milk and add the chopped bananas, raisins and vanilla.

Remove the amaranth from the heat, stir briskly and add in the milky mixture. Give it all a gentle stir.

Pour and scrape the pudding mix into a medium-sized pie dish (about the size of a magazine page). You're aiming for a pudding at least 1 inch deep, but no more than 2 inches. Pyrex rectangular glass dishes give the best result for custardy puds like this one. Cook for 40 minutes in a conventional oven. It should wobble slightly in the centre when removed. Halfway through cooking, mix the rapadura sugar and cinnamon together and sprinkle it on top.

CHIA AND CHAI BREAKFAST PUDDING

****

I make this for my little monsters and their mighty appetites. While chai tea is not essential, I recommend using it through the wintry months. Sweet chai contains cardamom, cinnamon, ginger, anise, fennel and cloves - all of which are warming spices for your belly.

Using a fork, whisk together the chia seeds, milk and coconut oil. Tear open the sweet chai teabag and stir it through. Allow the chia pudding to set overnight, either in the fridge or on the countertop. Serve in the morning with layers of banana and blueberries. A sneaky drizzle of brown rice syrup is awfully good too.

3/4 cup chia seeds
2 cups almond (or other) milk
1 tablespoon melted coconut oil
1 teabag sweet chai (or cinnamon)
1 banana, sliced
handful of blueberries
drizzle of brown rice syrup (optional)

Serves 3

BADASS BREAKFAST BARS

****

These fibre-rich breakfast bars are sure to have your arteries applauding. No butter, cream, sugar or stodgy white flour — just pure, unadulterated whole foods the way Mother N intended.

The attraction of low-glycemic food like oats is that it breaks down slowly, releasing a steady stream of energy into the body. Picture drip-feeding your diesel tank so that it never runs empty. This makes oats an excellent diabetic food, but also gold for athletes, weight watchers, hyper children and anxious cabinet ministers.

More geek speak? Oats' cargo of soluble and insoluble fibre has the nifty ability of servicing our pipes in more ways than one. There ain't nothing sexy about constipation, especially given that our skin often takes over as an excretory organ. Yes, oats will make you regular, but they'll also sat nav your pipes for cholesterol and escort it out of your body like a bad-tempered bodyguard.

It's important to note that oats need to be cooked or soaked in order to tap into their nutritional benefits. Muesli straight out of a bag with milk does not count.

4 1/2 cups combination of
  dried apricots, prunes and
  pitted dates
juice of 1 lime
4 tablespoons pumpkin seeds
  (optional)
5 cups oat flakes*
1 cup ground almonds
1 cup rye* flour
1/2 cup ground chia or
  ground flaxseeds
1 teaspoon unrefined organic
  salt
1 cup freshly squeezed
  orange juice
1 cup extra virgin coconut
  oil
5 tablespoons barley malt
  extract, maple syrup or
  brown rice syrup*

Makes 20-25 bars

Preheat the oven to 180°C/160°C fan/350°F. Line a 20cm square baking tin (or something similar) with greaseproof baking parchment.

Place your apricots, prunes and dates in a saucepan and pour in enough water to come just below the level of the fruit. Bring to the boil, then lower the heat and simmer for 15-20 minutes with the lid on. If steam escapes, add a touch more water. Once cooked, stir through the lime juice and mix until the fruits are almost smooth. Set aside.

While the fruits are doing their thing, briefly pulse the pumpkin seeds in a blender or a coffee grinder. You can chop them up with a sharp knife if you prefer less washing up, or buy them pre-milled.

* For the gluten-sensitive brigade, I find using brown rice flour, maple syrup and gluten-free oats works well.

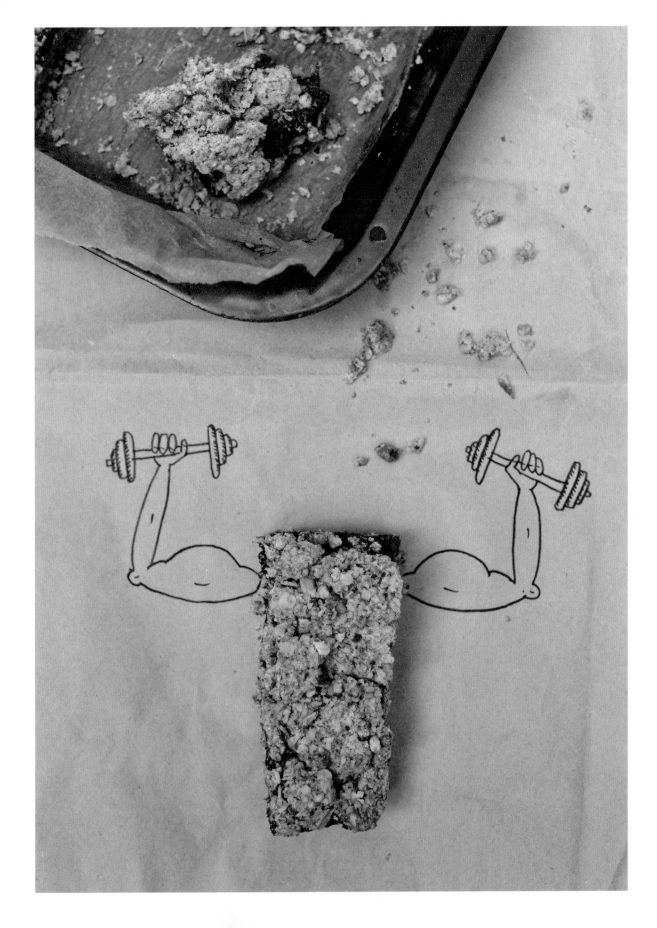

In a mixing bowl (and wearing a deliciously
frilly apron), mix together the pumpkin seeds,
oats, ground almonds, rye flour, chia/flaxseeds and
salt. If your oats are big, pulse them in a food
processor first with the pumpkin seeds. Finer oat
flakes give better results, but be careful not to
pulse into an oatmeal or flour.

In a separate bowl, mix the orange juice, oil
and sweetener and pour into the dry ingredients,
stirring until everything is glistening.

Using dampened fingers, press two-thirds of the
oat mix into the lined tin. It's really gooey and
sticky, so ramp up the radio to take the edge off
impatient fingers. Spread the jammy apricot mix
over this base. Gently press the remaining oat
mix on top of the apricot mix. You'll need to
do this with your fingers again. Take a curtsy -
only if you're wearing a frilly apron, otherwise
you'll look a bit silly - and admire your
brilliance.

Place on the centre shelf of the oven and bake
for 40 minutes, until lightly golden but not
browned. Allow to cool before slicing into
squares. Store on top of kitchen paper inside
an airtight tin or in the fridge. The smell of
these Badass Breakfast Bars will draw children
away from their Nintendo like the Pied Piper
- straight into an apron. Who knows, maybe
you'll have the next MasterChef hatching in your
kitchen?

These keep well in the fridge for up to 10 days.
In other words, a lot of happy breakfasts.

HIGH-OCTANE BANANA NUTMEG FLAPJACKS

****

Commercial breakfast bars are full of sugar, cheap hydrogenated fat and salt - none of which your brain cells will appreciate. With increasing financial pressure on producers to lower their production costs, it's hard to trust anything with a wrapper and a marketing department nowadays. These homemade breakfast bars are more like supersonic flapjacks and store really well in the fridge for 2 weeks.

Don't be put off by coconut oil's saturated fat content. These fats are in the form of medium chain triglycerides. MCTs readily convert to energy, in contrast to longer chain triglycerides such as sunflower oil. This is done through our cells' mitochondria - the gateway to our body's fuel. No wonder sporting stars choose this oil over any other. What a shame no one told Lance Armstrong.

1 cup Medjool dates or pre-soaked regular dates
2 cups oats
1 cup ground almonds
3/4 cup broken banana chips (not dried banana)
1/2 cup chopped pecans
1/2 cup raisins
handful of sunflower seeds
1-2 teaspoons grated nutmeg
1 teaspoon Maldon sea salt flakes
3/4 cup extra virgin coconut oil
1/2 cup honey, brown rice syrup or barley malt extract

Makes 20 flapjacks

Preheat the oven to 170°C/150°C fan/340°F. Line a tin no bigger than a magazine page with parchment paper.

Chop the dates and combine with the remaining dry ingredients in a large bowl. Merrily mix.

In a saucepan, gently melt the coconut oil with your choice of natural sweetener for around 5 minutes, until nicely melded. Strangely, maple syrup does not work in this recipe.

Create a hole in the centre of your dry ingredients and add the deliciously syrupy coconut oil. Energetically mix, preferably with sashaying hips and a bit of Bell X1. This helps every last bit of your gooey mix to glisten. Pour into the prepared tin and press down firmly with your fingers. Licking of utensils and bowl most definitely encouraged. Lightens the washing up.

Bake for 35 minutes, until lightly golden - any darker in colour and the oats will turn bitter. Remove from the oven and allow to rest for 10 minutes before refrigerating them. Resist cutting until they have chilled. Otherwise you will be left with a frustratingly messy affair, which no amount of Bell X1 can remedy.

MAPLE AND CARDAMOM PEACHES

****

Peaches are bursting with vitamins that keep our bodies jolly. Niacin in particular helps improve circulation to the brain - something most of us would appreciate on a Sunday morning.

And you know the disappointing, fluffy peaches you sink your teeth into? Those infuriating peach imposters? No need to hurl them in the bin. Collect yourself, and scald the living daylights out of them instead. A peach's sweetness will sing once heated. Such delicious reprisal.

If you're using fresh ginger in place of dried ginger, try peeling a thumb-sized piece and freezing until firm. This makes it super easy to grate and ensures the ginger's stringy fibres don't corrupt your brekkie. Grated frozen ginger gives any dish a heart-thumping ping - my number one tip for boring lentils and despondent salads.

4 massive peaches
2 tablespoons maple syrup
1/2 teaspoon ground cardamom
1 teaspoon fresh or dried
  ginger
cultured soya or coconut
  yoghurt, to serve
squeeze of lemon juice, to
  serve

Serves 4-8

Preheat your grill or barbecue. It's wise to clean any residue from yesterday's messy chicken wings - not a good companion to today's breakfast.

Cut the peaches in half and remove the stone. This is noticeably easier with ripe peaches, as under-ripe peaches refuse to let loose their centre stone. Then, using a lunchbox and lid, mix the maple syrup and spices together. Pop the peach halves inside and shake the box to coat the fruit.

Place the gooey, coated peaches under a grill or over the barbecue flames and cook for a few minutes on each side, depending on how hot it is. You'll be the judge of that. Remove each one gently, as they are decidedly delicate now. Tuck in with yoghurt and lemon juice. Chill for up to 3 days in the fridge.

6AM TODDLER COOKIES

****

Ever up at 6am with your teeny tots? These cookies will keep them quietly active while nourishing their little motors. There's hardly any mess - notice there's no flour or eggs.

Preheat the oven to 180°C/160°C fan/350°F. Line a baking tray with greaseproof paper.

Grate the apple into a large mixing bowl. If you're crafty enough to do this without getting your knuckles involved, high five your toddler. Toss through the remaining ingredients, coating everything really well with the mashed banana. Make approximately 16 cookies by taking a table-spoon of the dough and flattening it between your hands, just like Play-Doh. A bit of *Blue Peter* may be required.

Place on the lined baking tray and bake for 12 minutes, or a little longer if the cookies are a bit bigger. No need to cool on a wire wrack - let them find your breakfast table immediately. Minor caveat - scoff them all on the same day, as they tend to misbehave after 24 hours.

1 medium apple
1 cup porridge oats (not
  jumbo)
1/2 cup sultanas or raisins
1/2 cup mashed banana
2 teaspoons baking powder
1 teaspoon ground cinnamon

Makes 16 cookies

STICKY CINNAMON AND PRUNE CAKES

****

Unless you were born before 1945, a prune cupcake sounds as appealing as a jug of turnip juice. But balk not. My friend the prune has more antioxidants than a blueberry. Prunes are a lot cheaper too. Add to this the nutritional superpowers of flaxseeds, apples, bananas, pecans, olive oil, carrots, cinnamon and rye, and you've got yourself a love bomb. Just what your body needs to survive a morning in the office.

8 squishy prunes, destoned
  and chopped
1 medium banana, mashed
1/4 cup pecans
6 tablespoons freshly
  pressed apple juice
4 tablespoons raw agave,
  barley malt extract, maple
  or yacón syrup
2 tablespoons milled
  flaxseeds (linseeds)
2 tablespoons extra virgin
  olive oil
1 cup loosely packed grated
  carrots
1 1/4 cups rye flour
2 teaspoons baking powder
1 teaspoon ground cinnamon

Makes 9-12 muffins

Preheat the oven to 180°C/160°C fan/350°F. Line a muffin tray with 9-12 paper cases.

In a large bowl, mix the prunes, banana, pecans, apple juice, sweetener, flaxseeds and oil together. Stir through the grated carrots and set aside.

In a separate bowl, introduce the rye flour to the baking powder and cinnamon. Make sure the baking powder doesn't stick in one place. Make a well in the centre of the flour and scoop the wet prune mixture into it. Mix thoroughly. I always find singing loudly helps. Spoon into your prepared muffin tray, but don't fill the cases too high or they won't cook in the centre.

Bake for 30-35 minutes (or half that time if using a smaller fairy cake tray). Remove from the oven and watch hungry nostrils dance. These muffins benefit from cooling down for 20 minutes to solidify and rest. Very difficult to resist looting, so remove self from kitchen and find distraction elsewhere.

SCRAMBLED TOFU WITH CARAMELISED ONION AND SHIITAKE MUSHROOMS

****

This is vegan speak for a full fry. Good for lazy evenings and sedate brain cells. Just make sure your tofu is biodynamic and organic to avoid the dodgy mechanical isolation techniques many processors use. (For more on this, see pages 13-14).

Shiitake mushrooms are good for the immune system, according to Dale Pinnock, aka The Medicinal Chef. Their polysaccharides play funny games with our frontline defences, resulting in some serious moves against invading pathogens. The herb turmeric has been implicated in the reduction of tumours, amyloid plaque in Alzheimer's and many other inflammatory conditions, such as arthritis, so we've stuck a good tablespoon in for you. There's raw garlic too, vaunted for its healing powers. Think Pac-Man in your bloodstream. In other words, this is a good dish to have up your sleeve alongside your emergency Kleenex.

1 onion
about 8 shiitake (or other) mushrooms
2 tablespoons extra virgin olive or coconut oil
about 8 cherry tomatoes
splash of tamari, plus extra to serve
1 x 300g block firm biodynamic tofu (we use Demeter)
1 garlic clove, crushed
1 tablespoon ground turmeric
2 teaspoons ground cumin
1 teaspoon nutritional yeast flakes or a pinch of salt
cayenne pepper, to serve

Serves 3

Slice or dice the onion and shiitakes, depending how you like to eat them. In a warm frying pan, add the oil, onion, mushrooms and cherry tomatoes and cook for 10 minutes, until the onions turn glassy and translucent. If your frying pan looks overcrowded, watch out. Steam won't escape and will waterlog your breakfast instead of caramelising it. I like to roast or grill my tomatoes with a lick of balsamic vinegar and olive oil and add them to the mushrooms before plating up. While I find this method best, it does add to the washing up.

Once the onions and mushrooms are cooked, add a splash of tamari and stir briskly as the pan sizzles. This will dress the mushrooms in some finger-licking umami. Add the block of firm tofu and crumble it under a wooden spatula. Let the garlic, turmeric, cumin and yeast flakes join the party, digging any white pieces of tofu into the bright yellow turmeric glaze. As soon as it's warmed through, serve with cayenne pepper, tamari soya sauce and some cracking company.

BAKED SWEET POTATOES

****

Ambrosial, warm and comforting - everything a breakfast should be on a chilly morning. Sweet potatoes are superheroes of the soil. Expect to ramp up your frontline defences after breakfasting on these. You'll find lots of beta carotene, zinc, vitamin E and vitamin C within its amber flesh. These are the nutrients responsible for fancy immune ripostes. Think Catherine Zeta-Jones and Zorro. The sniffles won't stand a chance.

2 medium sweet potatoes
a little time

Serves 1-2

Throw the potatoes into the oven, whole and in their skins. Bake at 200°C/180°C fan/400°F for 60-90 minutes, depending on their size. There's no need to pierce or slit the potato skins. Sweet potatoes will steam beautifully in their own jackets if you leave them alone. Remove when very soft to touch. Sweet potatoes benefit from overcooking rather than undercooking.

GREEN EGGS

****

Matcha is the Rolls Royce of green teas. The whole tea leaf is ground into a powder, as opposed to diluted in a teabag. This might help explain why matcha has significantly more antioxidants and pomposity than regular green tea. This neon green powder also houses a gob-smacking amount of protective catechins. Health scientists get indecently excited about these compounds. Be careful not to fall for all the hype of 137 antioxidants per sip, bottomless libido and eternal life. But it does make scrambled eggs more interesting.

Green eggs take 3 minutes from start to finish. Double up to serve a friend.

Gently warm the coconut oil in a heavy-based pan on a medium heat, making sure the oil doesn't reach smoke point. Butter and cream are supposedly the best allies to making the perfect scrambled eggs, but something very special happens when they cavort with coconut oil instead. You're about to find out.

Break the eggs into a bowl and whisk briefly with a fork. Add them to the heated pan and let them cook halfway through before stirring them. I like my eggs luscious and floppy, so I take them off now and plate up. El Hubador prefers his fluffy and seriously scrambled, so I leave his on for a further 10 seconds and stir with a vigour usually reserved for rowing a sinking boat. Stir through the chives or chervil and season once cooked. Whatever way you like yours, just remember not to add the matcha powder until the scrambled eggs are served up. Use a sieve to sprinkle the green powder over them like angel dust.

2 teaspoons extra virgin coconut oil
3 eggs
2 teaspoons chopped chives or chervil
generous pinch of salt and crushed black peppercorns
1/4 teaspoon matcha green tea powder

Serves 1

MISO EGGS AND SOYA SAUCE

****

4 teaspoons extra virgin
  coconut oil
5 eggs
2 teaspoons live,
  unpasteurised miso
splash of tamari

Serves 2

Gently warm the coconut oil in a heavy-based pan on a medium heat, making sure the oil doesn't reach smoke point. Butter and cream are supposedly the best allies to making the perfect scrambled eggs, but something very special happens when eggs fraternise with coconut oil.

Break the eggs into a bowl and whisk briefly with the miso. Add to the heated pan and let the eggs cook halfway through before stirring them. I prefer mine soft and floppy, so I fold the eggs over like an omelette and plate up. If you prefer them cooked for longer, stir briskly until the eggs look fluffy. This usually makes the miso silky smooth as opposed to lumpy.

Whatever way you like yours, just remember not to add the tamari until the scrambled eggs are served up. Otherwise you'll end up with murky-looking eggs, which don't go well with hangovers.

IDEAS FOR BREAKFAST

MILLET AND CHESTNUT CRÊPES WITH PASSIONFRUIT SYRUP

****

This recipe is borrowed from Béatrice Peltre's award-winning blog, La Tartine Gourmande. Turns out Bea married my mother-in-law's cousin's son. That makes me practically French. Three times removed, of course, but what's a number, right?

Combine the flour, sugar and salt in a large bowl. The sugar is an important addition, so please do leave it in the recipe. Break the eggs into the centre of the flour and slowly whisk while pouring in the milk. Continue to whisk until the batter is silky. Stir in the coconut oil and vanilla. Cover with a plate and place in the fridge to rest for 1 hour, or overnight.

When ready to use, stir again. In a crêpe pan or frying pan, melt a little more coconut oil. Swirl to coat. Add enough batter to barely coat the bottom. You may have to shake the pan a little. Cook for 1-2 minutes on a medium to high heat. Once it starts bubbling and the batter looks cooked through, flip the crêpe and cook for 1 extra minute on the other side. Repeat until you run out of batter, adding a little coconut oil between each crêpe. Keep the crêpes warm on a plate as you work, covering them with a towel.

To make the syrup, just combine the pulp of the passionfruit with your choice of sweetener and drizzle over your creations. Homemade apple syrup is like a flavour grenade, so try to give the recipe on page 25 a go.

1/2 cup millet flour
1/4 cup chestnut flour
2 tablespoons cornflour
2 tablespoons rapadura or coconut sugar
pinch of sea salt
2 eggs
1 cup hemp, oat or almond milk
1 tablespoon extra virgin coconut oil, melted, plus extra to cook
1 teaspoon pure vanilla extract
2 passionfruit
2 tablespoons raw honey, apple or date syrup

Makes 10 crêpes

SMOKED SALMON BLINI WITH HEALTHIER HOLLANDAISE

****

If you could do one thing to improve your health this year, swap your nasty margarine and commercial salad dressing for this incredibly sumptuous mayonnaise. When made with warm coconut oil, it rivals the most heavenly hollandaise to ever kiss a blini.

For the 'hollandaise':
2 egg yolks
1/4 cup flaxseed oil or
  Udo's Oil
1/4 cup extra virgin coconut
  oil, melted
2 big garlic cloves, crushed
1-2 tablespoons
  unpasteurised cider
  vinegar
1/2 cup extra virgin olive
  oil
6-8 anchovies, roughly
  chopped

For the buckwheat blini:
1 cup buckwheat flour
1 teaspoon baking powder
salt and freshly ground
  black pepper
1 egg
2/3 cup almond, hemp or oat
  milk
extra virgin coconut oil,
  to fry
8-10 slices of smoked salmon

Makes 8-10 big blinis

To make the 'hollandaise', run the motor of your food processor with the egg yolks. Keeping the motor on low, gradually add a steady stream of flaxseed oil and watch it thicken ever so gradually. Add it drop by drop - don't rush or you will end up curdling it, as I have done through impatience and overexcitement many a time. This can take up to 4 minutes. Repeat with the coconut oil. When it gets very thick, it's time to add the crushed garlic and cider vinegar to thin it out and give it an edge. Keep the motor running.

Next, slowly add the olive oil, watching the mayo thicken again. Always add the olive oil after the coconut oil and not the other way around. Olive oil can turn bitter if overly whisked.

Finally, add the anchovies and pulse briefly - you don't want to pulverise the anchovies. Taste and adjust the sharpness of the cider vinegar to your preference. If it's too sharp, turn on the motor again and add a little more olive oil.

Scoop into a screw-top jar and refrigerate for up to 3 weeks. A jar is approximately 12 portions.

To make the blini, sieve the flour, baking powder and a generous amount of seasoning into a bowl. In a separate cup, beat the egg with the milk and gradually pour into the dry ingredients, whisking all the while to prevent lumps. The batter lasts for 2 days in the fridge, so advance preparation is easy.

Heat some extra virgin coconut oil in a large non-stick frying pan on a medium to high heat. Drop enough of the blini batter to form a drop scone and fry for 20-30 seconds, until set.

Several can be done at once. Flip to cook the
other side. The mixture is usually runny on one
side, so flip with haste. Try not to leave them
cooking too long or they will dry out. Taste the
first one when cooled and decide for yourself. Hot
blini will always taste moist, but they quickly
lose their juiciness upon cooling. Bear this in
mind too.

Repeat until there is no batter left. Dollop with
the hollandaise and a blanket of smoked salmon.
Pretty special stuff.

YOUR NEW WHEAT-FREE BREAD

****

Few pleasures in life can compete with tearing open a hot focaccia. I'm not suggesting you quarantine or banish such pleasures. On the contrary, let's celebrate these delights for what they are and enjoy them from time to time.

For a wholegrain and nourishing alternative, I recommend inaugurating this recipe to your life. And your freezer. It tastes like Irish brown bread, but without the bloating often associated with wheat.

Preheat the oven to 200°C/180°C fan/400°F. Line a shallow tin just smaller than a magazine page with greaseproof paper. We're going to bake this in a tray rather than a loaf tin, so when it's cooked, we'll cut it into squares. Each square can be used for a sambo, sliced horizontally like a bap.

Sieve the flours, baking powder, seasoning and spices into a large bowl to introduce air and make it fluffy. Try not to omit the spices, as they are central to this bread. Add the milk, millet flakes, sunflower seeds, whole buckwheat grains and honey (if using). It should be a pouring consistency and be quite runny. Pour the batter into the lined tin.

Bake for 35-40 minutes, depending on the depth of the tray you are using. Remove from the oven, allow to cool on a wire rack and divide into quarters. Looks really slick. Once you taste this buckwheat bread, you'll never want to buy bread again. Freeze in quarters, ready to split horizontally and toast every morning.

1/2 cup buckwheat flour
1/2 cup organic soya flour
2 teaspoons baking powder
1 teaspoon Herbamare seasoning, celery salt or sea salt
1 teaspoon ground ginger
1 teaspoon ground cinnamon
2 cups almond milk, oat milk or hemp milk
3/4 cup millet or barley flakes
3/4 cup sunflower seeds
1/2 cup whole buckwheat grains
1-2 tablespoons honey, barley malt or maple syrup (optional)

Makes 1 loaf

RYE BANANA BREAD WITH HOMEMADE NUTELLA

****

Rye is rich in B vitamins, the chaps that act as spark plugs for energy ignition. This grain is also thought to have a higher concentration of cancer-protective lignans than any other cereal crop. Even more interesting, rye is the grain of choice for body-builders because of its specific amino acid profile, which seems to fancy muscle mass. But don't worry – you won't end up looking like a Transformer by nibbling away on this banana bread. You've got to lift insatiable amounts of weights to do that.

If you're looking for a totally gluten-free or grain-free recipe, just swap the rye flour with more coconut flour. It will be a little drier, but still crazy delicious. Barley malt syrup also works well, but honey doesn't for some strange reason.

However tempted you may be, please don't add walnuts or pecans. Nuts dry out the mixture.

For the bread:
1/4 cup coconut flour
1/4 cup rye flour
handful of dried dates
2 teaspoons ground cinnamon
1 teaspoon baking powder
1/2 teaspoon Maldon sea salt
  flakes
3 eggs, beaten
1 cup roughly mashed bananas
  (about 3 bananas)
5 tablespoons melted coconut
  oil
2-3 tablespoons yacón, maple
  or date syrup
2 teaspoons apple cider
  vinegar
1 teaspoon vanilla extract

For the homemade Nutella:
1/3 cup hazelnut butter
  (about half a small jar)
3 tablespoons cacao or cocoa
  powder
2 tablespoons maple or brown
  rice syrup

Makes 1 loaf

Preheat the oven to 180°C/160°C fan/350°F. You'll need a small to medium bread tin, lined and ready.

To make the Nutella, whip the ingredients together in a cup using a fork.

For the banana bread, get two large bowls. In the first one, stir the flours, dates, cinnamon, baking powder and salt together. In the second bowl, add the remaining ingredients and blend well.

Using a balloon whisk, beat the wet mix into the dry mix and transfer to your loaf tin. If you have banana left over, a few thin slices on top give it the Martha Stewart treatment. They also turn sweet and squishy in the oven.

Bake for 40 minutes. Cool on a wire rack and smother with Nutella or reverence.

BLACK BREAD WITH SUN-DRIED TOMATOES

****

Omega-3 oils are to hormones what Edward is to Jedward: indispensable. Our bodies cannot make omega-3, so we need to regularly include it in our diet. As always, food sources are preferable to supplements. You'll find a decent supply of omega-3 fatty acids in this bread. Flaxseeds are also said to be one of nature's highest sources of cancer-protective plant lignans. These groovy compounds are linked to happy hormones, lower blood cholesterol and boisterous antioxidant behaviour. Quite the hat trick for a tiny seed.

If you know someone who is gluten intolerant or coeliac, please jot this recipe down and gift it to them. It contains no flour or grains, making it perfect for paleo disciples too. But you don't have to be a paleo geek to appreciate this bread - it's incredibly good for you and seriously tasty.

I prefer to use blackstrap molasses instead of honey for three reasons. First, it gives the best baking results. Second, it's super rich in iron and B vitamins for energy. And third, it's much cheaper.

2 cups milled flaxseeds
 (linseeds)
3 teaspoons dried oregano
2 teaspoons baking powder
4 eggs
1/2 cup hemp or almond milk
4 tablespoons extra virgin
 olive or macadamia oil
2 tablespoons blackstrap
 molasses or honey, warmed
 until runny
10-12 small sun-dried or
 sun-blushed tomatoes
handful of black olives,
 stones removed

Makes 1 loaf

Preheat the oven to 180°C/160°C fan/350°F. Lightly oil or line a small baking tray that's a few inches smaller in height than an A4 page. Brownie tins are perfect.

Combine the ground flax, oregano and baking powder together in a large bowl. Set aside.

In a separate bowl, mix the eggs, milk, oil and molasses until thoroughly united.

Chop up the sun-dried tomatoes and olives and add them to the wet ingredients. Now add wet to dry and immediately pour into your greased baking tray. Spread evenly and sprinkle a little more dried oregano on top.

Bake for about 25 minutes, then remove from the oven and its tin. Allow to cool for 25 minutes on a wire rack. Tickle with black olive tapenade, some super-garlicky hummus or serve alongside your favourite bowl of soup. This bread freezes exceptionally well, ready to grill when there's nothing in the cupboard.

See photo of Black Bread on page 96.

IDEAS FOR BREAKFAST

MULTISEED BREAD WITH CARAWAY SPICE

****

Trying to cut down on butter and baguettes? Difficult, isn't it? Now's a good time to create fresh associations with the food you eat in order to break the unhealthy ones.

David A. Kessler has written a gripping book about how junk food hijacks our brain chemistry and controls our behaviour. Reading even one chapter of Kessler's The End of Overeating feels so liberating and empowering. Kessler cautions us that certain cues activate brain circuits that guide behaviour. Instead of attacking the behaviour (overeating, smoking, reaching for more butter, insert vice here), recognise the cue.

For example, can you watch TV without reaching for a snack? Or have a coffee without smoking a cigarette? In other words, it's the cue that needs reformulating if we are to successfully ditch the junk in our diets. It's not enough to put a fatwa on the food. We need to acknowledge the prompts. So what are your cues?

Kessler's advice is to create fresh associations in an attempt to retrain our behaviour and palate. I recommend putting caraway and aniseed into your bread. Such a simple change will help keep your mitts off that errant butter dish. Caraway and aniseed are so much tastier when paired with olive oil. Your taste buds will breakdance.

Start by lightly toasting the pumpkin and sunflower seeds on a baking tray in the oven for 12 minutes at 180°C/350°F with no oil. Leave to cool. I recommend toasting more than you need, as hot, crunchy seeds are often looted in my house.

Once cooled, transfer the toasted seeds and linseeds into a large mixing bowl with the sugar, warm water and yeast. Let these guys laze for 10 minutes before adding the remaining ingredients. Mix into a firm dough and leave for another 10 minutes.

Now briefly and lightly knead the dough. Leave in the bowl, covered with a clean cloth, for 1 hour in a warm spot. Transfer to a suitable loaf tin lined with non-stick parchment. You'll need to squish in the sides a little. Leave to rise for another hour. This will depend on the type of yeast you have used, so as soon as it looks about 20% bigger, you're in business.

Bake for 45 minutes at 200°C/180°C fan/400°F. Remove from the oven and from its tin and cool on a wire rack. Best sliced thinly.

You'll love this multiseed bread. It tastes incredible warm from the oven, but you can gently toast some slices the next day to achieve similar results. For a funky change, add a teaspoon of ground fenugreek, aniseed and fennel seeds.

3/4 cup pumpkin seeds
3/4 cup sunflower seeds
3/4 cup linseeds
1/4 cup rapadura or coconut
  sugar
300ml warm water
2 teaspoons fast-action
  organic yeast
3 cups (400g) rye flour
2 tablespoons extra virgin
  olive or macadamia oil
1 tablespoon caraway seeds
1 teaspoon sea salt flakes

Makes 1 loaf

Snacks and Other Nutritional Hits

'Health is beauty. If someone takes care of themselves,
you can see the health shining from within them.'
Anna Friel, actress

The definition of madness is doing the same thing over and over again but expecting different results. If your body isn't functioning as well as you'd like it to, take a look at what you're putting into it. Eating foods that promote good health will have you on your tippy toes. Eating foods that promote poor health will have you on your knees. It's as simple as that.

Many of these snacks can be stored in the freezer, lined up like soldiers for when the munchies attack. This is an important feature of a clean diet. If you don't have back-up, you're sure to fall under enemy fire.

Of course, there will be occasions when we fraternise with the enemy (insert vice here). No matter. Move on and baptise a few of these recipes to get you back on track. Today is the first day of the rest of your life.

HOT AND SMOKY SEEDS

++++++++++++++++++++++++++++

Touche Éclat and espressos must be keeping our economy afloat. Over half of us reportedly suffer from some sort of sleep disorder. So when it comes to nodding off, what are the smarter options? If self-hypnosis and camomile tea never worked for you, take a close look at your diet and see if you are getting enough B vitamins (especially B6), zinc and the amino acid L-tryptophan.

Foods rich in tryptophan can be an effective sleep aid without having to subscribe to dodgy narcotics. Tryptophan is the building block for an important snoozy hormone called melatonin. Without it, our eyes will struggle to shut.

Here's the good news. You'll find tryptophan, B vitamins and zinc in pumpkin seeds. As a result, scientists have begun to put pumpkin seed extract in multivitamin pills and sleeping aids. Bear in mind that it's easier and cheaper to keep a stash of pumpkin seeds in your fridge. But don't expect to fall straight to sleep if you eat them. Think of pumpkin seeds as couriers, delivering the cargo your body needs later tonight.

roughly 1 1/2 cups
  combination of pumpkin and
  sunflower seeds
2 tablespoons tamari
1 tablespoon mirin
  (optional)
1 teaspoon dried chilli
  flakes
1 tablespoon dried nori
  flakes (optional calcium
  boost)

Makes 1 1/2 cups

Preheat the oven to 180°C/160°C fan/350°F.

Toss the sunflower and pumpkin seeds on a baking tray and roast for 8–10 minutes. Now it's time to add the tamari, mirin and chilli flakes. Coat well, using a wooden spatula to stir the seeds about so as not to scrape your tray. Return to the oven for an extra 1–2 minutes of toasting.

Remove from the oven to cool and stir through the nori flakes (if using). Shards of Crispy Kale (page 63) also work. Once cooled, the seeds become crunchy again. Refrigerate in a screw-top jar and sprinkle over salads and soups or keep a stash in your pocket. They can last for up to 6 weeks.

OFFICE BOMBS

+++++++++++++++

Office Bombs love lunchboxes, gym bunnies and little mitts. They take just minutes to prepare, but the benefits last all day. These snacks were designed to drip feed your battery consistently instead of one big sugar surge. Perfect fodder to help high jump that 3 o'clock afternoon trap.

If you can't find the large packets of milled sunflower and pumpkin seeds, just whizz enough of both seeds until they resemble fine breadcrumbs.

2 raspberry leaf teabags, opened
2 cups combination of milled pumpkin and sunflower seeds
1 cup raisins, chopped
1/2 cup ground almonds (or more ground seeds)
1/2 cup tahini
1/2 cup maple syrup, honey or brown rice syrup
1/4 cup raw cacao nibs
5 tablespoons carob powder
pinch of good-quality salt, like pink Himalayan
desiccated coconut, to coat

Makes 30

Blitz everything except the desiccated coconut in your food processor just long enough for the mixture to start clumping together. You may need to scrape down the sides as you go along. Alternatively, with the assistance of some tunes or tenacity, beat the ingredients together with a simple metal fork.

Roll the dough between your palms into golf ball-sized treats. Drop them into a bowl of desiccated coconut to turn them into Office Bombs. They'll keep for 3 weeks in the fridge, 3 months in the freezer or 3 seconds in your hands.

CRISPY KALE

++++++++++++++

I experimented with 19 batches of kale crisps and over 40 guinea piglets. My taste buds had to be validated. After all, kale is a green leafy vegetable, the kind that tends to repel even the intrepid herbivores among us. Suddenly it was casting a spell upon rambling little fingers.

Not one of my guinea piglets gagged when I divulged its core ingredient. A couple of gasps could be heard, and a few silent screams. The under-10s thought these 'crisps' were a really naughty snack. One plate later, they had wolfed down more greens than the entire week.

There are a couple of variations you could try. Below is the most basic. Nutritional yeast flakes have an umami buzz. It's cheese to vegans, and replete with that elusive vitamin B12. If your local health food store is out of yeast flakes, use garlic granules and smoked paprika instead.

Preheat the oven to 180°C/160°C fan/350°F.

Flatten the kale leaves and use the point of a knife to remove the tough centre ribs. Tear the leaves into bite-sized pieces.

Using your hands, massage oil into each leaf. Spread across a baking tray. Don't worry about flattening the leaves out; they're better bunched up. Bake for 8–12 minutes. Check after 6 minutes and toss to prevent charring.

Grind the yeast flakes into a powder using a pestle and mortar. Remove from the oven and sprinkle the powdered yeast over the now-crispy kale. Scoff while warm. I'm not sure if crispy kale keeps in a sealed container. It never gets that far. Also awesome with sweet brown rice, avocado and tamari as a swift supper.

2 good handfuls of bone-dry
curly kale
4 tablespoons extra virgin
olive or coconut oil
1 tablespoon nutritional
yeast flakes

Serves 4

CHIA BONBONS

+++++++++++++++

Chia seeds are an easy way to get those much-coveted omega-3 fats without having to neck back flax oil or pharma bullets.

What's so snazzy about omega-3s? A deficit in omega-3 fats has been linked to angry skin conditions, poor concentration levels and delinquent hormones. Without omega-3s, it seems we manufacture substandard cells. Not an attractive proposition. Think gazelle or tortoise: which would you rather be?

So will taking omega-3 fats cure mental atrophy, PMT and sagging boobs? No, but strong evidence suggests it can help. That's enough.

It's worth noting that the type of omega-3 fatty acids found in chia is slightly different to those found in oily fish. Chia contains ALA, the precursor to EPA and DHA fatty acids. You've probably come across these confusing terms at the pharmacy when choosing omega-3 supplements. In short, it has been argued that EPA and DHA are easier for the body to absorb. As a result, the omega-3s present in oily fish like mackerel are thought to be superior to those found in plants such as chia and flax. But chia offers a suite of other goodies, including more calcium than milk, banks of potassium, bone-building boron and cholesterol-reducing fibre.

1/4 cup tahini
nearly 1/4 cup maple syrup
1/2 cup milled chia seeds
1/4 cup ground almonds
2 tablespoons cocoa or raw
  cacao powder
5 tablespoons desiccated
  coconut

Makes about 30 bonbons

Beat the tahini and syrup together with a fork. Please note that honey won't work in this recipe. Once the tahini mixture is all glossy and luscious, measure in the chia seeds, ground almonds and cocoa powder and encourage them to party. A wooden spoon is useful.

Put the coconut in a bowl or shallow plate. Roll a small cherry-size ball of mixture between the palms of your hands to form a bonbon. Drop each one into the coconut and roll it around to coat, then let it set on a cold plate. You could try different coatings, like beetroot powder, lúcuma powder or ground hazelnuts. Store in the fridge and plunder at will.

BARLEY GRASS BALLS

Instead of those dodgy energy drinks, make a big batch of these and store them in the office fridge.

Barley grass is like a mini farm of nutrients. Is it exceptionally rich in any one nutrient? No, but its broad nutritional spectrum makes it a first-rate tonic for dull days. I suspect that eating profuse quantities of green leafy vegetables would offer similar results. Let's agree that barley grass is a lot quicker and easier to prepare.

4 tablespoons ground almonds
4 tablespoons milled pumpkin
  and sunflower seed combo
2 tablespoons tahini
1-2 tablespoons runny honey
1-2 tablespoons barley grass
  powder
sprinkle of goji berries
  (optional)

Makes about 16 big bonbons

Mush everything together with a fork until it looks like thick cookie dough. Roll a teaspoon of the mixture into little bonbons between your palms. Store in an airtight jar in the fridge and liberate when required.

DR SMOOTHIE

++++++++++++++

Here's an easy way to start the day with a halo on your head. It doesn't involve broccoli, lycra or resetting your alarm clock. Just fruit, live yoghurt, oats and an appetite. Okay, and maybe a sense of humour if you forget to put the lid on the blender.

1 very ripe banana or
   avocado
1 cup frozen berries
1 cup freshly pressed apple
   juice
1/2 cup organic live soya or
   coconut yoghurt
1/4 cup oat flakes
1 tablespoon ground chia or
   flaxseeds

Serves 2-3

The joy of this recipe is that you don't need a special juicer, just your magical whizzy machine. Blend everything together and leave for 1 hour or overnight before scoffing. Bring Dr Smoothie into work in a jam jar, or savour it on the road when your nerves begin to fray in the tailback traffic. Harness its happiness and you'll be surprised how mellow you'll feel by 8am.

PROTEIN GRENADES

+++++++++++++++++++++

These grenades will save you money, fuel your muscles and feed insatiable appetites. More importantly, they're unequivocally better than the commercial sports muck at supermarkets and specialist sports stores.

Hemp protein powder is outrageously tasty, and legal. It comes directly from the hemp plant and contains all eight essential amino acids as well as a nice dose of omega-3 and iron. Iron is responsible for making haemo-globin, which transports oxygen around the blood. No iron, no energy. Omega-3s are important post-training, as they help quench inflammatory markers and heal bruised tissue.

And finally, a word on linseeds. They help your pipes. A lot. And offer another round of omega-3 artillery.

Not bad for a bonbon.

Using a fork, mush everything together in a bowl. Sunwarrior's vegan protein powder is awesome too, but it may dent your bank account.

Roll into mini bonbons and maybe coat each protein grenade with more desiccated coconut. Store in the refrigerator, preferably behind the vegetables, where your housemates will never find them.

2 tablespoons crunchy peanut butter
1 tablespoon hemp seed (protein) powder
1 tablespoon pea protein powder (we use Pulsin)
1 tablespoon ground linseeds
1 tablespoon desiccated coconut
1 tablespoon raw agave, honey or maple syrup
1 tablespoon goji berries (optional)

Makes 8

APPLESAUCE AND CINNAMON COOKIES

++

Satisfying and chewy, these are designed as everyday cookies, the sort you throw in your bag as you dash out the door. Or sneak into tedious board-rooms.

Raisins are pumped with resveratrol, which acts as a free radical assassin. Free radicals cause damage to our skin and to our arteries by helping LDL cholesterol set up home. Nasty things.

Preheat the oven to 180°C/160°C fan/350°F. Line a large baking tray with parchment paper.

Chop the apples into bite-sized chunks and place in a small saucepan with 1/4 cup of water and your dates or prunes. Cover with a tight-fitting lid and boil for 15 minutes, being careful the apples don't stick to the bottom of the pan. Once the fruit is soft enough to mush, remove from the heat and blitz with a hand-held blender. Measure out 2/3 cup and set aside. Any leftover purée can be frozen for the next batch of cookies or served on top of yoghurt.

Next, finely chop the roasted hazelnuts. There's little point buying pre-chopped hazelnuts, as their good oils turn rancid much quicker. In a large bowl, stir together the chopped hazelnuts, oats, raisins, coconut, linseeds and cinnamon. In a smaller bowl, beat the fruit purée and nut butter together thoroughly, followed by the milk and vanilla. Fold this glossy batter into the dry ingredients and mix thoroughly.

Place a large cookie cutter on the paper-lined tray and spoon the dough into the cookie cutter, filling until it's at least 2cm deep. Press and smooth with the back of the spoon. Gently lift the cookie cutter up and repeat with the rest of the dough.

Bake for 30 minutes, before they turn brown. Remove from the oven and cool on a wire rack. They can be eaten right away if, like me, you don't have the willpower to wait.

2-3 apples
8 dates or prunes, destoned
1/4 cup roasted hazelnuts
1 3/4 cups jumbo oat flakes
3/4 cup raisins and/or dried
  cranberries
3/4 cup desiccated coconut
2 tablespoons milled
  linseeds or milled chia
  seeds
1-2 tablespoons ground
  cinnamon
1/4 cup nut butter, like
  hazelnut, almond or
  macadamia
1 cup organic soya yoghurt,
  almond milk or hemp milk
2 teaspoons vanilla extract

Makes about 12 big cookies

SPIRULINA SHOTS

++++++++++++++++++++

Ever heard of an algae called spirulina? It smells a bit like fermented horse urine. This is usually overlooked once its magic starts to kick in. A favourite among ambitious models, spirulina offers a shortcut to cleansing the body. This curious green powder is home to immodest amounts of protein, calcium, zinc, iron, essential fats and energy-releasing B vitamins. Spirulina is hailed for helping with everything from lazy limbs to waning libidos.

Manufacturers recommend adding spirulina to yoghurts or smoothies. Here's a better way to shoot it back without assaulting your senses, or the kitchen floor.

2 apples (or 1 cup freshly
  pressed apple juice)
2 teaspoons spirulina powder

Serves 1

Juice your apples if you have one of those groovy machines. Cucumber is also good. Spirulina powder clings to the bottom of cups, so I recommend pouring half the juice into a cup, followed by the spirulina, then the remaining juice. Whisk with a fork. No need to hold your nose - it's surprisingly nice. Or perhaps I'm still asleep when I knock it back.

NUT MILK

++++++++++

Brazil nut milk is gorgeous. A Vitamix is the ultimate accessory when making it - and a clean muslin from Mothercare. Since I don't have a Vitamix, my kitchen walls are regularly redecorated. It hasn't stopped me making nut milk every other week. I drink the milk straight away or soak muesli in it overnight.

Start by soaking the Brazil nuts overnight or for 24 hours. Rinse and drain. Add 4 fresh cups of water to your Vitamix or food processor along with the vanilla and blitz until silky smooth. In theory you could add a drop of maple syrup, but I don't think it needs it.

Pour this messy lot into a large jug, using the muslin cloth as a strainer to catch the shards of nuts. A very fine sieve also works. That's it.

1 cup Brazil nuts
1/2 teaspoon vanilla extract
  or powder (optional)

Makes 1 litre

STRAWBERRY AND BANANA SHOELACES

+++++++++++++++++++++++++++++++++++++++

These popular children's snacks are called fruit leathers in the US and are usually pumped with sugar and preservatives. DIY versions are easy to make and noticeably tastier. The downside is that they take 6 hours to slow cook. The upside? A strawberry-scented house!

2 cups strawberries, stems
  removed
1 banana
1 tablespoon milled flaxseeds
  or milled chia seeds

Makes 15 shoelaces

Blitz all the ingredients in a powerful blender until smooth and glossy. If your strawberries are not fully ripe, you may need to add 1 tablespoon of honey to compensate for any bitterness. I also tried an apple and strawberry combo, which didn't work so well. Looks like banana might be key.

Line a Swiss roll tin (a roasting tray with a lip) with parchment paper. Spread the banana and strawberry mix evenly over the parchment with a spatula, making sure it's as smooth as smooth can be. This is the most important step.

If you are lucky enough to own a dehydrator, use your Teflex tray and dehydrate at 42°C for 5-6 hours. I use my oven at 60°C/40°C fan/140°F. Depending on the thickness (5mm is perfect), I cook it for 6–8 hours. You will know when it is done - touch and see whether it is still tacky. Remove from the oven once it feels dry to touch. Allow to cool on the parchment before cutting into shoelaces with a scissors, paper and all. The parchment can be removed straight away or later, when the chislers attack them.

SNACKS AND OTHER NUTRITIONAL HITS

BUCKWHEAT PANCAKES

+++++++++++++++++++++++++

Buckwheat pancakes taste sweeter and more wholesome than regular pancakes, and are unquestionably more interesting. White flour is nutritionally bland in comparison.

If you're a fan of Japanese take-out, chances are you've already tasted buckwheat in the form of soba noodles. Buckwheat, despite its name, is not wheat at all. It appears to be a relative of rhubarb and is entirely gluten free.

Russians make blini from buckwheat flour (see page 48) and smother them in caviar for their elevenses. Certainly beats a KitKat.

1 cup buckwheat flour
generous pinch of seasoning,
 like Herbamare
2 cups water
extra virgin coconut oil,
 to fry

Makes 9 x 20cm pancakes

Stir the flour and seasoning together in a deep jug. Add a little of the water until it forms a smooth paste. Add the remaining water and whisk, ensuring no lumps appear. Leave to settle for at least 20 minutes. This makes flipping the pancake much easier when you go to cook the batter.

Heat your non-stick frying pan (non-stick is essential) with 1/2 tablespoon of coconut oil for each pancake. Using a soup ladle, pour just enough batter onto your hot pan to coat the whole surface. Too much batter will make the pancake too thick to flip. You may need to tilt the pan to cover the whole surface with the batter.

Flip when the underside is cooked. A few practice shots are generally necessary - this is pretty common, so don't beat yourself up over it. The added bonus is munching the unsuccessful ones! By the third or fourth pancake, your results will be flawless.

While the other side of the pancake is cooking, go make yourself some scrambled eggs as a filling. Serve on top of a buckwheat pancake and roll up like a wrap. Any leftover pancakes can be used as cold wraps for lunch at school or the office tomorrow. Try boiling baby potatoes and stirring through crunchy peanut butter, crushing a few spuds along the way to help create a softer filling. A couple of torn salad leaves or fresh coriander will make it look like you hired Gordon Ramsay to make your lunch.

SUPERFOOD SPREADS - BRAZIL NUT RED PESTO

+++

*Traditionally, a pesto is made by crushing ingredients to a smooth paste.
We're speeding things up here with a cheat's version. The addition of
anchovies provides omega-3 oils to our diet as well as boosting brain power
with its DMAE phospholipid content. DMAE is believed to convert into the
brain nutrient choline, which is useful for remembering important things
like the boss's dog's name or where you parked the cursed car. Pregnant
mothers feeding on choline-rich foods can also raise their baby's chances of
becoming the next president of Mensa.*

Throw all the ingredients into a food processor
and pulse until it's nicely chopped up and
chunky. If the tomatoes were jarred, you won't
need additional olive oil. Refrigerate in a
screw-top jar until ready to ravage.

12 sun-dried tomatoes
1 x 50g tin of anchovies
handful of Brazil nuts
drizzle of extra virgin
  olive oil

Makes 5 portions

SUPERFOOD SPREADS - DIBIS W'RASHI

+++

*This is an Iraqi dish that children love to eat with smashed banana or
bread. You can make your own date paste by boiling the fruit in a little
water for 15 minutes, then whizz until sumptuously smooth.*

Whip the tahini and date syrup together with a
fork. Add a spot of sea salt if it's not going to
find your toddler's mouth. This is good enough to
eat straight from a spoon. If stored in a jar in
the fridge, this dip will keep for 2 weeks.

1/4 cup tahini
2 tablespoons date syrup or
  homemade date paste (see
  above)
pinch of sea salt

Makes 6 portions

Sweet and Salty Chilli Sauce

Fig and Sesame Butter

Dibis W'rashi

Masala Walnut Butter

Avonnaise

Brazil Nut Red Pesto

SUPERFOOD SPREADS - MASALA WALNUT BUTTER

+++

When pounded to a pulp in a pestle and mortar, walnuts' natural omega oils are released and meld together to make a decadent butter, heaps healthier than the dairy equivalent. While it's true that walnuts are made up of approximately 60% fat, their natural omega-3 oils power your brain, not your waistline.

Look out for stale or oxidised walnuts. They're about as bitter as Simon Cowell. Try to keep walnuts in the fridge and source from reputable stores with a high turnover.

1 good mugful of walnuts
1 garlic clove
1 teaspoon garam masala
sprinkle of Maldon sea salt
  flakes
1 teaspoon lemon juice
raw carrots, cucumbers or
  peppers, as dippers

Makes 5 portions

Break up the walnuts and add to your trusty pestle and mortar alongside the garlic, spice and salt. Pound for about 5 minutes, until you've got an oily butter. If it's still crumbly, keep on going.

Add 1 tablespoon of water and the lemon juice. Water tends to change the colour of the mixture from biscuity brown to light beige. Don't worry - you're on the right track. It's really up to you how creamy or thick you want it. As a guide, 2 tablespoons of water should be ample. Taste and decide if you'd like more spice or crushed garlic.

Tuck in using strips of carrot, cucumber or pepper. As a dinky starter for a supper party, you can make great pass-aroundies by filling a teeny Brussels sprout leaf with this whip and crown with a juicy redcurrant.

SNACKS AND OTHER NUTRITIONAL HITS

SUPERFOOD SPREADS - OMEGA PARSLEY BUTTER

+++

Think about it - your skin is made from the inside, not the outside. This recipe specifically combines pumpkin seeds' rich source of zinc, lemon's vitamin C, hemp's protein, the essential omega fats from seeds and parsley's stock of chlorophyll. In other words, it's a real beauty bullet.

Mince the garlic, or grate it with the teeny-tiny part of your grater. Follow with the lemon rind, then squeeze its juice. Give everything a jolly good whizz in the blender until smooth. Store in a scrupulously clean jam jar, with an extra drizzle of olive oil on top. In theory, it should keep for 2 weeks in the fridge. In practice, well, that's another thing. Super tasty on avocados, oatcakes, sliced cucumber, tomato, bread sticks or Sunday's roast chicken.

1 small garlic clove
1/2 unwaxed lemon
bunch of parsley, finely
  chopped
3 tablespoons hemp seeds
3 tablespoons pumpkin seeds
2 tablespoons extra virgin
  olive oil
1 tablespoon hemp or linseed
  oil
1 tablespoon sunflower seeds
1/2 teaspoon good-quality
  sea salt

Makes 6 portions

SUPERFOOD SPREADS - FIG AND SESAME BUTTER

++++++++++++++++++++++

Great source of calcium, iron and finger-licking. Oh, and beautiful bowels. My little ones take it to nursery in place of peanut butter.

Remove any stalks from the dried figs, then whizz all the ingredients together in a food processor. Add 1-2 tablespoons of water if you fancy a softer finish. Water won't thin the spread down, but rather, reduce its richness.

6 dried figs, soaked
  overnight
4 tablespoons raw tahini
1-2 tablespoons honey or
  maple syrup (optional)

Makes 6-8 portions

SUPERFOOD SPREADS - SWEET AND SALTY CHILLI SAUCE

+++

This is a smashing dip for chicken wings and dunky thangs.

2-3 tablespoons barley malt
  extract, raw agave or
  yacón syrup
2 tablespoons fresh miso
  paste
2 tablespoons cold-pressed
  toasted sesame oil
1/2 teaspoon cayenne pepper

Makes 5-6 portions

Whip the ingredients together in a cup with a fork. Serve in a soup bowl to facilitate easy dunking. Leftovers can be stored for 1 week in the fridge.

SUPERFOOD SPREADS - AVONNAISE

+++++++++++++++++++++++++++++++++++++++

Fairly deadly with tinned tuna, raw carrots and flax crackers. I love using Herbamare veggie salt in this, from the Swiss naturopath Alfred Vogel. Find it in most good health food shops.

1 large ripe avocado
2-3 tablespoons water
1 teaspoon lemon juice or
  cider vinegar
black pepper, to taste
celery salt, to taste

Makes 2 portions

Purée all the ingredients together. You'll need to use a hand-held blender to achieve a super-smooth consistency, like mayonnaise. Taste and adjust the seasoning to your preference. Eat straight away, as avocados tend to discolour quickly.

SUPERFOOD SPREADS - HOMEMADE NUTELLA

++

Makes a great gift to someone feeling poorly.

Whip the ingredients together in a cup using a
fork. If you're not planning to eat this DIY
Nutella straight away, you can refrigerate it in
a clean jam jar for up to 3 weeks. Once chilled,
it can be difficult to spread, so add a teaspoon
of hot water and beat the Nutella until it's
glossy again.

1/3 cup hazelnut butter
  (about half a small jar)
3 tablespoons cacao, cocoa
  or carob powder
2 tablespoons maple syrup

Makes 6 portions

SUPERFOOD SPREADS - PEANUT BUTTER, BANANA AND MAPLE SPREAD

++

I usually sneak leftover beans into the mix when I have them. My son is
none the wiser, but his bowels certainly are.

Mash all the ingredients together and serve
on oatcakes. This spread is best scoffed right
away, as the mashed banana starts to darken with
oxidation.

1 ripe banana
2 tablespoons pure peanut
  butter
a drop of maple syrup
oatcakes, to serve

Serves 2-4

Soups

'It's better to pay the grocer than the doctor.'
Michael Pollan

Soups are magical potions. They can resuscitate flat
batteries and pump life through our bodies faster than a
voodoo drum. There's something special about slurping a
hot bowl of sunshine and feeling your veins ignite. When
food is in liquid form, we not only digest it rapidly, we
also absorb nutrients much quicker. Here are some of my
favourite recipes to get your toes tingling. No need for
cream, butter or flour - just a little love and a
wooden spoon.

LEMONGRASS, COCONUT AND SWEET POTATO SOUP

==============================

Lemongrass is the easiest of exotic Asian herbs to deal with in a Western kitchen. I tend to have problems pronouncing the others, let alone soliciting them into a pan. Lemongrass is widely available in supermarkets now, which either means we are becoming more courageous behind the apron or more mournful of our carefree days backpacking around Thailand.

Organic coconut milk is best, otherwise the milk can be hijacked with all sorts of preservatives and stabilisers. If you think this is just claptrap, I urge you to buy both and compare. You'll notice a trippy purple hue in many non-organic milks.

Gently warm a dollop of extra virgin coconut oil in a sauté pan. Add the sweet potatoes, onions and garlic and leave to sweat quietly while you prepare the remaining ingredients. This process sweetens the veg naturally as long as you don't brown them.

Bash the fat, fibrous end of the lemongrass stalks with the base of a saucepan or heavy object. Of course, a pestle and mortar would be perfect, but not as cathartic as a flying saucepan after a long day in the office. Add the smashed stalks to the sweet potatoes and onions along with the stock and coconut milk. Bring to a simmer and cook for 10 minutes, until soft.

Remove the lemongrass and discard. Purée the soup with a hand-held blender until delectably smooth. Tickle with cayenne to give delicious heat and a splash of lime for a sharp kick. Finally, dazzle with the torn coriander, a splash of tamari and your holiday photo album. Guaranteed to transport you straight back to the coconut-lined beaches of Koh Samui.

good blob of extra virgin coconut oil
2 sweet potatoes, peeled and diced
1 onion, diced
3 garlic cloves, chopped
1-2 lemongrass stalks
2 cups vegetable stock or water
1 x 400g can organic coconut milk
pinch of cayenne (optional)
squeeze of lime juice
handful of fresh coriander leaves, torn
tamari, to serve

Serves 4

HITCHCOCK AND NUTMEG SOUP

==================================

Thank goodness you can now buy raw pumpkin from supermarkets in wedges, just like melon. Hacking into a whole one is a little too Hitchcock for me. Besides, you'd need to be Mr Universe to dice up a pumpkin.

Roasted, this saffron-coloured vegetable is deliciously sweet and mapley to taste. As soon as you socialise it with your palate, you'll wonder why we only eat it at Halloween. Be careful not to buy the monstrous decorative pumpkins, which are only good for ghoulish faces.

Nuts like me - short for nutritionists - love pumpkin because of its super-sonic carotenoids, its liver-loving antioxidants and astral amounts of vitamins C and A. Winter bugs won't stand a chance. Of particular impor-tance to the hypertension-istas or balding men among us, pumpkin sports more potassium than the humble banana: five times as much.

2 onions, chopped
5 garlic cloves, left in
  their paper houses
1 x 1-1.5kg pumpkin
good splash of extra virgin
  olive or coconut oil
3-4 cups chicken or
  vegetable stock
whole nutmeg, to garnish
buckwheat blinis (page 48)
  to serve

Serves 8

Preheat the oven to 200°C/180°C fan/400°F.

Toss the chopped onions onto a large baking tray with the whole cloves of garlic in their papery pods. Slice the pumpkin into wedges, discard its stringy nest and seeds and dice the flesh into bite-sized pieces. Leave the skin on if it's an organic pumpkin. Tumble with the onions and garlic, giving it all a good lick of oil. (You may need to use 2 trays to avoid overcrowding.) Roast for 45 minutes, or until the pumpkin is soft and caramelised around the edges. Shake the tray once or twice during roasting, just so your nostrils can party.

Once the pumpkin is seriously tender and sweet, scoop into your food processor alongside your onions. You'll need to squeeze the garlic from their papery shells - swipe a little taste for yourself. It's pretty cosmic roasted this way. Blend on high. Add enough stock to give the desired consistency of your soup. Whizz carefully now, trying not to scald yourself or redecorate the kitchen walls. Pour into big bowls and grate fresh nutmeg on top.

SOUPS

ROASTED GARLIC AND WILD NETTLE SOUP

==

Children are fascinated with nettle soup because it curiously fails to sting their tongue. Use this alleged sorcery to your advantage. If the nippers stay up later than bedtime, threaten to turn them into purple ferrets. In the meantime, learn this recipe by heart so that when you return from the fields, this ingenious alchemy can begin.

1 whole head of garlic, cloves peeled
glug of extra virgin olive oil
Maldon sea salt flakes
a crack of black pepper
4 onions, diced
1 leek, chopped any old way
roughly 1/2 carrier bag of nettle leaves*
2 litres homemade chicken or vegetable stock
1 cup frozen petits pois (optional)

Serves 12

* *Please use rubber gloves when you pick the nettles!*

To roast the garlic, preheat your oven to 180°C/160°C fan/350°F.

Toss the garlic cloves in a bowl with the olive oil and seasoning. Stack 6 squares of tinfoil on a work surface and place a sheet of parchment paper on top. This prevents the garlic from colouring or burning and turning bitter. Put the cloves in the middle of the paper and fold the parchment and foil over it like a tent, scrunching the edges. Make sure it's sealed well. Place the package in the centre of the oven and roast for 45 minutes.

Remove from the oven and allow to cool for at least 30 minutes. If you open the package too early, you will lose all that fabulous juice or burn yourself with plumes of steam.

If this all seems a little much, feel free to use crushed raw garlic in place of creamy roasted garlic. They taste very different, but are both fabulous in their own ways.

To make the nettle soup, sweat the onions and leek in olive oil over a gentle heat for 10 minutes, until the onions look translucent. If the veg catches on the bottom of the pan and starts burning, splash some water in and turn the heat down. Using a heavy-based saucepan is best.

Rinse the nettles under running water and remember to wear your rubber gloves. Spring nettles are sweetest. Toss the nettles into your pot of veg and add the stock, salt flakes and cracked pepper. Bring to the boil, immediately reduce the heat to a gurgling simmer and cook for 5-6 minutes. Any longer, and you risk murdering the taste. Remove from the heat and sprinkle in

the petit pois (if using). So sweet and juicy
when fresh, baby peas will cook rapidly in the
residual heat of the soup. Take out your soup gun
and whizz everything until delectably smooth.
Mash the roasted garlic and stir it through. This
soup also freezes well and sings beside a slice
of toasted rye sourdough.

PICNIC GAZPACHO

====================

Tomatoes practically blush with virtue, like a rosy cherub with puppy fat. You've probably noticed the praise they enjoy in medical circles. In fact, the European Commission is backing a five-year research project called Lycocard to explore the role that tomatoes play in reducing the risk of developing cardiovascular disease and prostate cancer.

Lycopene, a carotenoid found in tomatoes, is thought to have raging antioxidant properties. We like antioxidants because they help to counteract mischief-making oxidants in our bloodstream. These meddlesome oxidants are often the result of poor dietary choices like processed fats, sugar, artificial additives and synthetically created preservatives. Cheap pre-packaged meals are full of the above, making your blood feel like sludge.

Now that we know lycopene can help zap villainous oxidants, we should be plotting to take more. Gazpacho is a chilled tomato soup. It's absurdly refreshing on a summer's day, especially if heat tends to muffle your appetite. When temperatures soar, the Spanish swill pitchers of gazpacho. Their tickers are all the merrier for it.

Too simple, really – whizz and serve. You'll need to start with the cherry tomatoes and garlic. Just give them a jolly good whizz in a high-speed blender until they're really smooth. Add in the spring onions, red pepper, cucumber, passata, lemon juice and a crack of black pepper and pulse very briefly. Gazpacho is best when it's thick and chunky, like a soupy salsa. If you accidently purée until kingdom come, don't panic. Blame heat stroke. Garnish with a smile and crumbled egg, announcing it is in fact salmorejo.

Chill in the refrigerator for at least 1 hour and spoon into 4 shallow soup bowls. Serve with a drizzle of top-quality olive oil, ice cubes, a few basil leaves and The Gypsy Kings' greatest hits.

1 small punnet (250g) cherry
  tomatoes, quartered
2 garlic cloves,
  crushed
3 spring onions, sliced
1 red pepper, deseeded and
  diced
1 cup diced cucumber
500ml tomato passata
juice of 1 small lemon
fresh crack of black pepper
top-quality extra virgin
  olive oil, to serve
ice cubes, to serve
basil leaves, to garnish
  (optional)

Serves 4

SMOKY BLACK BEAN SOUP

===========================

I love this soup. Your taste buds will back flip and your cardiologist is sure to wildly applaud. We already know the virtues of beans. Add to this tomatoes' heart-protective carotenoids, olive oil's cholesterol-busting tendencies and yeast flakes' cargo of B vitamins and you've got yourself a defibrillator in a kitchen pot. Just don't leave out the cumin or smoked paprika. They give this soup an extraterrestrial kick.

2-3 cups chopped leeks
1 garlic clove, sliced (not crushed)
4 tablespoons extra virgin olive oil
1 teaspoon ground cumin
1 teaspoon smoked paprika
2 x 400g tins black beans, drained and rinsed
1 x 400g tin cherry tomatoes
6 cups vegetable stock or seasoned water
1 tablespoon tomato purée
1 tablespoon nutritional yeast flakes (optional)
1-2 teaspoons honey or coconut sugar
splash of tamari

For the pseudo crème fraîche:
1 cup natural or coconut milk yoghurt
1 garlic clove, crushed
handful of parsley, chopped
a few turns of the black pepper mill

Serves 6-8

Using a large heavy-based saucepan on a low heat, sweat the leeks, garlic and olive oil for 8-10 minutes, until soft and sweet. Toss in your cumin and smoked paprika and stir briskly, allowing their aroma to hit your hungry nostrils, then add the remaining ingredients. Turn the heat up until the soup starts to gurgle, cover and lower the heat again. Allow to putter away for 5 minutes.

Ladle into large bowls and top with a pseudo 'crème fraîche' made from natural yoghurt, crushed garlic, parsley and smashed black pepper.

CHILLED AVOCADO AND WATERCRESS SOUP

===

Instead of artery-clogging cream, you'll find that avocado can deliciously thicken soup while cranking up your meal's nutritional value. Avocados are especially high in vitamin E, nature's antidote to damaged skin. Combined with this soup's stellar vitamin C content, you're looking at an anti-ageing elixir. Although I'm not suggesting you apply it as a face mask.

Many of us need to increase our calcium intake from alternative sources to dairy. Watercress should help.

Start by gently warming the olive oil in a large pan. Add your onion and garlic to the oil and cook on low for around 10 minutes, until the onion looks fairly translucent. This process is called sweating and helps to sweeten root vegetables for soups.

Add the petits pois, watercress and stock. Cook for 5 minutes, until the water starts to violently boil. Remove from the heat and pulse with a hand-held blender. It will turn a brilliant green. Pour into a wide-brimmed, pre-chilled bowl and allow to cool in the fridge for 1 hour. An ice bath is helpful.

Preheat the oven to 180°C/160°C fan/350°F. Toast the almond flakes on a flat oven tray for 4–6 minutes, until lightly coloured but not brown. Set aside.

Once the soup is chilled, scoop out the flesh of your chilled avocado and add before serving. Give everything another blitz and serve immediately with an untidy smattering of toasted almond flakes.

2 tablespoons extra virgin olive oil
1 onion, diced
2 garlic cloves, minced
450g frozen petits pois
125g watercress
4 cups homemade vegetable or chicken stock
flaked almonds, to serve (optional)
1 medium avocado, chilled

Serves 4

90-SECOND BARLEY MISO SOUP

===================================

Miso is one of Japan's culinary trophies. Made from fermenting soya beans or grains with a live culture, miso is high in enzymes, good bacteria, female-friendly isoflavones, cancer-fighting selenium and that elusive vitamin B12. Look for unpasteurised miso in the refrigerator section of all good food stores. You'll notice there are lots of varieties and grains to choose from, a bit like wine. Some are sweet, others are earthy and full bodied. I've even noticed happy versions with fermented hemp for the die-hard hippies among us.

Miso paste is my secret weapon in the kitchen. When a sauce, soup or dressing misbehaves, in goes a tablespoon of barley miso and out comes Beethoven's seventh symphony.

A small nutritional caveat - never boil fresh miso. Its flavour and bacterial culture will get the guillotine. Instead, add a little of the liquid to a cup with the miso and dissolve into a smooth paste. Pour this brew back into the soup or sauce and then serve without any further cooking.

1-2 teaspoons unpasteurised
  barley (or other) miso
1 spring onion, sliced
sprinkle of petits pois
1 quail's egg (optional)
pinch of arame seaweed
  (soaked for 10 minutes) or
  nori flakes

Serves 1

Mix the miso paste in a soup bowl with 2 table-spoons of hot water until dissolved. Pour over boiled water from the kettle and add the spring onions and peas. Crack a raw quail's egg into the centre (if using). The heat from the soup will quickly cook the teeny tiny egg. It's pretty awesome to watch.

If that doesn't appeal, play with additions such as warm almond milk, soaked arame or nori flakes. Reach into the freezer and grab a slice of Your New Wheat-free Bread (page 51). No need to cook tonight.

JEWISH PENICILLIN

=========================

There's nothing quite like a bubbling cauldron of chicken stock wafting through the kitchen on a Baltic winter evening. Sends my nostrils into a frenzy of hunger. Stock is quite happy to sit on the hob and gurgle away for several hours, enveloping your senses while you get going on that bumper box set of The Wire.

Let's be honest: most of us still grab ready-made stock cubes instead of making our own. But that's like comparing Peter Andre to Damien Rice. The first ingredient in an average chicken stock cube is salt. What a rip-off. Then comes artery-clogging hydrogenated fat, followed by sugar - exclamation mark - unspecified starch (aka more sugar), monosodium glutamate (MSG) and dubious 'flavourings' are star ingredients. Even the canned varieties are based on these cheap, phony stocks.

This recipe is liquid gold. Simmering the bones helps draw out the chicken's natural minerals and collagen to fuel our bodies. Its potency is further enhanced with garlic, ginger and turmeric's anti-viral, anti-bacterial and anti-inflammatory compounds. Our grannies and our granny's grannies used it to soothe indolent limbs and hazy eyes in place of popping flu pills.

Ask your local butcher to save his free-range or organic chicken carcasses for you instead of dumping them. Just make sure to return his generosity with a great big flask of steaming hot goodness and a seraphic smile.

Break up your chicken carcass as much as you can and cover with cold filtered water in a large saucepan. Add all the ingredients to the pot and bring to a bubbling simmer, uncovered. Lower the heat so that the liquid is only shuddering. Skim off and discard the foam that appears on the surface over the next 60 minutes - there's no need to become a slave to it, however.

Once the broth has a rich, chickeny flavour, usually in 4-8 hours, turn off the heat. Strain. Allow the broth to settle and throw out the bones and veg. Store in the freezer to make soup at a later date or tuck straight in.

Give this stock your own signature stamp by adding grilled mushrooms, slices of avocado and chilli, broken buckwheat noodles or freshly chopped parsley before serving. Although it's so darn delicious on its own, it rarely needs any doctoring.

1 organic chicken carcass
3 onions, peeled and roughly
  chopped
3 celery sticks, roughly
  chopped
5 garlic cloves, peeled
2 bay leaves
thumb-sized piece of fresh
  ginger, peeled and chopped
3cm piece of fresh turmeric
  root, peeled
1 teaspoon unrefined salt
  flakes
freshly cracked black
  pepper, to serve

Makes 1-2 litres

Salads

Healthy eating should never tax your taste buds.

Relax. You're in the right place. Cleaning up your diet
doesn't need to involve neon leotards or cauliflower
smoothies. No one should be threatened with that.
This chapter is more about pleasure than denial. We could
all improve our diets, but we don't have to sacrifice
flavour.

The food we eat is inescapably linked to our concentration
levels, our mood, our libido and yes, our love handles.
We eat about five times a day. That's over 1,800 opportu-
nities each year to positively affect our energy and weight.
Salads are a great place to start. Let me prove it.

SPIRALISER RECIPES - MAKING SPAGHETTI FROM COURGETTES

I love spiralisers. These dinky machines make you feel like Handy Manny in the kitchen. Instead of prepping pasta, you can grab a courgette, fix it to a spiraliser, and kaboom! Courgette spaghetti! And if you don't fancy forking out for another kitchen gadget, you could use a potato peeler to scrape ribbons from the vegetables instead.

A naturally shy vegetable, courgettes carry flavour rather than provide it. The trick is to avoid the large, bitter ones. You can dress courgette spaghetti up with your usual tomato passata, a bit of garlic, olives, spinach and look! That's your five a day busted in less time than it takes to reheat a dodgy take-out. Investing in a spiraliser might be the best €40 you'll spend this year.

SPIRALISER RECIPES - THE HAPPY COURGETTE

○○○

Crunchy, chewy, smooth yet zippy, this is one happy courgette.

1 fat carrot
1 small to medium courgette
1/4 cup walnuts
1/4 cup dried cranberries
handful of flat-leaf parsley,
  dill or chervil

For the dressing:
3 tablespoons organic
  natural soya yoghurt
2 tablespoons red wine
  vinegar or apple cider
  vinegar
1 tablespoon Dijon mustard
1/2 garlic clove, minced

Serves 2 as a salad or 3 as
  a side

Spiralise the carrot and courgette into a large bowl. Loosely toss together with the walnuts, cranberries (raisins and grapes love this recipe too) and herbs.

To make the dressing, whisk together the yoghurt, vinegar, mustard and garlic. Tumble into the prepared carrot and courgette. Dig in.

SPIRALISER RECIPES – WASABI PEA CARBONARA

○○○

This is a good creamy dish with a delicious sting of wasabi. When you're rehydrating dried mango, just add enough water for them to soak it up. Leave for a few hours, or overnight if possible.

Pour boiling hot water on top of the frozen peas and leave to sit while you spiralise the courgette and carrot into a bowl. Drain and add the peas to your courgette and carrot spaghetti.

In a separate bowl, purée the avocado, the rehydrated mango pieces and their soaking liquid, the wasabi, green tea (if using) and the lemon or lime juice. Taste, and add a dash more juice if you think it's required. Pour this sumptuous green ganache over the courgette spaghetti and coat it thoroughly. If you think there is too much sauce, spiralise another carrot into the mix.

Divide between bowls and have your friends guess the ingredients!

1/2 cup frozen petits pois
1 small to medium courgette
1 fat carrot
flesh of 1 avocado
handful of dried mango, rehydrated in water (see note above)
2 teaspoons organic wasabi paste
1 teaspoon matcha green tea powder (optional)
squeeze of lemon or lime juice

Serves 4-5 as a starter or side

SPIRALISER RECIPES - FLAKED SALMON WITH SPICY POMEGRANATE NOODLES

ooooooooooooooooooooooooooooooooooooooooooooooooooooooooooooooooooo

One of my all-time favourite salads. The key lies in good-quality pomegranate molasses, so beware of imposters!

2 fillets organic salmon or wild trout

extra virgin raw coconut oil (or whatever oil you prefer)

1 fat carrot

1 small to medium courgette

2 tablespoons pomegranate molasses

2 tablespoons almond butter

2 tablespoons cold-pressed toasted sesame oil

2 tablespoons Bragg Liquid Aminos or 1 tablespoon tamari

1 small garlic clove, minced or crushed

good pinch of cayenne pepper

pomegranate seeds, to garnish

Serves 2

Preheat the oven to 200°C/180°C fan/400°F.

Prepare the salmon by wrapping the fillets in a parcel of tinfoil and drizzle with the oil. I use extra virgin raw coconut oil, but use whatever you're happiest with. Make sure there's lots of space above the fillets - it's more like a tent than a parcel. They steam in their own juices this way.

Transfer the tent of salmon onto a baking tray and roast for 10-15 minutes, depending on how big the fillets are. Check by pulling the flesh apart. If they're not done, just reseal your tent and pop them in the oven again. When you've become familiar with this method of cooking, crank it up another level by adding smashed lemongrass, maple syrup, chilli, cumin, kaffir lime leaves or whatever tickles your appetite on any given evening.

While the salmon is cooking, spiralise the carrot and courgette. In a separate bowl, beat together the remaining ingredients to make your spicy dressing. Toss through your spiralised noodles and divide between 2 bowls. When the salmon is done to your liking, flake the flesh over each bowl of noodles, then sprinkle over the pomegranate seeds. Awesome meal on a warm summer evening.

SPIRALISER RECIPES - GARLICKY TAGLIATELLE WITH BLACK OLIVES AND PINE NUT RICOTTA

○○

Sick of stodgy pasta and cheese? Preparing courgette and carrot tagliatelle takes less time than boiling pasta, and also delivers your entire vegetable RDA. Admittedly the pine nut ricotta demands a bit of Mary Poppins in the kitchen, but if you plug in some Ricky Martin he'll visit your fingertips. My hubby sneaks some diced anchovies and tomatoes in here too.

Put the courgette and carrot through the middle blade of your spiraliser or use a potato peeler to create long, thin ribbons.

In a separate glass, whisk together the parsley, garlic, olive oil and lemon juice. You won't need it all, so freeze the remainder for another evening.

Tumble enough of the dressing into your tagliatelle and toss thoroughly to coat each strand. Sprinkle in the chopped olives. Crown with a generous drop of pine nut ricotta and a few turns of the black pepper mill. A simple smattering of pumpkin seeds is a filling alternative to the ricotta.

1 courgette
1 carrot
roughly 1/2 cup flat-leaf
  parsley or chervil
3 garlic cloves, crushed or
  finely grated
1/2 cup extra virgin olive
  oil
juice and zest of 2 small
  lemons
handful of black olives,
  roughly chopped
pine nut ricotta (page 143)
  or pumpkin seeds

Serves 2

SPIRALISER RECIPES - RED PEPPER AND WALNUT (MUHAMMARA) NOODLES

○○

Last time I made these noodles, I necked the entire batch. My husband's roar was heard several postcodes away.

2 fat carrots
2 small to medium courgettes
3 red peppers (or 1 jar of roasted peppers)
1 cup walnuts
1/3 cup wheat-free breadcrumbs
3 garlic cloves, minced and mashed to a paste with 1/2 teaspoon salt flakes
4 tablespoons tomato purée
1 tablespoon pomegranate molasses
1 teaspoon ground cumin
pinch of dried chilli flakes
1/2 cup extra virgin olive oil
fresh lemon juice, to taste (optional)

Serves 6 as a starter or side

Spiralise the carrots and courgettes. Large courgettes can taste bitter and fluffy, so it's worth hunting down the smaller ones.

Let's get making the muhammara. To prep the peppers, place them directly on the middle shelf in a very hot oven. Let them roast for around 40 minutes, until they're on the brink of collapse. Don't worry if their skin is blistered or black. It's what's inside that counts. Gently remove the roasted peppers from the oven by pulling the stalk of each one and catching them in a large bowl. Cover the bowl with cling film for 10 minutes. This makes it much easier to remove their skins. Without ouching yourself, pinch off the skin and discard along with the stalks and seeds.

To prep the walnuts, smash them in a pestle and mortar until their natural oils begin to be released. Or you could use the base of a saucepan, so long as the neighbours aren't in.

Purée the rest of the ingredients except the olive oil and lemon juice to a smooth, creamy dip. Now stir through the olive oil. Any sooner, and your muhammara will look like something Peppa Pig has expelled. Stir through the walnuts.

Taste, and adjust with a squeeze of lemon or more chilli flakes if you fancy. Tumble into your prepped noodles and divide between your serving bowls. Black olives and hummus make for groovy companions.

SPIRALISER RECIPES - CURLY CARROTS

○○○

My boys chase each other with giant shoelaces of raw carrot. They think it's hilarious. I look on with the wonder of an astronomer sighting a new galaxy. Who would have thought raw carrots could be so much fun?

When they have playdates, Benjamin and Marty beg me to make 'curly carrots' for their unsuspecting guests. Everyone ditches the Lego, sits on the floor and chomps on ribbons of carrots as if they were liquorice laces.

Use the smallest plate on your spiraliser to make carrot laces. The carrot needs to be fat, or else you'll be left with brief curls of carrots instead of long, curly laces.

1 fat carrot
some currants or pomegranate
  seeds

Makes 3-4 snack portions

SPIRALISER RECIPES - CARROT RIBBONS AND SPRING PESTO

○○○

Leftover pesto can be frozen in jars. Make sure to press the pesto down firmly with the back of a spoon to remove any pockets of air (trapped air can cause contamination and foul tempers). Top the pesto with a little more oil, making a seal.

Start by picking the wild garlic leaves over and discarding any coarse stalks and grass. Whizz in a food processor along with the pumpkin seeds, olive oil, salt and lemon juice. Transfer to a scrupulously clean jar and set aside. This takes 6 minutes, tops.

Head and tail the carrots. Make sure they are straight to facilitate smooth spiralising. Put them through your spiraliser and collect the curly carrots in a bowl. Toss through the wild garlic pesto and tuck in. It's honkingly good stuff.

50g freshly picked wild
  garlic leaves
25g pumpkin seeds
1/2 cup extra virgin olive
  oil
1/2 teaspoon Maldon salt
  flakes
small squeeze of lemon or
  lime juice
2 fat carrots

Serves 2

MOON-DRIED TOMATOES AND SPROUTED HUMMUS

ooooooooooooooooooooooooooooooooooooooooooooooo

I'm a devotee of buying local and organic. This doesn't make me a sermon-ising tree-hugger or a hemp-wearing hippy (although I do have a crush on Woody Harrelson). I'm a fan because organic farming nourishes the soil naturally without the use and abuse of chemicals. Organic methods help protect Mother Nature's playground and preserve nature's biodiversity. (Though science is rarely ever that simple.)

By now you've probably heard about colony collapse disorder and the disap-pearance of honeybees in many parts of France, Britain and the United States. This phenomenon has been increasingly linked to neonicotinoid insecticides. Not good news. Honeybees are critical for the pollination of many of our favourite foods, such as almonds, apples, beetroot, asparagus and blueberries. Scientists say the disruption of pollination could wipe out entire crops, threaten our agriculture and bring the world into an ecological crisis. According to the USDA, one-third of the American diet relies on bee pollination.

So what can we do? For a start, we can choose to support farmers who grow vegetables without the indiscriminate use of agrichemicals. Check out local organic farmers' markets. By doing so, we not only support our winged friends, we also support nature, our local economy, our health and even our taste buds. Secondly, think about becoming a beekeeper. (The first might be easier to manage.) For more information, visit the beautiful site www.helpsavebees.co.uk.

For the moon-dried tomatoes:
about 16 cherry tomatoes, halved
1 garlic clove, finely chopped
3 tablespoons extra virgin olive oil
1 teaspoon coconut blossom sugar or maple syrup
1/2 teaspoon sea salt flakes
handful of fresh coriander leaves

For the sprouted hummus:
1 mug dried chickpeas
1-2 garlic cloves, crushed
1/2 cup chilled water
4-8 tablespoons lemon juice
4 tablespoons tahini or cashew nut butter
2-3 tablespoons ground cumin
2 tablespoons extra virgin olive oil
1 tablespoon tamari
1/2 cup finely chopped parsley, coriander, basil or black olives

Serves 4

Preheat the oven to 220°C/200°fan/425°F.

Coat the halved tomatoes generously with the garlic, oil, sugar and salt. Sit the tomatoes cut side up in an ovenproof dish and pour the remaining juices over. Pop in the oven and immediately turn off the heat. Leave overnight or for a day without opening the door.

For the sprouted hummus, simply sprout your dried chickpeas by soaking them in water overnight. Drain them the following morning and place the chickpeas on damp kitchen paper along the windowsill for the day. When you return from the office, you can canter straight into your kitchen and whizz up this hummus. Purée everything except the herbs in your food processor for 3 minutes. Add more iced water to help loosen it up if necessary.

Herbs are best chopped finely and stirred through the hummus instead of blending them. Otherwise, it can look as if Kermit the Frog crawled into your blender. The green tops of spring onions are a stealthy money-saver instead of using pricey fresh herbs.

Serve the tomatoes with loads of freshly chopped coriander leaves and the sprouted hummus.

IRISH SUPERFOOD SALAD

OOOOOOOOOOOOOOOOOOOOOOOO

This is a cosmic combo of truly tasty, local ingredients. It happens to be healthier and cheaper than popping vitamin pills. Plus you get to soak up the applause showered upon you by your dinner guests.

If you're feeling particularly lazy, use vacuum-packed beetroot in place of potatoes. No need for cooking.

Scrub and wash the baby potatoes, cover in cold salted water and bring to the boil for 15-20 minutes. Pierce them with a fork to check whether they are cooked. For the last 5 minutes of cooking the potatoes, add the eggs to cook simultaneously as a nifty time-saver. Once the eggs are boiled and the potatoes are cooked, drain and discard the cooking water. Allow to cool.

While the spuds are cooking, flake the mackerel fillet into a bowl with your chosen salad leaves, olive oil, the juice of half the lemon, lemon zest, nori flakes and capers (if using).

Halve the cooked baby potatoes. Peel and quarter the boiled eggs. Gently toss everything together and serve straight away or divide into paper deli boxes for lunch. Try not to reuse your old Tupperware if you're having lunch with that hottie from the office next door. You'll find smart recyclable containers by the salad counters in food stores and delicatessens. Politely, er, borrow them on your next shopping trip.

handful of baby Irish
  potatoes
2 large eggs
1 fillet smoked mackerel
handful of fresh rocket or
  watercress
decent splash of extra
  virgin olive oil
zest and juice of 1 small
  unwaxed lemon
sprinkle of dried nori flakes
  (optional)
a few capers (optional)

Serves 3

Leabharlanna Poibli Chathair Bhaile Átha Cliath
Dublin City Public Libraries

BASIL BUTTERBEANS

ooooooooooooooooooo

We love butterbeans because they look like something out of a Roald Dahl storybook. They're also cheap and keep in the cupboard for over a year. The trick with cooking beans is to soak them overnight. Unsoaked beans can taste dry and crunchy, even if you double the cooking time.

Here are a couple of tips to help you introduce butterbeans to the dinner table: Toddlers will eat them whole. Teens don't notice them mixed through a can of baked beans. And leery grandparents won't suspect anything different in their mashed potato (FYI, butterbeans mash beautifully). For everyone else, this recipe is sure to convert them.

1 cup dried butterbeans
3 tablespoons extra virgin
  olive oil
zest of 1 small lemon
a few basil leaves, chopped

Serves 4 as a side

Cover the butterbeans with water and soak overnight. The next day, drain the beans, cover with fresh unsalted water and boil for 90 minutes, until very tender. Taste a bean - you're aiming for the texture of a baked potato. When you're satisfied, drain the beans and stir through the remaining ingredients. Also excellent with dribbly tomatoes and mint.

DINING AL DESKO BEET SALAD

○○○○○○○○○○○○○○○○○○○○○○○○○○○○○

I love the summer. It's probably my favourite day of the year. I queue up to sit in the park and sear my beautiful blue skin. For the other 364 days of the Irish calendar, I like to keep toasty indoors and dine al desko. Loads of us do it.

But keep those sambos away from me or I'll be snoring by 3pm. Food should give you energy, not take it away. Try this recipe and see for yourself. The ginger will give your circulation a good giddy up.

Chop the veggies into bite-sized chunks. Two or three beets from a vacuum packet should suffice, depending on their size. Quantities are up to you.

Steam the chunks of carrot until tender. It won't need more than 5 minutes in a pot with a tightly covered lid and a minimum amount of water. You could also leave it raw for extra nutrition and crunch, but this renders talking over lunchtime next to impossible.

Toss the veggies, apple and walnuts together with a splash of olive oil and a squeeze of lemon juice. Grate some ginger over everything using the same part of the grater that you would use for lemon zest. Taste, and adjust the seasoning to your liking. Wrestle into a plastic lunchbox or empty container. Just don't forget the fork.

1 vacuum packet of beetroot
1 large carrot
1 celery stick
1/2 apple, diced
handful of walnuts
splash of olive oil
squeeze of lemon juice
3cm piece of fresh ginger,
  peeled
salt and pepper

Serves 2

'F%*K ME' SALAD

ooooooooooooooooo

*Here's a fragrant supper of fiery prawns, honeyed papaya and mint, all kissed with toasted sesame oil. Anyone who tastes it usually responds with a whispered 'f%*k me!'*

Chillis are devious little vegetables. They raise our body temperature and help release natural endorphins to keep our blood gurgling with excitement. I recommend the powdered form to give your lips a delicious sting and swell the senses. Guessing the heat of a fresh chilli is riskier than cycling backwards in a Grand Prix. Double the quantities if you plan on sharing this dish.

rice or mung noodles for 1
1 small papaya
1/4 cucumber
1/4 red onion
handful of cooked prawns
freshly torn mint leaves

For the Thai dressing:
juice of 1 lime
1 tablespoon fish sauce (nam pla)
1 tablespoon toasted sesame oil
2 teaspoons raw honey or maple syrup
pinch of cayenne or freshly sliced chilli

Serves 1

Cook the noodles according to the manufacturer's instructions on the packet (these can vary greatly). Cut the papaya in half, and again into slices. This will make it easier to cut into chunks for the salad. Treat it like a melon. While the seeds are deemed edible, they are deeply unpleasant. Known for its rich enzymes and potent anti-inflammatory compounds, papaya will help keep your liver on speaking terms with you. Especially if you're Irish.

Slice the cucumber thickly, then cut each slice into quarters. Slice the red onion thinly into rings. Toss the papaya, cucumber and red onion joyfully together with the prawns and mint.

Whisk together the remaining ingredients to make a Thai dressing good enough to drink. Pour over your medley of papaya and allow the flavours to infuse. By now, your noodles will be ready. Drain and rinse briefly with cold water to separate the starchy bits. Tumble into the happy medley and serve with a fork and straw. If you're bringing this into work, expect office pillagers to descend. Arm yourself with an extra sharp fork.

SAY HELLO TO OPRAH'S OCEAN VEG

○○○○○○○○○○○○○○○○○○○○○○○○○○○○○○○○○○

Seaweed is the next big thing. Our dear Oprah is a massive
fan of these 'ocean vegetables'. We Irish seem to think
it's only useful for deflecting annoying children on the
beach. In fact, seaweed is full of anti-ageing nutrients
and disease-fighting lignans.

Listen up, rusty bones! Sea veggies' calcium supply is good
for healthy bones and teeth, without the artery-clogging
effects that dairy-rich diets can yield. Then there's iron
- a mere 10 grams of mixed sea vegetables can give you
just under half the recommended daily allowance of this
blood-building mineral. Ocean veg are also a good source of
vitamin B12. Meat-eaters get lots of B12, but vegetarians
struggle to keep up. Spirulina, an edible water alga,
provides plenty of this elusive vitamin.

There are many types of sea vegetables to choose from,
guaranteed to make Brittas Bay more exciting this year.
Here are a few to get you started. All are harvested wild
and are free from chemicals, preservatives and, yes,
sometimes taste.

The most common type of sea vegetable on our menus is <u>nori</u>, the shiny green wrapping around sushi. Nori is unusually rich in protein. You'll get loads of nori in Asian food stores for a fraction of the high street price. Best crumbled on top of brown rice.

<u>Agar</u> and <u>carrageen</u> are used in place of artificial stabilisers and gelling agents. I use them to set panna cotta and fruit jellies - a crafty way of getting important minerals into children's party food.

<u>Kombu</u> and <u>sugar kelp</u> are the dark ones that gave me nightmares as a nipper. Thick, slippery strands of goodness. Who would have thought? Pop them into slow-cooking stews at the very beginning. I find they can take a long time to break down. It's rumoured that adding kombu to beans can help reduce the incidences of trouser-trumpets. That's Latin for flatulence.

<u>Kuzu</u> is surprisingly powdery. This ocean veg is traditionally used to thicken stews, broths and sauces in place of flour. Wholefood chef Jude Blereau does a fabulous kuzu gravy made from shiitake mushrooms, designed for those days when your body feels like a petri dish.

We always add <u>wakame</u> to stews about 30 minutes before cooking is finished. It brings a good smack of umami for the taste buds as well as a suite of fancy minerals. Like most ocean veg, a packet of wakame will last 3 years in the cupboard.

<u>Dulse</u> is particular to Ireland. This sea veggie has a chewy texture and deep purple hue. Best purchased in powdered form and sprinkled on food. The more courageous cooks can play with it in broths and soups. Cornucopia Café in Dublin has an excellent one on their menu.

<u>Arame</u> is the sweetest and most elegant of the sea vegetables. Jet-black angel strands of goodness. No need to cook - simply soak for 10 minutes and socialise them with broccoli, Brazil nuts and soya sauce for a speedy lunch, or with sautéed garlic mushrooms as a side.

SESAME SEA SALAD

ooooooooooooooooo

Arame doesn't taste as weird as it sounds. It is the easiest and prettiest seaweed to prepare. Consider it essential for your kitchen's emergency programme, especially designed for occasions when the oven decides to misbehave and you have a hot date to feed. Or a starving in-law. Equally as terrifying. The result is Ready Steady Cook meets Heston Blumenthal.

a handful (20g) of dried
  arame
3 carrots, grated
3 spring onions, chopped
1/2 apple, grated
juice of 1/2 lemon
3 tablespoons sesame seeds
3 tablespoons currants
3 tablespoons extra virgin
  olive or sesame oil

Serves 4 as a side dish

Soak the arame in cool filtered water for 10-15 minutes.

Meanwhile, toss the grated carrots, spring onions, apple, lemon juice, sesame seeds and currants together. Gloss it up with a good splash of olive or sesame oil. When the sea veggie has swelled to twice its size, discard the water and comb through the salad. Serve alongside fish or hummus. Watch out, though - kids tend to spit out the spring onions!

SPROUTING - THE BEAN ZOO

ooooooooooooooooooooooooooo

Here's a new hobby for a healthier, glossier you.

The task? (1) Purchase a Vogel three-tier germinator for about the same price as a yoga class. (2) Stock up on dried mung beans, alfalfa seeds and whole lentils. These are the easiest chaps to start with. (3) In each tier, sprinkle 2 tablespoons of your chosen bean, seed or lentil. (4) Let the germinator pay homage to the natural sunlight adorning your windowsill and tickle with water twice daily. Ta-da! Your very own bean zoo, providing oodles of entertainment, fascination and nutrition.

Depending on the bean, seed or lentil, sprouting can take from as little as 36 hours to 7 days. Your jolly germi-nator will come with an index of sprouting timelines. The trick is to refrigerate them as soon as they have sprouted, preventing them from growing too large and bitter. The shorter the sprouting time, the crunchier and sweeter they taste.

Bean sprouts provide a talented array of protein, vitamins, minerals and raw enzymes without the hassle of cooking. This is what I call *real* fast food. Word of wisdom – don't bother trying egg, fish or linseed oil with sprouts. Something alarmingly unpleasant happens.

SUPERMAN'S SALAD

○○○○○○○○○○○○○○○○○○

Choose from eight different varieties of sprouts to vivify your lunchtime and your liver. All sprouts need is a little lick of olive oil, juicy fruit and chopped herbs before throwing them into Tupperware.

Take about 4 segments of grapefruit and peel the white pith away from their juicy flesh. Chop each segment into approximately 4 pieces. This could take a while - my grapefruit usually finds its way into my mouth. Roughly tear your chosen herbs and toss with the grapefruit, sprouts and olive oil.

Further combos to try:
In place of pink grapefruit and chives, try olives, lemon juice and parsley; chopped banana, coconut flakes and coriander; Brazil nuts, steamed broccoli and soya sauce; roasted veg and rocket; yoghurt, curry powder, raisins and grated carrot; tofu, rice noodles, chilli and sesame oil; or avocado, pistachios and dried apricots.

1 pink grapefruit
handful of fresh chives,
  mint or coriander
1 mug of sprouted beans
2 tablespoons extra virgin
  olive oil

Serves 1-2

NECTARINE AND LITTLE GEM SALAD WITH GOJI BERRY CREAM

○○

1-2 Little Gem lettuces
1/2 apple or nectarine,
 depending on the season
handful of pumpkin seeds
handful of sunflower seeds
a few turns of the black
 pepper mill

For the dressing:
6 tablespoons extra virgin
 olive oil
2 tablespoons lemon juice or
 apple cider vinegar
2 tablespoons goji berries
1 tablespoon raw honey,
 brown rice syrup or raw
 agave
pinch of cayenne

Serves 2

Break the leaves from the lettuce heads into the largest bowl you have. Gently tumble with the chopped apple, seeds and black pepper. You can toast the seeds to bring out their nuttiness: heat a non-stick pan on high and toast the seeds for 30 seconds. They are done when you hear the pumpkin seeds pop off the pan. A few chilli flakes will give a delicious nip.

Using a hand-held blender, purée the dressing ingredients to make a glossy sauce almost like a mayo but lighter in consistency. If your blender is as contrary as mine, it's worth soaking the goji berries in a little water first for 25 minutes. This should make the ride a little smoother. Pour over the salad and lightly toss together using your fingertips. An implement like a spoon or fork can bruise the leaves and make a salad quickly look tired.

Pile on the centre of a large plate. A turn or two of the black pepper mill is all it needs now. And maybe a bit of adulation. The pine nut ricotta on page 143 is fairly swell on top.

BOND GIRL SALAD

ooooooooooooooooo

If we are what we eat, then most people are cheap, fast and easy. But good nutrition doesn't have to compromise your wallet or your wristwatch. Raging hot actress Halle Berry swears by her 5-factor rule: meals have to use 5 different ingredients and be ready to eat in 5 minutes.

A few examples: smoked salmon, poached egg, fresh cress, cucumber and jarred capers; grated raw carrot, coconut, sultanas, curry powder and sesame oil; or tinned mackerel, spring onion, rocket leaf, tomato and avocado. Your brain gets a good workout! No refined muck, of course, just 5 wholesome ingredients. That means if you couldn't find a particular ingredient 100 years ago, it doesn't count.

Try this Indonesian-style slaw to get you started. It takes a lot less than 5 minutes to make and is a great side dish with fish.

3 handfuls of finely sliced
  red cabbage
1 cup chopped pineapple
1/2 cup natural yoghurt
1/4 cup sultanas
1 tablespoon curry powder
sprinkling of red-skinned
  peanuts

Serves 2-3

Tumble all the ingredients together. If you have a red onion loitering in the larder, throw that in too. Use whatever natural yoghurt you have - coconut, soya, goat, sheep. The hotter the curry powder is, the better. Something cosmic happens to pineapple when fire touches its orbit.

PROBIOTIC CELERIAC SLAW

○○○○○○○○○○○○○○○○○○○○○○○○○○○

Celeriac may look like a Harry Potter concoction, but it's actually as common as turnip. Watch out for it on your next trip to the grocers. You'll notice that the rest of these ingredients are probably resident in your fridge already, save the offensive-sounding berry. Physalis look like massive amber raisins and have a sherbety smack.

Sprightly little berries buzzing with goodness and charm, physalis supply immune-enhancing beta carotene and vitamin C to help slay bugs. Throw them into salads and conversation to impress. However, it would be prudent to enunciate carefully. Get it wrong, and you will sound as if you enjoy STDs.

If you want to upgrade the quantities of this slaw for a party, the ratio of apple to carrot to celeriac is 3:2:1. In other words, remember to grate three times the amount of apple to the amount of grated celeriac. You're in control.

Let all the ingredients converse in a large bowl. If you're planning on having leftovers the next day, dunk more yoghurt into the slaw before plating up. There's no need for additional probiotic powder – you'll get plenty in the natural yoghurt. I originally devised this recipe for a client finishing several courses of antibiotics, so we whacked up the probiotic element to nourish her intestinal flora.

3/4 cup grated apple
1/2 cup grated carrot
1/2 cup whole walnuts, finely
  chopped
1/2 cup natural soya yoghurt
  or coconut milk yoghurt
1/4 cup grated celeriac
3 tablespoons sultanas and/
  or dried physalis
1 tablespoon chia seeds
  (optional)
1 tablespoon smooth or
  wholegrain mustard
1/2 tablespoon probiotic
  powder, like Udo's
  (optional)

Serves 2 for lunch or 3 as
  a side

CURRIED CAULI, BANANA AND SPINACH WITH FLAKED FISH

○○○

Use any fish you like, but we find salmon, mackerel, hake and cod easiest to flake. Prawns work deliciously well and can be thrown in a hot oven on a separate roasting tray to the cauli. Pan-fried squid is quickest - only 90 seconds to flash-fry in a little extra virgin coconut oil. Ask the fishmonger to prep your squid into rings for you.

Jack up the oven to 210°C/190°C fan/410°F.

Find your biggest roasting tray and briefly melt the oil in it in the oven for a few moments.

Meanwhile, split your cauliflower in half and break into clumsy chunks. Peel and chop the blackened bananas. Remove your roasting tray from the oven, tumble in the cauli, banana, curry powder and turmeric and coat everything really well. Roast for 20-25 minutes, shaking from time to time if you remember to. When the cauliflower starts to char, she's done. Remove the tray and mix through the baby spinach.

Meanwhile, to cook the fish, dot a large piece of tinfoil with coconut oil or your favourite oil. Place the hake or cod on top, fold the edges of the foil towards each other and seal them together, leaving lots of air above the fish. The fish will steam naturally in this 'tent' as long as both sides are sealed. Bake in the same oven as the cauliflower for 15 minutes, until the flesh can be pulled away. It's easy to overcook fish - I find the alarm on my phone to be a good ally in the kitchen. Once you reckon the fish is cooked, remove from its foil tent, season well and sprinkle with extra spices if you fancy. Set aside until the cauli is ready.

To serve, flake your hake or cod on top of the tray of cauliflower and add a little squeeze of lemon or lime if you have it.

3 tablespoons extra virgin coconut oil
1/2 large head of cauliflower
2 blackened, over-ripe bananas
3 tablespoons Indian curry powder
1-2 teaspoons ground turmeric (optional for colour and nutrition)
handful of baby spinach leaves
1 large fillet of hake or cod, bones removed
salt and pepper
squeeze of lemon or lime juice (optional)

Serves 3

BEGINNER'S BUCKWHEAT WITH GRATED APPLE, CHILLI AND PUMPKIN SEEDS

ooooooooooooooooooooooooooooooooooooooooooooooooooooooooooooooooooo

Instead of boring pasta, which often tastes more like soggy Kleenex than good-quality wheat, give buckwheat a shot. It's a teeny triangular grain, confused by shades of red, brown and green. The all-familiar Japanese soba noodles and Russian blini are made from buckwheat. Chances are you already like its nutty flavour.

Despite its name, buckwheat is not wheat. Hollywood's glitterati love its slow-release carbs and avalanche of beautifying bioflavonoids. Buckwheat even has lysine, that elusive amino acid responsible for preventing outbreaks of cold sores.

More good news? Once you have the ingredients sourced, this dish takes a mere 12 minutes to rustle up from package to plate.

A handy habit is to store fresh ginger, skin peeled, in your freezer so you never run out of it. Then, with the part of the grater that you normally use for zesting lemons, grate the ginger straight from frozen. Fresh ginger can be a little fibrous, overpowering and stringy. Frozen ginger is not.

1/4 cup pumpkin seeds
1/2 teaspoon chilli flakes
1 cup whole buckwheat grain,
 rinsed
2 red apples, grated
up to 1 cup gooey, dark,
 dried apricots, chopped
splash of extra virgin
 sesame oil
good lump of fresh ginger,
 peeled and frozen (see
 note above)
lime juice, to serve
tamari, to serve
dried nori flakes, to serve

Serves 4 as a side

Toast the pumpkin seeds with the chilli flakes by heating a dry frying pan or wok over a flame and listening for the pumpkin seeds to start popping. Stir briskly and remove when they look pregnant and crispy. Try not to let the pan smoke on a high heat.

Bring 1 1/2 cups seasoned water to the boil. Reduce the heat to a rolling simmer, add the freshly rinsed buckwheat and cook with a lid on for 8-10 minutes, until all the water has been absorbed. Turn off the heat and let the grain steam with the lid on for another few minutes. It should have a bite to it, but not a crunch. Drain any excess liquid and rinse with cold water.

Toss the buckwheat with the toasted pumpkin seeds, grated apple, chopped apricots, a splash of sesame oil and plenty of grated ginger. Serve with a squeeze of lime if you have one or a trickle of tamari and dried nori flakes.

Suppers

One month of eating like this will have you feeling
like you're plugged into an electrical socket.

Cooking has never been just about the recipes. It's about navigating your creativity and flirting with flavours. It's about sensuality as much as science. To me, it's the ultimate form of self-expression, where you set out to nourish your body and those you love.

Self-love is distilled in healthy eating. Feeding your body with nutrient-rich food is like plugging into an electrical socket. It has the ability to transform energy levels and resurrect brain cells. Athletes see food as their body's artillery. It's probably about time we did too. Processed food has little nutritional purchase, leaving the body bereft of the vital nutrients necessary for us to function well. Think three-toed sloth or puma: which would you prefer?

So how can you clean up your diet without losing your personality or taste buds? It's easier than you think. Here are a couple of tips.

Get your hands on a copy of Wham's greatest hits. I'm not sure if their groove transfers to my fingers, but something cosmic happens to my serotonin and my pies. Turn up the volume and get jiggy with it.

Next step is to share the results of your kitchen adventures with friends. Everyone loves to be fed. There's no easier way of getting hooked on a new habit than receiving rampant adulation.

The more you surround yourself with healthy people, the more you start to think like them. I subscribe to great blogs to get ideas for healthy eating in my inbox every week. Think of it as a form of helpful 'advertising'. Cleaning up your diet may seem slow in the beginning, but persistence will make way for a new and better you. Just think: if you make one of my recipes every week, you'll have mastered 52 seriously healthy dishes by this time next year. Your body is sure to levitate. Ready?

BROWN RICE AND HIS COUSINS

xxxxxxxxxxxxxxxxxxxxxxxxxxxxxxxxxxxxxxxxxxxx

At one stage, American actress Mariel Hemingway made brown rice so fashionable that Californian grocers struggled to keep it in stock. Mariel is a bit of a beaut, so it's hardly surprising to find brown rice, lentils and chickpeas at the heart of her diet.

You see, whole grains like brown rice contain those mighty B vitamins responsible for fuelling our batteries and busy bods. Vitamin B3 in particular can help lift your mood, like daydreaming about James McEvoy or making small changes to politicians' Wikipedia pages. There's far less B3, fibre and manganese in the white starchy stuff. We need fibre to service our pipes and regulate our poops. Nothing nice about constipation. Manganese seems crucial to an antioxidant enzyme called SOD, the maestro of all antioxidants. One cup of brown rice delivers almost 100% of our daily manga-needs! Manganese comes from the Greek word for magic. Nuff said.

There are legions of whole grain rice to choose from; here are the best ones. Soaking rice apparently improves digestibility and shortens cooking time. There's no downside to soaking rice, so it's probably a sensible thing to do.

I use my rice cooker all the time. Exact cooking times and instructions are on my blog: www.susanjanewhite.com.

Wild rice

Very expensive, so it's advisable to add 1 tablespoon into other varieties of rice instead of serving it straight. Cooks in 45 minutes.

Brown jasmine

Rinse. Simmer 2 parts water to just over 1 part rice and a pinch of salt. Follow the directions on the packet, but 30-40 minutes should be just about right. Brown jasmine rice usually takes less time to cook than long grain rice. During the final few minutes of cooking, remove the lid and boil off any remaining water.

Brown basmati

This is the fastest brown rice to cook. Rinse and simmer 1 cup brown basmati with 1 3/4 cups seasoned water. Ready in 22 minutes (check the cooking time suggested by the manufacturer on the packet). Add 1 teaspoon of caraway seeds for a smack of Bombay.

Brown long grain

Most popular but least impressive. Simmer 2 parts water to 1 part rice. You can add 1 tablespoon of millet, quinoa, wild rice or amaranth to 1 cup of long grain brown rice and cook for 45 minutes. It will be stickier than regular long grain rice, but very nourishing alongside a curry or stew.

Short grain

Rinse. Simmer 2 parts seasoned water to 1 part rice. Ready in 45 minutes. Soaking rice apparently improves digestibility and shortens cooking time. We often do 1 1/2 cups short grain rice with 1/2 cup whole barley in the rice cooker. Works beautifully.

Sticky brown sushi rice

Wash sushi rice very well in cold water. Transfer to a saucepan with 1 3/4 cups cold water to 1 cup sushi rice. Soak for 30 minutes, then boil for 35 minutes. Remove from the heat and leave to dry-steam until all the water is absorbed. It's best to use a plastic spatula to avoid splitting the grain and mushing it.

Red (camargue) rice

Good for beginners. Rinse and simmer in 2 parts seasoned water to just under 1 part rice for 40-50 minutes. Be watchful of the final few minutes to avoid burning.

Sweet brown rice

Our absolute favourite. It's a cross between sticky white rice and short grain brown rice. Rinse. Simmer 1 part rice to 2 parts water. Cook for 35 minutes or until all the water is absorbed. Remove from the heat and allow to dry-steam with the lid on for a further 10 minutes.

EGGY FRIED RICE

xxxxxxxxxxxxxxxxxxxxxxxxx

Every time you make rice, try to remember to make enough for this meal the following day. Then you can high five your genius when you come home from work and spend 90 seconds whizzing up your supper.

Black garlic keeps for a year in the fridge and is useful for days when you can't dart to the grocers for fresh stuff. In fact, most of these ingredients will already be lurking in your kitchen. And therein lies its USP.

There's a knack to good fried rice. The first is to cook the eggs completely before adding the rice. The second is never to add soya sauce - it should be served alongside the dish instead. Ready? Let's see if we can get this from fridge to plate in 90 seconds.

1 tablespoon extra virgin
   coconut oil
1/2 cup frozen petits pois
3 eggs
2 cups leftover rice
3 black or fresh garlic
   cloves, chopped
pinch of arame ocean veg
   (optional)
tamari soya sauce, to serve

Serves 2

Melt the coconut oil on a medium heat in your best frying pan. Make sure the heat isn't too high. While the oil is melting, place the peas in a separate bowl and pour boiling water over them.

Crack the eggs into the pan and poke the yolks so they break. Coat the pan with the eggs. Don't scramble or mix them, but allow them to slowly cook through (around 20 seconds). Now add the rice and stir to coat. Drain the peas and pop them in with the garlic. The arame is optional if you have it in your cupboard (this is an ocean veggie that lasts for up to 3 years in the packet, so it's very handy for suppers like this). Arame demands 10 minutes of soaking too, which would hamper our 90-second challenge right now. But it's something to consider for next time.

Plate up once hot and serve with a bottle of tamari.

BUCKWHEAT CRÊPES WITH PINE NUT RICOTTA AND SPINACH

xxxxxxxxxxxxxxxxxxxxxxxxxxxxxxxxxxxxxxxxxxxxxxxxxxxxxxxxxxxxxxxxxxxxxxxxxxxx

I never get my fill on Pancake Tuesday, partly because I always forget it's coming - bit like Mother's Day and Visa deadlines. Pancakes are so darn delicious, it's rather puzzling why we don't tuck into them every Tuesday. Why reserve them for one special day a year?

To make the pine nut ricotta, drain the soaked cashews. Whizz everything together in a mini blender or food processor. A hand-held soup gun won't work - something more powerful is needed. Scoop into a glass jar and top with crushed black peppercorns.

Boil the frozen spinach in 2cm of water for 5 minutes. Drain thoroughly. Salt and pepper it up. Keep warm in the oven or on top of the cooker until the pancakes are ready to rock.

As you cook each crêpe, keep them warm on a wire rack and cover with a tea towel. Tinfoil will make the crêpes sweat and turn them soggy. At home, I just serve as I go. There's usually a queue of children at my ankles.

When everyone is seated, dish up the pancakes and dot with pine nut ricotta and a generous dollop of spinach.

1 x crêpe recipe on page 78
600g frozen spinach

For the pine nut ricotta:
1 cup raw cashew nuts,
  soaked overnight
1/2 cup pine nuts
1-2 garlic cloves
3 tablespoons water
2 tablespoons extra virgin
  olive oil
2 tablespoons lemon juice
3/4 teaspoon good-quality
  sea salt
a few turns of the black
  pepper mill

Makes 8 crêpes

CHILDREN'S STICKY RICE WITH CAULIFLOWER CONFETTI

xxxxxxxxxxxxxxxxxxxxxxxxxxxxxxxxxxxxxxxxxxxxxxxxxxxxxxxxxxxxxxxxx

1 cup cooked short grain,
   sweet or brown sushi rice
3 tablespoons cultured
   coconut yoghurt
floret of purple cauliflower

Serves 2

Rice and quinoa can be tricky for children to master. You can make a 'glue' by using mashed sweet potato or coconut yoghurt to bind it all together. Using a zester or microplane, grate the purple cauliflower over each bowl of sticky rice to make purple confetti. Cauliflower has never been so cool!

SNAZZY BROCCOLI AND SOBA NOODLES

xxxxxxxxxxxxxxxxxxxxxxxxxxxxxxxxxxxxxxxxxxxxxxxxxx

Broccoli is a crusader, backing up your front line defences with vitamin C, chlorophyll, antioxidants and other handsome phytonutrients. I tell my boys broccoli are edible Lego trees and then they plunder the entire plate.

Famed for its cancer-fighting properties, broccoli is an affordable superfood. When choosing a head, just make sure the florets have not turned yellowish or look limp and tired. With age, broccoli loses those supersonic nutrients.

Cook the soba noodles according to the instructions on the packet. They usually take 8 minutes.

Meanwhile, break the broccoli into bite-sized pieces. Steam for 3–4 minutes.

Whisk the garlic with the sesame oil, tamari, Brazil nuts, miso and cayenne. Reverently drizzle over the warm broccoli, toss with the cooked noodles and watch your friends and family go bonkers.

1 portion 100% buckwheat
  soba noodles
1/2 head of broccoli
2 garlic cloves, crushed
1 tablespoon sesame oil
1 tablespoon tamari
1 tablespoon roughly chopped
  Brazil nuts (optional)
1 teaspoon miso paste
pinch of cayenne pepper

Serves 2–3

BEGINNER'S QUINOA

xxxxxxxxxxxxxxxxxxxxxx

The rapid increase in wheat and gluten sensitivities is good news for quinoa. This grain practically swaggers with its impressive stash of B vitamins (energy), protein (repair), iron (strength), magnesium (circulation) and zinc (sexy skin). Quinoa is really quite the starlet and should be given centre stage on your shopping list. The United Nation's Food and Agriculture Organisation considers it to be as nutritionally complete as whole milk.

Quinoa is ideal for picnics, packed lunches, alongside curries, tossed in salads, scattered into soups or to accompany a tray of roasted veg on indolent evenings.

1 cup quinoa
1 1/2 cups stock or
  seasoned water
8-12 juicy baby tomatoes,
  halved
flesh of 1 avocado, roughly
  chopped
1 mild chilli, deseeded and
  sliced (optional)
handful of rocket, chives,
  cress or coriander,
  roughly torn
3-4 tablespoons extra virgin
  olive oil
1 tablespoon finely chopped
  red onion
sea salt flakes and a few
  twists of the black
  pepper mill

Serves 2

Wash the quinoa very well in a sieve under running water. Transfer to a heavy-based saucepan. Bring to the boil with the stock or seasoned water and cook for 12-15 minutes with a lid on. The longer you cook it, the softer and stickier it becomes. Take the pan off the heat as soon as the quinoa has drunk up all the water. Let it sit on the countertop and fluff up in the residual heat of the lidded saucepan. Some rice cookers have a special 'grain' setting that works perfectly for quinoa.

Leave the quinoa to cool a little before stirring through the remaining ingredients. Give the black pepper mill a few twists and add a smattering of sea salt flakes. You could pack the quinoa into an empty container for lunch at the office. I use the cardboard ones from my local deli's salad counter. They seem far snazzier than my manky old Tupperware.

NOTHING-IN-MY-CUPBOARD QUINOA

xxxxxxxxxxxxxxxxxxxxxxxxxxxxxxxxxxxxxxxxxxxxxxxxx

When the fridge looks bare and you can't find the energy to resuscitate your sleepy brain cells, reach for a packet of quinoa. Uncooked, quinoa will store for ages in your cupboard, making it a very attractive last-minute meal. Here's one to get you started. Cooked quinoa will happily samba in the fridge for a few days.

Soak the arame in water for 10 minutes if using. Drain, and set aside for the quinoa collection. The arame is optional if you have it in your cupboard. Arame is an ocean veggie and lasts for up to 3 years in the packet, so it's very handy for suppers like this.

Thoroughly rinse the quinoa in a sieve under running water. You'll be tempted to skip this step, but try not to or you'll end up with a bitter residue. Drop the rinsed quinoa into your saucepan of boiling salted water. Add the turmeric if you have it and simmer for 12-15 minutes with a lid on it. Drain any excess water from the pan by manoeuvring the lid very slightly so that you can pour off the liquid into the sink without losing the heat from the pan. Let the quinoa dry-steam in the saucepan on your countertop for a few more minutes. This step eliminates the threat of soggy quinoa.

When it's done (taste and see), let the quinoa cool a little and toss through the remaining ingredients. The coconut looks better tickled on top. Add as much curry powder as you fancy and a spot of citrus if you feel like it. Olives, capers, pomegranate seeds and herbs are cracking additions should you find any loitering in your pantry.

pinch of arame ocean veg
  (optional)
1 1/2 cups quinoa
2 cups seasoned water
1 teaspoon ground turmeric
  (optional)
1/2 cup raisins
1/4 cup desiccated coconut
2 garlic cloves, crushed or
  minced
1 tall spring onion, sliced
zest of 1/2 orange
1 tablespoon Madras curry
  powder
good glug of extra virgin
  olive oil
smattering of pistachios or
  any other nut

Serves 3 as a main or 6 as
  a side

SMOKED PAPRIKA AND CUMIN QUINOA

xxxxxxxxxxxxxxxxxxxxxxxxxxxxxxxxxxxxxxxxxxxxxxxxxxxx

Cooking quinoa is a lot easier than pronouncing it. Insiders call it keen-wah rather than quin-oh-ah, but nobody seems to care what I call it. This curious carb looks and feels the same as couscous, except that it tastes a whole lot nicer. Once you give quinoa a shot, you'll be outraged that couscous ever seduced you.

With its encyclopaedic mineral and vitamin profile, quinoa is by far the healthiest grain in my cupboard. It's real fast food with a nutritional halo. Each seed is host to an army of minerals to help service our adrenal glands. These are the call centres for stress and mood. Athletes love quinoa for its low glycemic value. All this means is that a bowl of quinoa can drip feed your body, brain and dimples for longer than white bread or pasta. Apparently, it also has higher levels of calcium and protein than dairy. Hail quinoa!

1 cup quinoa
1 1/2 cups hot chicken stock
  or boiling water
2 teaspoons ground cumin
1 teaspoon smoked paprika
2-3 eggs
generous splash of extra
  virgin olive oil
a few turns of the black
  pepper mill
bunch of rocket, dill,
  chives, parsley or
  coriander

Serves 2-3

Rinse the quinoa in a sieve under running cold water for a good 30 seconds (some grains have a bitter coating). Knock the wet quinoa into a small saucepan. (Bits will stick to the sieve. No matter.) Add the hot chicken stock or boiling water to the quinoa, sprinkle in the spices and simmer on a medium heat for 15 minutes with a lid on. The kitchen will smell incredible. You can tell quinoa is cooked once the tail of the seed comes away from the grain. A nifty trick is to remove the pot from the heat after 12 minutes, drain all the water and cover the pot with a tightly sealed lid for another 5 minutes. This way, the quinoa won't stick to the base or burn. Any residual heat left in the pot should fluff the grains up nicely.

To poach eggs, make sure you have the freshest eggs possible, left at room temperature, otherwise the eggs may become very disobedient. Using a small heavy-based saucepan, bring 8cm of water to a simmer. Swirl the water in a circular motion like a whirlpool and slide the raw egg into the middle. Many chefs swear that adding cider vinegar to the water will make the egg white behave. Your call. Watch carefully, and remove with a slotted spoon after 60-90 seconds to drain the water off your plump little treasure. Don't worry if it looks like half the egg white is floating in the saucepan. That always happens

to me and yet the eggs turn out beautifully.
To serve, add a good lick of extra virgin
olive oil and a few turns of the pepper mill
to the quinoa. Chop up any rocket or herbs you
can resuscitate from the fridge and stir them
through. Divide between 2 or 3 bowls and crown
with a perfectly poached egg. Poke the egg yolk a
little so its lava oozes out.

HARISSA QUINOA WITH ROASTED LEMON FENNEL

xxxxxxxxxxxxxxxxxxxxxxxxxxxxxxxxxxxxxxxxxxxxxxxxxxxxxxxxxxxxxxx

Harissa is a spicy North African paste guaranteed to send your blood beating like a bodhrán. While it looks like a lot of ingredients, you'll find most of them in your cupboard. This should make enough harissa to last 2 weeks in the fridge or 4 months in the freezer.

For the lemon fennel:
4 fennel bulbs
splash of olive oil
zest and juice of 1/2 lemon

For the quinoa:
2 cups quinoa, well rinsed
3 cups vegetable stock or
   seasoned water

For the harissa:
3-4 red peppers
6 red chillies
4 garlic cloves
1 tablespoon cumin seeds,
   ground
1 tablespoon caraway seeds,
   ground
1 tablespoon smoked paprika
1 tablespoon tomato purée
1/2 teaspoon sea salt flakes
1 tablespoon red wine or
   apple cider vinegar
3-5 tablespoons extra virgin
   hemp seed or olive oil

Serves 4-6

Preheat the oven to 180°C/160°C fan/350°F.

Cut each fennel bulb lengthways into quarters. Don't be tempted to slice the bum off, as the bulb will fall apart and you will be left with loads of bitty pieces rather than thick wedges. Throw onto a large baking tray.

Now slice the red peppers for the harissa into chunks, discarding the inner white film, stalk and seeds. Toss on the baking tray with the fennel and a splash of olive oil. Roast for 30 minutes.

While the peppers and fennel cook, bring the quinoa and stock to a rolling boil. Reduce the heat until it's puttering away politely. Put a lid on it and cook for about 12 minutes. Drain (if the stock is not thoroughly absorbed), place the lid back on and let the grains fluff up from the residual heat of the saucepan for another 5 minutes.

While the quinoa and roasted veg do their thing,
let's get going on the fresh harissa. Wearing
disposable gloves, cut the chillies down the side
and scoop out the seeds and pith with a teaspoon.
Discard. Or rub on husband's toothbrush if he
hasn't taken out the bins. Blitz the chillies
with the garlic, spices, tomato purée and salt
until it forms a smooth paste. I find a hand-held
blender much better than a food processor for
this. Now, and no sooner, add the roasted red
peppers (pick them out from the tray of roasted
fennel) and the vinegar. Pulverise to your satisfaction. Stir through the hemp oil or olive oil
and scoop into your serving dish. Avoid adding
the oil while pulverising the rest of the ingredients or the harissa will turn pink and no one
will eat it, not even your Barbie-loving toddler.

To serve the whole lot, gloss up the quinoa with
a smidge of olive oil. Divide between 4-6 plates,
top with a couple of fennel wedges, the zest and
juice of a little lemon and a royal dollop of
harissa.

QUINOA WITH STRAWBERRY AND MINT GREMOLATA

xxxxxxxxxxxxxxxxxxxxxxxxxxxxxxxxxxxxxxxxxxxxxxxxxxxxxxxxxxxxxxxx

This is the kind of dish that will make you purer simply by looking at it. If you haven't cooked quinoa before, it's the perfect food for taking into work and dining al desko. Bring an extra fork to ward off envious colleagues forced to queue for manky canteen food.

If you're worried about evacuating the office at lunchtime with your honking breath, fear not: parsley can help neutralise garlic breath. Crushed walnuts are another stealthy trick to remember. Failing that, peppermint oil capsules from health food stores are a winner and will make you giggle when you have gloriously refreshing burps.

2 cups quinoa

3 cups stock or seasoned water

1 teaspoon ground turmeric (optional for colour and nutrition)

For the strawberry mint gremolata:

2 garlic cloves

1 lemon

1/2 cup extra virgin olive oil

generous helping of salt flakes and crushed black pepper

25g curly parsley

25g mint leaves

1/4 cup dried strawberries (fresh won't work)

Serves 2 as a main or 4 as a side

Rinse the quinoa under running water for 30 seconds, rubbing the grains together with your fingers. A sieve is helpful. Knock the rinsed quinoa into a saucepan (don't worry about the bits that stick to the sieve, these are designed to test your patience and are destined for the kitchen sink). Add the stock and turmeric. Bring to a rolling boil, lower the heat and fit a lid on top. Cook for 10-15 minutes, until all the liquid is absorbed. You'll know it's cooked as soon as you see a little tail on each grain. If you like it soft, keep the lid on and let it dry-steam on the counter for a further 5-10 minutes. This will make the grain nice and fluffy without the risk of burning.

To make the strawberry mint gremolata while the quinoa cooks, finely grate the garlic and lemon rind. Squeeze a tiny bit of juice from the lemon into a jam jar and add the olive oil, salt and pepper. Chop the parsley and mint into it. Give everything a jolly good mix in the jar by shaking it all wildly.

Let the quinoa cool a little before dressing it up. I find hot quinoa always absorbs more than I'd like it to, resulting in disappointing, squidgy quinoa. When it feels cooler, tumble in the dressing and dried strawberries.

KATE MOSS QUINOA

xxxxxxxxxxxxxxxxxxxxxxxxx

Every time I eat quinoa, I feel like a supermodel. This elegant grain contains around 17% complete protein, making it white-hot for vegans, athletes and professional nuts (nutritionists). Celebs love the stuff. Bloggers are possessed by it. And over-priced restaurants have hijacked its pulling power with an excitement usually reserved for a Disney premiere. This grain is going places.

Quinoa is perfect to bring in for lunch at the office. Black+Blum sell dinky bento boxes and lunch sets online (see page 253). Purchase one, and you'll save a fortune on junk food and dodgy sangers.

Rinse the quinoa under cold running water for at least 30 seconds, using your fingers to rub the grains together. Plonk the now-wet grain into a small saucepan and add the stock and turmeric. Bring to boiling point, cover with a lid, turn down the heat slightly and cook for 12 minutes, until all the liquid has been soaked up. Remove from the heat and allow the saucepan to stand on the kitchen counter for a further 5 minutes with the lid on. This step is important if you like fluffy quinoa. Taste and decide for yourself. As soon as you're happy with it, let the grain cool down (I spread it out on a large flat plate).

While your quinoa is puttering away, prep the remaining ingredients. Slice the red onion in half and thinly shave into semi-circles using a sharp knife. Soak in the red wine vinegar for 15 minutes. Cut the pomegranate into quarters and peel back the white pith to reveal lots of ruby-red seeds. You're aiming for about 1/4 cup of pomegranate seeds.

In a large bowl, add the pom seeds, blueberries, dill, garlic and olive oil. I recommend using 8 cloves of creamy roasted garlic and mashing them into a paste with the oil. Drain the red onion before adding it to the remaining ingredients (you'll need to discard the vinegar).

Once you're satisfied with the texture of your quinoa, add to your prepped ingredients and give it a nice tumble and tickle. Crown with extra blueberries, or lamb cutlets for carnivores.

1 cup quinoa
1 1/2 cups vegetable stock
  or seasoned water
1/4 teaspoon ground turmeric
1 small red onion
3 tablespoons red wine
  vinegar
1 small pomegranate
1/4 cup blueberries
1 bunch (30g) dill, stems
  removed
1 clove freshly minced
  garlic or 8 cloves roasted
  garlic (see page 94)
4 tablespoons extra virgin
  olive oil

Serves 2 as a main or 5
  as a side

CHILDREN'S QUINOA

xxxxxxxxxxxxxxxxxxxxxxxxxxx

Quinoa is a carb indigenous to Peru. As a grain, it's sort of like couscous only nuttier in taste and significantly healthier. Quinoa provides essential amino acids that the body requires for optimum functioning, making it a first-class plant protein. No wonder those wily Peruvians can skip up the Incan altitudes with the ease of greyhounds at a marathon. My children love the stuff.

Quinoa is even powdered down and sold in capsule form, such is its nutritional bounty. This children's recipe has a stash of other immune-enhancing superfoods, such as sweet potato, mango, goji berries, virgin coconut oil and turmeric. No nursery bug will stand a chance!

1 cup quinoa
1 1/2 cups filtered water
2 tablespoons goji berries
  (optional nutrition)
1 teaspoon ground turmeric
2 tablespoons extra virgin
  coconut oil
1 sweet potato, baked whole
1/2 mango (optional
  nutrition)

Serves 2-4

Rinse the quinoa very well under running water. A sieve is useful. Knock the wet quinoa grains into a saucepan (don't worry about the bits that stick to the sieve, these are designed to test your patience and are destined for the kitchen sink). Add the water, goji berries (if using) and turmeric. Bring to a rolling boil, lower the heat and fit a lid on top. Cook for 12-15 minutes, until all the liquid is absorbed. You'll know it's cooked as soon as you see a little tail on each grain. Children like it soft, so keep the lid on and let it dry-steam on the counter for a further 10 minutes. This will make the grain nice and fluffy without the risk of burning. Add the coconut oil and replace the lid.

Peel and roughly mash the baked sweet potato (it won't matter what size it is). Finely chop the mango. Mix into the fluffy quinoa. The mash acts like a glue to bind the quinoa together, making it easier for children to eat.

BASIC LENTILS

xxxxxxxxxxxxxxxxxxxxx

Heart disease is Ireland's biggest killer, chased closely by bowel cancer. If you're worried about either condition, make friends with your health insurer. Or lentils. You don't have to be a member of the Green Party to enjoy them or start campaigning against animal cruelty. Just a little mustard and garlic, and in no time you'll be the best of friends.

Lentils are the heavyweight champion of fibre. Why is this important to you? Fibre helps maintain a healthy cholesterol range by deporting excess bile from the body. The lower your cholesterol range, the lower your risk of heart disease (CVD, in doctor speak). At the same time, fibre gives your pipes a first-rate servicing. A cup of lentils holds a stonking 17 grams of fibre. That's more than half our recommended daily intake. These tiny legumes have other salubrious gifts for your ticker, such as potassium and magnesium. See ya later, paltry pasta!

The Blue Zones Diet, also dubbed the Centenarian's Diet, is a compilation of foods we should be paying close attention to if we are planning to cavort well into our nineties. The diet reveals how centenarians across the world manage to live longer and better and still look buff at 99 without pills or Crème de la Mer. And you know what? Beans and lentils are among their top foods. Here are a few good recipes to bring into the office with you. Lentils love dining al desko.

Simmer the lentils gently with a lid on for 15-20 minutes (if you're using Canadian or brown lentils, they'll need more water and an extra 10-15 minutes). Lentils are cooked when they look like they're yawning. A bit like mussels, only 20 times smaller. Puy lentils cook rapidly and hold their shape very well compared to other varieties.

Try not to add salt until afterwards, or the lentils' skin can toughen. Once cooked, or when the cooking liquid has evaporated, lick with extra virgin olive oil, raw cider vinegar and a smattering of celery salt. They're not very demanding.

1 cup Puy lentils
1 1/2 cups stock or water
extra virgin olive oil
raw cider vinegar
celery salt

Serves 2

MAPLE MUSTARD LENTILS

xxxxxxxxxxxxxxxxxxxxxxxxxxxxxxxxx

1 x Basic Lentils recipe
  (page 157)

For the dressing:
1 small garlic clove,
  crushed
3 tablespoons extra virgin
  olive oil
2 tablespoons balsamic or
  raw cider vinegar
1-2 teaspoons maple syrup
1 tablespoon smooth Dijon
  mustard
1 teaspoon black or mixed
  peppercorns, crushed
handful of salad leaves or
  fresh herbs

Serves 2 as a side

Cook the lentils as outlined on page 157. Combine all the dressing ingredients (except the herbs) together before pouring over the warm lentils and then stirring through some herbs. A great side plate to fish and meat. We tend to add finely chopped anchovies to ours, but I realise not everyone shares our anchovy fetish.

Leftover dressing can be refrigerated in a clean jam jar for 2 weeks.

PUMPKIN AND BLACK GARLIC LENTILS

xxxxxxxxxxxxxxxxxxxxxxxxxxxxxxxxxxxxxxxxxxxxxxxxxxx

1 small organic pumpkin
extra virgin coconut or
  olive oil
1 x Basic Lentils recipe
  (page 157)
6 cloves of black aged
  garlic, finely sliced
a couple of anchovies, finely
  sliced (optional)
coconut yoghurt, to serve

Serves 6 as a side

Preheat the oven to 220°C/200°C fan/425°F.

Quarter the pumpkin using a sharp knife (and even sharper concentration - no one wants roasted fingers). Deseed the flesh and roughly chop into 5cm pieces - no need to peel the skin. Splash with coconut or olive oil and make sure every-thing is well coated. Roast on a baking tray for 45 minutes, shaking the tray halfway through the cooking time. Remove the pumpkin once the sides start to caramelise. Tumble into the cooked lentils and sprinkle with the black garlic and anchovies (if using). Tuck your creation into a lunch carton, ready to pack into your briefcase the next day. Try not to scoff it all at the bus stop in the morning or you'll weep at lunchtime.

TINNED SARDINES FIVE WAYS

xxxxxxxxxxxxxxxxxxxxxxxxxxxxxxxxxxxxxxxx

Tinned sardines are an excellent source of omega-3, calcium, protein and vitamin D. Let's not go into bone density here, but suffice it to say that if you want to groove on the dance floor well into your sixties, get 'em into ya! There ain't nothing sexy about brittle bones. Here are a couple of ideas to get you foxtrotting with sardines again.

Chermoula-kissed Sardines

This North African chermoula has been Irishified with a touch of seaweed. Arame only requires a little soaking before it's ready to dance. Don't be afraid of using seaweed in your cuisine - it's easier than opening a can of beans!

good pinch of arame seaweed
4 garlic cloves
1 teaspoon whole black peppercorns
1 cup flat-leaf parsley, chopped
1 cup coriander, chopped
1/2 cup extra virgin olive oil
2 tablespoons ground cumin
2 tablespoons lemon juice
1/2 teaspoon cayenne

Soak the arame seaweed in water for 10 minutes while you prep the other ingredients.

Crush the garlic and peppercorns in a pestle and mortar. Briskly stir in the remaining ingredients with a fork. This is traditional chermoula.

Drain the arame and discard the soaking liquid. Finely chop and stir through the chermoula. Moroccans love it on hardboiled eggs, white fish or tumbled into chickpeas. I think it's cosmic with sarnies.

Smoky Sarnies

Drain the tinned sardines. Mash with crushed garlic and a good pinch of smoked paprika. Serve on top of half an avocado.

Mediterranean Sardines

Drain the tinned sardines and mash with chopped sun-dried tomatoes, olives, parsley and lemon zest. Tastes great on dehydrated linseed crackers if you can find them. My boys eat these every week.

Balsamic Sardines

Drain the sardines of their oil or brine and combine with a splash of balsamic vinegar and chopped chives (or any herb from your window farm). Use celery sticks and red pepper strips as edible spoons.

Curried Mayo and Sarnies

You can make your own curried mayo using health-enhancing oils (see page 48 and add 3 tablespoons of curry powder at the beginning). The mayo will last for 3 weeks in the fridge. Just reach for a tin of sarnies and crown on top of a simple salad of Cos lettuce leaves and chopped apple. Go for papaya or mango if you're dead fancy.

MACKEREL PÂTÉ WITH ANCHOVY AIOLI

xxxxxxxxxxxxxxxxxxxxxxxxxxxxxxxxxxxxxxxxxxxxxxxxxxxx

This is the short-top-and-sides of evening meals.

It's clear we need to look for sustainable fish if we want our grandchildren's kids to know what tuna and salmon taste like. Overfishing is leading to extinction. Our choices affect real-time demand in the marketplace, and fishing is a demand-driven industry. If you're unsure, look for the Marine Stewardship Council (MSC) label of approval or the Responsible Irish Fish logo.

Mackerel is on tap in Ireland. It has to be the tastiest, cheapest and most plentiful fish I can get my greedy mitts on. If gutting or filleting fresh fish is too much for your blood pressure, ask Mr Terribly Kind Fishmonger to do it for you.

2 hardboiled eggs
1 large fillet cooked/smoked
  mackerel or 1 x 125g tin
  of mackerel
3 tablespoons anchovy aioli
  (page 48) or coconut
  yoghurt
1-2 tablespoons chopped
  spring onion or fresh dill

Serves 2

Pulse the eggs, fish and aioli or yoghurt in a food processor before adding the chopped herbs. Make it as chunky or smooth as you wish, but don't whizz the herbs or you'll end up with what looks like remnants of Kermit the Frog.

Tinned mackerel works best with aioli and smoked mackerel with yoghurt. It's great on half an avocado or the Your New Wheat-free Bread (page 51). Bring leftovers into work the next day in a jar for a sneaky mid-morning dining al desko experience. Fishavores might like to alternate mackerel with kippers or tinned wild salmon and capers.

BAKED HAKE WITH LEMONGRASS SALSA

xxxxxxxxxxxxxxxxxxxxxxxxxxxxxxxxxxxxxxxxxxxxxxxxxxxx

Farmers know all about the importance of nutrient-rich soil to grow top-quality produce. It's no different for us - nourish your body and your body will nourish you.

With that in mind, get your entire five a day with this mango and lemongrass salsa. It's also ace to bring to a BBQ. Word of caution - this salsa is the prima donna of accompaniments, made to outshine all others. Your host will hate you.

Preheat the oven to 200°C/180°C fan/400°F.

Season the hake with salt and pepper and place onto a piece of tinfoil. Secure into a tent-like parcel, transfer the tent onto a baking tray and cook for approximately 15 minutes. I always dot the fish with extra virgin coconut oil and a splash of mirin or ume, but you decide. The basic message I want to convey is that cooking fish is easy peasy. The razzmatazz is up to you.

You'll know it's cooked when it falls apart with pressure from your thumb. Raw fish won't. While the hake bakes, get going on your salsa.

There's no need to peel your mango straight away. Using a sharp knife, slice down either side of its flat, oblong stone. Cut each slice into 5 or 6 strips. Similar to a slice of melon, run your knife along the skin of each strip of mango to free its flesh. Lick your fingers and chop into small chunks. The mango, not your fingers. Peel the ginger, discarding its gnarly skin, and freeze its core for 15 minutes. Freezing fresh ginger makes it easier to grate straight into salads.

Gently toss all the salsa ingredients together. Remove the ginger from the freezer and grate it over the salsa.

When your hake is happy, serve on a big plate with the salsa running over the fish. It will end up like a large cross on the plate - the idea is not to hide the fish under the salsa. If you have any black olives lurking in your cupboards, scatter a couple over the fish for a touch of *Blue Peter*.

1 large piece of hake
a few turns of the salt and
 peppercorn mill

For the salsa:
1 mango
thumb-sized piece of fresh
 ginger
1 cup cherry tomatoes,
 quartered
3 spring onions, chopped
1 red chilli, deseeded and
 sliced into circles
1 lemongrass stalk, white
 part finely minced
1/3 cucumber, cut into small
 chunks
handful of chopped coriander
juice and zest of 1 lime
decent glug of extra virgin
 olive oil

Serves 2

SIMPLE SALMON WITH ASPARAGUS SOLDIERS AND WHIPPED GREEN TEA

xxxxxxxxxxxxxxxxxxxxxxxxxxxxxxxxxxxxxxxxxxxxxxxxxxxxxxxxxxxxxxxxxxxxxxxxxxxxxxxxxxxxxxxxx

The latest research on folic acid is rather titillating. Sufficient quantities of this B vitamin can help prolong sexual orgasms. I wonder who signed up for those trials. And whether the placebo group were just plain boring? Suddenly, folic acid seems as important to my hedonistic rights as my favourite chocolate pie.

Where can we stock up on this much-coveted substance? Your local grocery store. Asparagus is full of folate (folic acid). That's why they call it vegans' Viagra.

2 salmon or trout fillets
  (certifiably sustainable if
  possible)
dot of extra virgin coconut
  or sesame oil
large bunch of asparagus
2 tablespoons toasted sesame
  oil

For the whipped green tea:
flesh of 1 large, ripe
  avocado
juice of 1 orange
1 teaspoon wasabi powder or
  paste (Dijon mustard will
  do)
1 teaspoon matcha green tea
salt and pepper

Serves 2

Preheat the oven to 200°C/180°C fan/400°F.

Prepare the salmon by wrapping the fillets in a parcel of tinfoil and dotting with the oil. I use extra virgin raw coconut oil, but use whatever you're happiest with. Make sure there's lots of space above the fillets - it's more like a tent than a parcel. This way the fish steams in its own juices.

Transfer the tent of salmon onto a baking tray and roast for 10-15 minutes, depending on how big the fillets are. Check by pulling the flesh apart. If they're not done, just reseal your tent and pop them in the oven again. When you've become familiar with this method of cooking, crank it up another level by adding smashed lemongrass, maple syrup, chilli, cumin, kaffir lime leaves or whatever tickles your appetite on any given evening.

To roast the asparagus, start by removing the tougher ends of each asparagus spear. Gently bend each spear until it snaps. Trust the veg - it's sort of like natural selection. Discard the stalky parts and tumble the tender heads in a baking tray with the sesame oil. Roast for 10-15 minutes (same as the salmon tents), which should make them tender but not squishy.

To make the green tea whip, give the avocado, orange juice, wasabi, matcha and a touch of seasoning a jolly fine whizz with a hand-held blender. That's all there is to it. Taste, and add more wasabi if you need to ignite a dull evening or a vexatious guest.

Smear your dinner plates with a generous serving of the whip and place a fillet on top. You can arrange the asparagus on top of the salmon Jenga-style if you're brave enough.

SALMON FISHCAKES WITH CURRIED COCONUT YOGHURT

xxxxxxxxxxxxxxxxxxxxxxxxxxxxxxxxxxxxxxxxxxxxxxxxxxxxxxxxxxxxxxxxxxxxxxxx

Wild salmon is the Rob Kearney of the ocean: indecently tasty and hard to catch. Not bad for the heart and circulation either.

This supersonic fish is hailed for its cargo of omega-3, vitamin D and niacin. But before I get too misty eyed about the benefits of eating salmon, I should stress that not all salmon 'products' are created equally. Smoked, tinned, farmed or wild - each has a different nutritional purchase. While smoked might be the tastiest and the most popular, its tinned counterpart offers a lot more calcium without the smoky nitrates. Nitrates are under the watchful eye of food scientists, given their possible correlation to an increased risk of certain cancers. But then, we also have to temper our love of tinned food with questions hanging over the chemicals used in the cans. Put down the iPhone. Nothing to tweet about. Just something to be aware of should you be gobbling industrial quantities of the stuff.

Then there's the ubiquitous farmed or caged salmon, most of which are fed with dodgy colourings and antibiotics. Farmers in the US choose how pink or red they want their salmon from a colour wheel called the Salmofan. Nostril-flaring stuff. However, unlike its wilder cousin, farmed salmon is a fraction of the price and available fresh all year round. Two important factors for prudent parents.

So what does the savvy shopper do? Look out for organically farmed Irish salmon or Marine Stewardship Council endorsements, eat moderate amounts of the smoked stuff and drop into your nearest four-letter German supermarket to stock up on frozen wild salmon cutlets.

These are definitely better and cheaper than any fancy fishcake we've sunk our teeth into at restaurants. You can easily personalise this basic recipe by introducing your favourite spice: try some crushed cumin seeds, nutritional yeast flakes, caraway and fenugreek, coriander or pummelled black onion seed.

With a fork, stir the potato, spring onions,
salmon, chilli, garlic, egg, lemon zest, ginger
and salt and pepper together.

Heat your frying pan with a blob of extra virgin
coconut oil. When your pan is sufficiently hot,
drop a dessertspoonful of the fishcake mixture
onto the pan, pat with a fish slice and turn down
the heat a little to prevent it from burning.
Cook both sides until lightly coloured.

Meanwhile, mix together the yoghurt and the
curry powder. Serve the fishcakes cold or at
room temperature (not hot) with a dollop of
spicy yoghurt. The Vietnamese mint dipping sauce
on page 170 is pretty special too. Chill them
overnight if packing for a sneaky breakfast on
the bus to work.

1 1/2 cups lightly mashed
  potato
2 spring onions, chopped
1 fillet cooked salmon, flaked
  (see page 164)
1 chilli, sliced (not chilli
  powder)
1 fat garlic clove, minced
1 small egg, beaten
zest of 1/2 unwaxed lemon
good hunk of fresh ginger,
  peeled and minced
generous seasoning
extra virgin coconut oil,
  for frying

For the curried coconut
  yoghurt:
1 small tub of natural or
  coconut yoghurt, like CoYo
1 tablespoon sweet curry
  powder

Makes 8 fishcakes

CHIA CRAB CAKES WITH VIETNAMESE MINT DIPPING SAUCE

xxxxxxxxxxxxxxxxxxxxxxxxxxxxxxxxxxxxxxxxxxxxxxxxxxxxxxxxxxxxxxxxxxxxxxxxxxxx

Chia is an optional lah-di-dah. These tinchy seeds deliver a whackload of omega-3 brainpower. But if you can still remember how to solve a polynomial root with the factor theorem, you can probably leave them out.

The Vietnamese dipping sauce will leave a really refreshing taste in your mouth. If you can't be bothered making it, just add some miso paste to the mashed potatoes and wrestle some dill in there too.

For the Vietnamese mint dipping sauce:
1 red chilli, seeds removed and finely sliced
juice of 1 lime
4-6 tablespoons very finely chopped mint
1 tablespoon fish sauce (nam pla)
1 tablespoon sesame oil
1 tablespoon tamari
1 tablespoon raw honey, raw agave or yacón syrup

For the crab cakes:
2 tablespoons chopped dried mango, soaked overnight
1 1/2 cups lightly mashed potatoes
1/2-1 cup crabmeat
1 fat garlic clove, crushed
1 tablespoon chia seeds soaked in 2 tablespoons water
1 teaspoon Szechuan or black peppercorns, crushed
squeeze of lime juice
generous seasoning
2 tablespoons brown rice flour, to dust (optional)
extra virgin coconut oil, to fry
bean sprouts, to serve
Little Gem lettuces, to serve

Makes 10 small crab cakes

To make the dipping sauce, whisk everything together. Honey can be sticky, but don't worry, it eventually submits.

To make the crab cakes, start by draining the soaked mango pieces. Fresh mango won't work quite as well as its dried equivalent. Using a fork, crush with the remaining crab cake ingredients except the brown rice flour and coconut oil. If you're not making the dipping sauce, be sure to add some miso or nutritional yeast flakes to the mix for oomph. Mould into 10 small crab cakes and dust with brown rice flour (if using).

Heat a large frying pan with a little coconut oil and briefly brown each crab cake. Allow to cool completely before serving, otherwise they'll fall apart in your hands and you'll curse me. Really tasty served alongside bean sprouts and Little Gem lettuce - use the lettuce leaves to scoop up the minty mess.

FISH FINGERS WITH BEETROOT KETCHUP

xxxxxxxxxxxxxxxxxxxxxxxxxxxxxxxxxxxxxxxxxxxxxxxxxxxxxxx

Beetroot is still ranked as one of the most underused and misunderstood veggies. It's easy to find in supermarkets, yet it doesn't always mosey its way into our baskets. Dr Jonny Bowden, nutritional adviser to Hollywood's elite, rates it amongst his top superfoods. Good news for recessionistas and eco warriors because it's cheap, plentiful and comes with a low carbon footprint. We make ketchup from it. It goes devastatingly well with a salad of grated carrots, celeriac, pear and hazelnuts, for example, and keeps very well in the fridge.

You don't have to use nutritional yeast flakes in the crumb coating, but they're seriously handy to have in your cupboard. Dubbed the vegan's Parmesan, yeast flakes give your dish a nutritional upgrade and some real spine. There's also seaweed, which may sound gross but is in fact outrageously healthy. It helps bring the classic fish finger to another cosmos. Without it, we'd only hit the clouds.

These freeze exceptionally well (provided you're not using frozen fillets), so try to double the batch. They're the quickest healthy supper you can have for growing children without breaking into a sweat.

Preheat the oven to 200°C/180°C fan/400°F. Line a baking tray with parchment paper.

To make the beetroot ketchup, dice the beetroot. If using vacuum-packed beetroot, ensure there is no vinegar added as a preservative. Purée the ketchup ingredients with a hand-held blender until sumptuously smooth. Adjust the sweetness or sharpness to your preference. The honey or agave will sweeten the ketchup, while cider vinegar gives it attitude. A tiny amount of each makes a noticeable difference. Season.

To make the fish fingers, whizz the seaweed, yeast flakes and lemon zest in a food processor until they are uniform. Now stir through your almonds and transfer the mixture onto a large plate.

On another plate, lay out your chosen flour - rye, quinoa, oat, whatever you have. Pour the beaten egg onto a third plate and the pieces of fish on a fourth plate. You're ready to rock.

Using a fork - your hands need to be dry - scoop up a piece of fish, dust with flour, dip into the egg and dunk into the crumb coating. That's one fish finger. Settle on the lined baking tray and repeat until all the pieces of fish are coated.

Cook in the oven for 8-16 minutes, depending on the thickness of your fish. Lemon sole will only take 8 minutes, while thicker wedges of fish can take up to 16 minutes. Serve with the beetroot ketchup, a mini bowl of peas or diced avocado. Seriously snazzy.

For the fish fingers:
1/2 cup mixed dried seaweed, finely chopped (we use Clearspring)
1/2 cup nutritional yeast flakes (optional)
zest of 1 lemon (optional)
2 1/2 cups ground almonds or wheat-free breadcrumbs
1/2 cup flour of choice (chickpea flour doesn't work)
1 large egg, beaten
4 fillets wild salmon, pollock or lemon sole, cut into strips

For the beetroot ketchup:
4 medium-sized cooked or vacuum-packed beetroots
1 garlic clove, crushed
1 tablespoon cider vinegar
1 tablespoon raw honey or brown rice syrup
2 teaspoons organic soya or coconut yoghurt
salt and pepper

Makes 16-20 fish fingers

CHOPPED HERRING AND THE LAUREATES

xxxxxxxxxxxxxxxxxxxxxxxxxxxxxxxxxxxxxxxxxxxxxxxxxxxx

This is a classic Jewish recipe. Considering 58% of Nobel Prize winners in economics are of Jewish descent, it would be fair to conclude that Jewish mamas know how to nourish their brood.

Mood and activity in the brain are dependent on a series of chemical signals that cross each membrane with the help of neurotransmitters. This intricate process is referred to as transduction - sort of like a messaging service or a call centre. Now that we know omega-3 fats are a core component in every cell membrane, they are deemed crucial for signal trans-duction. In other words, happy call centre staff.

If, like me, you'd rather supplement your diet naturally with food and not pharma, then fill your shopping basket with foods rich in omega-3: herring, mackerel, wild salmon, sardines, anchovies, flaxseeds, chia seeds or hemp seeds. All provide better flavour and fun than those fish-oil bullets. This book sets out to help you include them in your diet. After all, where's the decadence in a tablet?

Not just an antidote to depression, the omega-3 fats in herring guard against cognitive decline (what we Irish refer to as our senior moments). No need to agonise over a pesky Rubik's cube every day. Go boost your brainpower with this laureate-loving recipe instead.

4 pickled herrings (rollmops
  will do)
2 hardboiled eggs
1 small red onion
1/2 apple
mega bunch of flat-leaf
  parsley
toast, to serve (try Your
  New Wheat-free Bread on
  page 51)

Serves 2-3

With your sharpest knife, finely dice the herring. Repeat with the eggs, onion and apple. Roughly chop the parsley and tumble everything together. You may want a little yoghurt to bring it all together, but this is not considered authentic.

SOLE AND SATAY

xxxxxxxxxxxxxxxxxxxxx

Getting teens to eat oily fish can be as easy as stuffing toothpaste back into its tube. That's why we've come up with a satay sauce using nutritious Udo's Oil. They'll get a sneaky dose of omega-3 while tucking into this stonkingly good dish. Shhh.

Chop the baby potatoes in half and steam for 20 minutes.

Meanwhile, finely chop your ginger and crush to a paste in a pestle and mortar. The base of a heavy object can sometimes work too, but can worry the neighbours and end up unreasonably messy. Mix with the remaining satay ingredients.

As soon as the potatoes are done, spoon the satay sauce over them and give it all a clumsy stir. The mess is half the charm.

Now is the time to flash-fry each sole fillet. Heat a pan on high. Dot with coconut oil and place each fillet on top. Let the teens do this part - with a bit of luck they'll surprise you one evening in the near future! Lemon sole is delicate, so gently turn after 30 seconds and flash fry the other side without letting it turn brown. If the pan is not sufficiently hot, the fish may need longer and will brown in the interim. It's a matter of taste I suppose, but I prefer mine snow white.

Plate up, sprinkle with anything green you may have lurking in the fridge (coriander? chives? rocket?) and serve with the potato satay. This is *real* fast food, to nourish your body and your creativity.

1 fillet lemon sole per
  person
extra virgin coconut oil, to
  flash fry

For the potato satay:
enough baby potatoes for 4
1 x 2.5cm piece of fresh
  ginger, peeled
6-8 tablespoons crunchy
  peanut butter
4 tablespoons Udo's Oil
3 tablespoons tamari
2 tablespoons mirin
1-2 tablespoons raw honey or
  barley malt extract
1 garlic clove, crushed
juice of 1/2 lime

Serves 4

CORIANDER AND POMEGRANATE CEVICHE WITH BOWLS OF FLOPPY FENNEL

xxxxxxxxxxxxxxxxxxxxxxxxxxxxxxxxxxxxxxxxxxxxxxxxxxxxxxxxxxxxxxxxxxxxxxxxxxxxxxxx

Freshly torn from its plant, coriander transforms a sad excuse of a salad into a party on a plate. And you're invited.

Unless you have a hotline to Diarmuid Gavin's brain, growing coriander can be a trifle tricky. Best tip? Don't bother with the supermarket plants. They are merely dejected relatives of the real thing and never live longer than their first haircut. Instead, follow these cinchy steps: (1) Sow salad seeds in a 25cm deep, well-drained pot. (2) Feed with at least 8 hours' sunlight on a windowsill. (3) Keep well watered. (4) Brag to everyone in the office that you GYO and let them rub your halo.

This will feed 4, but we double the quantities for supper parties. Very little work involved.

For the floppy fennel:
juice of 2 limes
1 tablespoon fish sauce (nam pla)
1 tablespoon toasted sesame oil
2 teaspoons maple syrup
1-2 red onions, finely sliced into semi-circles
1 fennel, topped and tailed and finely sliced

For the ceviche:
400g super-fresh fish like wild sea bass, cod, mackerel or salmon
juice of 1 blood orange
juice of 1 lime
2 tablespoons extra virgin olive oil
1 tablespoon Maldon sea salt flakes
bunch of fresh coriander, leaves only
a few tablespoons pomegranate seeds

Serves 4

To make the floppy fennel, whisk together the lime juice, fish sauce, sesame oil and maple syrup with a fork. Depending on the size of your limes, you may need to adjust the tartness by adding a smidgeon more sesame oil. Taste. Hover. Leap. Prostrate.

Pour over the thinly sliced red onions and fennel. In a few minutes, the vegetables will turn floppy and sweet, as if inebriated by the dressing. Leave them be and get going on the ceviche.

Ask your fishmonger to skin and bone the fish. If he's really nice, he'll cut them into bite-sized pieces for you too. Otherwise, you'll have to see to all three steps yourself before making the ceviche. Tumble the fish with the citrus juice, olive oil and flakes of salt. Allow to infuse for 1 hour or more in the fridge, but anything past 4 hours will turn the fish rubbery.

Tumble through the torn coriander and pomegranate seeds. Serve in a large glass bowl and have everyone help themselves alongside the bowls of floppy fennel. Plain quinoa is a great side too with a couple tablespoons of desiccated coconut.

TOMATO AND BANANA BEAN CURRY

xxxxxxxxxxxxxxxxxxxxxxxxxxxxxxxxxxxxxxxxxxxxxxx

A recent study of half a million people confirmed that eating more than 20g of processed meat a day was linked to early death. Twenty grams! That's a lick of chorizo. The research covered 10 European countries over 13 years. In other words, it's fairly bulletproof.

This news was announced in the wake of the horsemeat scandal. The clamour of worried shoppers scrambling towards the vegetarian aisles in super-markets is, frankly, unprecedented. Sales of tofu rocketed by 500%.

It's clear that our love affair with sausie sangers and shish kebabs has long needed a re-evaluation. And possibly even a P45. It takes up to seven fields of grain to feed one field of cows. No wonder there isn't enough food to feed the world - Daisy's scoffing most of it. With the intensifi-cation of global warming and the planet's population ever escalating, never has the case for cutting down on meat been more compelling. But quitting altogether? No thank you.

This is our RDA curry, squeezing loads of nutrient-dense fruit and veg into one small pot. It's enough for 5 tummies, freezes well and also keeps in the fridge for a few days. It's pretty dishy served on a bed of wilted spinach and doesn't require Birkenstocks to enjoy it. Beans are one of the most common foods found in a centenarian's diet, so if you want to live longer and look like vegan superstar Alicia Silverstone, start by Sello-taping this recipe to your cupboard door.

1 large onion, diced
2-3 tablespoons extra virgin
  olive oil
2 x 400g tins chopped
  tomatoes
1 x 400g tin mixed beans
5 dried apricots, chopped
2 bananas, sliced into rounds
2 tablespoons raisins
2 tablespoons curry powder
squeeze of lemon juice
2-3 garlic cloves, crushed
great handful of fresh
  parsley, to garnish
dollop of natural coconut
  yoghurt, to serve
a few turns of the black
  pepper mill
sweet brown rice (see page
  141), to serve

Serves 5

Normally the best way to begin a curry is by sweating the onion in olive oil on a low heat in a heavy-based saucepan until translucent, but on those seriously swift evenings, just bung it all in together. Add the tomatoes to the onion and bring to a low simmer, at which point you can add the beans, apricots, bananas, raisins, curry powder and lemon juice. Cook for 15 minutes.

The key to this recipe is to stir through the crushed garlic as soon as the curry is ready, and not before. Divide between 5 plates and drizzle reverently with extra virgin olive oil and torn parsley. Crown with a dollop of live coconut yoghurt and maybe a few turns of the black pepper mill and serve with short grain or sweet brown rice. You will feel your toes sing.

CENTENARIAN'S PINEAPPLE AND GOJI BERRY CURRY WITH RAITA AND SPINACH

xxxxxxxxxxxxxxxxxxxxxxxxxxxxxxxxxxxxxxxxxxxxxxxxxxxxxxxxxxxxxxxxxxxxxxxxxxxxxxxxxxxxxxxxxx

Gastroenterologists (the specialists who look after your pipes) recommend eating 30-35g of dietary fibre every day. That's because they know that high-fibre diets can lower the risk of developing colon and gastric cancers by 40%. One cup of cooked red kidney beans provides 11g, while adzuki beans ring in at 17g per serving. Want to know the average daily intake in Ireland? A measly 10g. So forget that hideous childhood rhyme and start loving beans. They love you.

There's a secret bonus in this recipe. Pineapple, goji berries, red onions, ginger, garlic, chilli and turmeric are all members of an anti-inflammatory squad. Many are flush with flavonoids too, otherwise known as heavyweight antioxidants that fight ageing and disease.

You can play around with the flavours here - try vindaloo, Bengali or Chinese five spice blend. The Green Saffron spice specialists do over 30 different Indian spice mixes. Let your taste buds vote. No need to stick to canned beans either. We often cook adzuki beans for 20 minutes or butter-beans for 90 minutes before adding them to the tomato base.

For the bean curry:
3 cups chopped butternut squash or sweet potato
splash of extra virgin coconut oil
3 red onions
2 red peppers, deseeded and chopped
2 x 400g tins whole tomatoes
1 cup chicken or vegetable stock
1 x 400g tin mixed beans, drained
4 slices of pineapple, skin removed and chopped
1/2 cup dried goji berries
2 tablespoons hot curry powder
1 teaspoon fresh or ground turmeric
2 garlic cloves
1 red chilli, deseeded if necessary
1 x 8cm piece of fresh ginger, peeled
sea salt flakes

For the spinach:
1 x 450g packet of frozen spinach for every 2 people
salt and pepper
extra virgin olive oil
1 garlic clove, crushed

For the raita:
cucumber
mint leaves
squeeze of lemon juice
1 teaspoon honey
natural or coconut yoghurt

Serves 8

Preheat the oven to 180°C/160°C fan/350°F.

The method employed here is more practical than traditional. Tumble the chopped butternut or sweet potato with a little oil and roast for 40 minutes, until caramelised and soft. You can leave the skin on the butternut if it's organic. Quarter the red onions and toss with the chunks of pepper and a splash of oil. Roast on a separate tray from the butternut or sweet potato for 20 minutes, until semi-soft. I keep a little raw red onion to mix through the curry before serving. It's up to you.

While the veg softens in the oven, find your largest casserole dish or stockpot and heat up the tinned tomatoes and stock. Add the drained beans, chopped pineapple, goji berries, curry powder and turmeric. Let this gurgle away for 10-15 minutes, by which time the roasted onions and peppers will be ready.

Remove the tray from the oven and shake the veg into your pot of spicy tomatoes. Your nostrils should be levitating by now. Turn down the heat very low and prep the last few ingredients while the butternut is finishing off in the oven.

Crush the garlic, chilli and ginger together with a sprinkle of sea salt flakes in a pestle and mortar to make a seriously fragrant paste. These are heroic immune-boosting anti-inflammatory foods. Stir the paste through the curry. The idea is not to cook these ingredients, but rather warm them so their medicinal qualities are not significantly diminished.

Pour 3cm of boiling water over the spinach and boil for 2 minutes in a small saucepan with a fitted lid. When it's defrosted (no need to murder it), drain very well in a sieve, give it a few turns of the salt and pepper mill, tickle with olive oil and maybe another lick of garlic.

The raita is a cinch - chop a bit of cucumber and mint. Add a spot of lemon juice and/or honey to natural yoghurt, taste, and adjust to your preferences. Spinach and raita are pretty special additions to this meal. Without them, think gin with no tonic.

As soon as the butternut or potato is soft, add it to the tomato curry, ramp up the heat and roar at everyone to take their places at the dinner table. Time to plate up.

PUMPKIN FALAFEL

It's a shame Halloween has monopolised the pumpkin. They're far too fabulous to be dismissed for 11 months of the year.

This vegetable's buttery flesh is stuffed with goodness. There's potassium for hangovers, vitamins A and C to slay superbugs (think Uma Thurman in Kill Bill) and extra carotenoids for those who can't afford to keep up their Botox instalments. That's a lot of ammunition for a supposedly ghoulish vegetable.

On the antioxidant radar, pumpkins are almost up there with blueberries and spinach. We like antioxidants because they help prevent the bad LDL cholesterol in our bloodstream from oxidising. Once oxidation occurs, the likelihood of cholesterol depositing onto blood vessel walls significantly increases. Not sure I like the sound of that.

Heart surgeon Dr Oz Mehmet has even devised a recipe for pumpkin brownies to entice his clients into eating more of this useful vegetable. According to Dr Oz, pumpkins are probably one of the best foods we ain't eatin'.

Here's our recipe, based on Allegra McEvedy's (one of my favourite chefs). Deep-frying falafel may taste delish, but isn't recommended for our waist-lines or arteries. Shame. More alarmingly, deep-frying food can make your mouth feel like a camel's armpit. Luckily, Allegra designed hers to be baked.

around 500g roasted pumpkin pieces
125g chickpea flour (aka gram flour) or chestnut flour
2 garlic cloves, crushed
zest and juice of 1/2 lemon
2-3 tablespoons extra virgin coconut or olive oil
2 tablespoons chopped spring onions
2 teaspoons ground cumin
black sesame seeds, to garnish

Makes 8-12 falafel

Preheat the oven to 170°C/150°C fan/340°F.

This recipe isn't a science. You're aiming for the falafel to be one-quarter chickpea or chestnut flour. It's really that simple, so use whatever amount of pumpkin you have and adjust the recipe as appropriate.

Roasting pumpkin is a cinch too - no peeling necessary. Just make sure to avoid the monstrous Cinderella ones. Start by cautiously hacking the side of the pumpkin. Chop this flesh into matchbox-sized pieces and continue to work your way around the pumpkin. The hardest part is that first slice. Tumble the pieces into a roasting tray with a good splash of coconut or olive oil. Cover with foil. Roast for 45-60 minutes, until sweet and tender. Pumpkin is better overcooked rather than undercooked.

Remove the tray of pumpkin and let the pieces cool completely before handling. If you've roasted more than you need, count yourself lucky. Whizz any leftover pieces with coconut milk, sautéed onions and a pinch of curry powder to make soup. Or freeze a batch for your next falafel craving.

Raise the oven temperature to 200°C/180°C fan/400°F. Line a baking tray with parchment paper or grease with a lick of olive oil.

Using clean hands, mash all the falafel ingredients except the black sesame seeds together. Put the falafel mix in the freezer for 15-30 minutes to firm up. Mould the chilled mixture into falafels and place on the lined baking tray. I find an ice cream scoop is the best way to shape falafel. If you use teaspoons and patience, you'll double the portions and halve the baking time. Sprinkle with black sesame seeds and cook in the oven for 20-45 minutes, depending on their size.

Try serving alongside thick natural or coconut yoghurt, smooth hummus, Maple Mustard Lentils (page 158) or a big bowl of peas. The messier, the better.

ANTI-INFLAMMATORY ALOO

xxxxxxxxxxxxxxxxxxxxxxxxx

This famous dish gets its psychedelic glow from poor man's saffron (turmeric). Its high veggie content also helps it feel like a big bowl of sunshine. Anti-inflammatory Aloo isn't the sexiest of names for a Saturday night curry, but did you know that inflammation relates to heaps of common conditions, such as psoriasis, bruising, swelling, hay fever, joint pain, chest infections, IBS and asthma?

You'll find a hub of ingredients in this aloo to help reduce menacing prostaglandins in the body. There are good prostaglandins and bad prostaglandins. Both manage the inflammatory process. The bad ones morph into inflammatory markers in your bloodstream and can make your body feel like a rusty BMX with a 20-ton rhino on the Tour de France. Anti-inflammatory foods like turmeric, ginger, goji berries, onions and chilli can help interrupt the life cycle of bad prostaglandins so that less of them end up circulating in your body. Pretty nifty, huh?

Start by peeling and finely chopping the onion and ginger. Heat a heavy-based casserole pot on your lowest setting with a few tablespoons of oil and add your chopped onion, ginger, chilli, cumin, mustard seeds and turmeric. Sweat for 10 minutes. Your nostrils will applaud.

Cut the baby potatoes into generous mouthfuls. Prepare your cauliflower by discarding the outer leaves, breaking into Lego-sized florets and cutting the centre stalk into rough cubes. Be sure not to throw this part out - it adds wonderful texture to your aloo. Toss the potatoes, cauliflower and butterbeans with the sautéed onion, coating everything with the spice's golden glow. Pour over the stock and add the goji berries (if using). Bring to the boil, cover with a lid and let it gurgle for 20-25 minutes, until the veggies are soft but not soggy. They will joyously soak up most of the stock while simmering away. Taste, and season with sea salt and a few turns of the black pepper mill. Serve with fresh coriander stirred through the gobi.

Other aloo gobi variations include a tablespoon of garam masala, shrimp, peanuts, desiccated coconut or raw minced garlic stirred through at the end, or a squeeze of lemon just before serving. Let your taste buds vote.

1 large red onion
thumb-sized piece of fresh
  ginger
splash of extra virgin
  coconut or peanut oil
1 green chilli, deseeded and
  finely chopped
1 tablespoon ground cumin
1 tablespoon black mustard
  seeds (optional)
2 teaspoons ground turmeric
6 baby potatoes
1/2 head of cauliflower
1 cup cooked (see page 118)
  or tinned butterbeans,
  drained
2 cups chicken, fish or
  veggie stock
1/4 cup goji berries
  (optional)
salt and pepper
fresh coriander, to serve

Serves 4

RED DAAL WITH WILTED SPINACH AND A PLUMP POACHED EGG

xxxxxxxxxxxxxxxxxxxxxxxxxxxxxxxxxxxxxxxxxxxxxxxxxxxxxxxxxxxxxxxxxxxxxxxxxxxxxx

This dish requires little or no kitchen experience. Unlike beans, red lentils do not need pre-soaking or hours of patience. You'll find most of the ingredients already lurking in your cupboard, making it particularly attractive for unexpected callers.

Research from the British Journal of Pharmacology shows that garlic and ginger contain anti-bacterial and anti-inflammatory compounds to help soothe anything from swollen tonsils to achy limbs. Did you know most common skin complaints involve inflammation? Dandruff, psoriasis, acne and eczema - all would benefit from a good frolic with garlic and ginger. Besides, they're outrageously tasty, dead cheap and will vastly improve a dull date.

1 onion, diced

2 tablespoons extra virgin coconut or olive oil

1 cup dried red lentils, washed

6-8 cloves

2 garlic cloves, finely chopped

1 tablespoon mustard seeds (wholegrain mustard would do)

1 tablespoon minced ginger

1 teaspoon whole black or white peppercorns, smashed

chicken stock or water

3 handfuls of baby spinach leaves

3 poached eggs (see page 150)

nice squeeze of lemon juice (optional)

Serves 3

Start by sweating the onion in the oil on a low setting for 10 minutes, until they appear slightly glassy. A heavy-based saucepan is perfect to avoid the onions 'catching' on the bottom of the pan and burning. If you fry the onions at a higher temperature, the oil will chemically change and play with your arteries. It doesn't matter if you use the best cold-pressed extra virgin oil money can buy. High heat, as opposed to gentle warmth, chemically disfigures oil and spoils most of the health benefits it carries. If you suffer from cholesterol or weight problems, it might be worth writing this on the inside of your kitchen cupboard to remind you!

As the onions sweat, in another medium-sized saucepan combine the lentils, cloves, garlic, mustard seeds, ginger and peppercorns. Add enough chicken stock or water to cover the lentils by about 2cm and bring to a boil. Sometimes we do a blend of carrot juice and water to give the lentils a fabulously rich colour and sweetness. Adjust the heat so that the lentils putter away rather than violently bubble. Cover and cook for about 12 minutes, then remove from the heat, keep the lid on and allow to stand on the countertop until tender. Ideally, daal should be saucy, not soupy, so keeping the lid on the pan will naturally steam the lentils for another couple of minutes.

Remove the cloves from the cooked lentils (it helps if you remember exactly how many you popped in) and add the baby spinach and the sautéed onion. Divide between 3 bowls and slip your poached egg on top. Finish off with a generous squeeze of lemon and love.

FLASH-FRIED PLAICE WITH PINK PEPPERCORN SALT AND LEMON DUST

xxxxxxxxxxxxxxxxxxxxxxxxxxxxxxxxxxxxxxxxxxxxxxxxxxxxxxxxxxxxxxxxxxxxxxxxxxxxxxxxxxxxxxxxxx

That gorgeous Italian Laura Santtini has bewitched me with her Flash Cooking. It's not a diet or a fad. It's a masterclass in creativity and time poverty. Santtini's mission is to arm your kitchen with an arsenal of explosively tasty spices, finishing salts and scented yoghurts. They are guaranteed to transform your meals, and possibly even your life.

Plaice is a super-slim fish that cooks in less than 90 seconds. Not so good from the freezer, so make sure your plaice is hyper-fresh. I buy the white-bellied fillets as opposed to the black side because the soft white skin is the best part. Plaice camouflage themselves in the ocean - one side is dark and mottled so that predators above the plaice can't differentiate them from the ocean floor. Their underbelly is white so that predators below them think they are shards of light glistening in the water. Poor things never accounted for crafty fishermen.

a dot of extra virgin
  coconut oil
2 x plaice fillets
zest of 1 small lemon
1 teaspoon pink peppercorns
pinch of sea salt flakes,
  like Maldon
black olives, to serve
roasted fennel (page 152),
  to serve

Serves 2

Heat a large frying pan on high. When the pan is piping hot, dot with coconut oil and immediately drop the fillets over the oil. Each side should only take 20-40 seconds to cook, during which time you can zest the lemon and crush the pink peppercorns in a pestle and mortar. Mix the zest and peppercorns with the flakes of salt and dust each fillet with this finishing touch as soon as you plate up. You'll need to work at an inflammable speed.

Plaice is too delicate for lemon juice, so the zest is perfect. A simple bowl of black olives and lightly roasted fennel serves us well.

UMAMI BEEF STEW

xxxxxxxxxxxxxxxxxxxxxxxx

Domini Kemp is a badass Irish chef who women want to be and men want to meet. This is her flavour bomb. One of Domini's restaurants, Hatch & Sons Irish Kitchen, pencils it on the menu from time to time. I've seen fans bless themselves in its presence.

Umami is our fifth taste sensation, often underserviced. Scientists refer to this neglected fifth taste bud as the lip-smacking point. Think anchovies, Parmesan cheese, miso, tamari soya sauce and prosciutto. Domini uses streaky rashers in the original recipe, but given the fatwa on piggies in our house, we subbed it with umami-rich seaweed and mushrooms.

This freezes really well, so tuck some away for those evenings when you couldn't be bothered to knock up a meal from scratch.

a good few splashes of extra
  virgin olive oil
800g stewing beef or lamb,
  cut into 2-3cm chunks
500g wild mixed mushrooms
  (dried won't work)
2 large onions, chopped
1/2 head of garlic, peeled
  and sliced
large glass of red wine
strip of dried wakame or
  kombu (optional)
1.5 litres stock
1 x 50g tin anchovy fillets
2 heaped tablespoons tomato
  purée
3 bay leaves

For the sweet potato purée:
6 large sweet potatoes
seasoning

Or a carrot and mango purée:
8 medium carrots, unpeeled
handful of dried mango
  pieces
extra virgin coconut oil

Serves 8

Preheat the oven to 160°C/140°C fan/325°F.

It's quicker to have 2 pans frying simultaneously. Using a heavy-based pan, brown the meat all over in batches. This should take 10-15 minutes. Make sure the meat almost looks caramelised.

Take your biggest ovenproof pot (ideally a cast iron, heavy-bottomed casserole dish like Le Creuset) and sauté the mushrooms, onions and garlic in small batches in some oil. As they soften and colour, transfer to a large plate with the browned meat. Work like this for 15 minutes, until all the beef, mushrooms and onions are coloured and ready to rock. The reason we don't bung them all into one pan is because they will sweat rather than caramelise.

Once the beef has finished browning, deglaze the pan with a large glass of red wine and transfer to the ovenproof pot. Let the mushrooms, onions, garlic and kombu or wakame (if using) join the party. Add the stock, anchovies, tomato purée and bay leaves and bring to a simmer.

Pop it into the oven and cook for about 2 hours with a lid on. Turn the heat way down to 120°C/100°C fan/250°F. Cook for another 60 minutes.

To make the sweet potato purée, pop the spuds
whole into a hot oven for 1 hour. They will
naturally steam in their skins, provided they
are not cut or slit. If the potatoes are massive,
you'll need an extra 30 minutes' cooking time.
Adjust as you feel fit. Sweet potatoes are best
when they are really soft, and not al dente.
Once they are properly cooked, their skins will
peel off easily. Mash with tasty seasoning like
Herbamare or celery salt. You can purée them in a
food processor to achieve a silky-smooth finish.
Sweet potatoes behave differently to regular white
spuds and can be put through a blender without
turning into glue.

For the carrot and mango purée, chop up the
carrots and steam with the dried mango for 10-15
minutes. Make sure they are very soft before
whizzing in a food processor or a hand-held
blender. Add a drop of coconut oil for cream-
iness.

All 3 dishes can be made 1 or 2 days in advance
of a dinner party and reheated when required. In
fact, the stew tastes even better when the beef
gets a chance to absorb all those umami semi-
quavers. Amen.

LICKY-STICKY WINGS WITH CHILLI SAUCE

xxxxxxxxxxxxxxxxxxxxxxxxxxxxxxxxxxxxxxxxxxxxxxxxxxxxxxxxxxxx

*I think cutlery is really odd. Touch is a sense that can heighten taste.
Try this recipe and see for yourself. Serve with your favourite bean
sprouts, dressed with freshly juiced ginger if possible or a tray of
roasted parsnip and carrot.*

Preheat the oven to 200°C/180°C fan/400°F.

Carefully remove any stray feathers from the
wings and discard. Throw the wings onto a
roasting tray and drizzle with the lemon juice,
honey, oil and peppercorns. Give everything a
jolly good tumble to coat well. Roast for
40 minutes, shaking the tray whenever you
remember to.

If you are cooking enough wings for 4 people, you
will need 2 trays. The magic in browning wings is
to give them plenty of space and independence on
the roasting tray. The same principle applies to
roasting veg – an overcrowded tray generates too
much steam between the ingredients, resulting in
a soggy, insipid meal.

To make the chilli sauce, knock it up with a
hand-held blender or stir together with a fork
and strength. The wings are sufficiently tasty on
their own, but the sauce amps up the reverie.
There's something so primal about chicken wings
and great big bowls of licky-sticky yummy.

around 12 chicken wings
juice of 1 large lemon
2 tablespoons honey (not
  agave)
2 tablespoons extra virgin
  coconut oil
1 tablespoon black or
  Szechuan peppercorns,
  smashed

For the chilli sauce:
2-3 tablespoons barley malt
  extract, raw agave or
  yacón syrup
2 tablespoons fresh miso
  paste
2 tablespoons cold-pressed
  toasted sesame oil
1/2 teaspoon cayenne

Serves 2-3

ROAST CHICKEN WITH IRISH GREMOLATA AND CHARRED PUMPKIN

xxxxxxxxxxxxxxxxxxxxxxxxxxxxxxxxxxxxxxxxxxxxxxxxxxxxxxxxxxxxxxxxxxxxxxxxxxxxxxxxxxxxxx

Chicken is a special treat in our home, when an occasion demands. We don't think meat is evil. I like Mark Bittman's idea of using meat as a garnish instead of giving meat the lead role. Hugh Fearnley-Whittingstall built on Bittman's idea by publishing a book with vegetables as its entire cast. This may not seem unusual, except that Hugh is Britain's High Priest of Carnivore-ville.

Scientists warn that the amount of meat we eat is unhealthy and unsustainable. Therein lies the problem. If Bittman's resolution seems too darn difficult, another smart option is to only buy meat when it is free range and unprocessed. Meat piracy is a curse.

1 large organic, free-range or higher-welfare chicken
1 large fennel bulb (optional)
1 large, juicy lemon
2 tablespoons extra virgin coconut oil
sea salt flakes

For the Irish gremolata:
pinch of sea veg (arame is excellent)
4 garlic cloves
zest and juice of 2 lemons
1 cup extra virgin olive oil
50g parsley, finely chopped

For the charred pumpkin:
1 small organic pumpkin
extra virgin coconut or olive oil

Serves 6

Take your chicken out of the fridge 40 minutes before cooking. It's also a good idea to clear the kitchen sink so that when you wash your hands after touching the bird, you don't transfer bacteria to your dishes.

Preheat the oven to 230°C/210°C fan/450°F. Quarter the fennel (if using) and place in the centre of a roasting tray. Carefully remove the chicken's packaging and gently place the bird on top of the fennel. Wash your hands thoroughly after handling the bird, especially if you have children dancing at your heels.

Roll the lemon under the palm of your hand (an Aga or microwave will briefly warm it up to get the juices spilling). Halve the lemon and rub the bird all over with it. Squeeze the juice into the tray and pop the empty lemon halves in the bird's cavity. Dot with the coconut oil and season with a flurry of salt flakes.

Place the tray into the oven and turn it down to 200°C/180°C fan/400°F. Cook a 1.6kg bird for approximately 1 hour 20 minutes. The top of the chicken leg bones will look dry and prominent once the bird is cooked and the meat should easily come away from the bone. If not, leave in the oven for longer.

Meanwhile, to make the Irish gremolata, soak the arame in water for 10 minutes to rehydrate.

If you've chosen a different sea veg, follow the
instructions on the packet. Discard the soaking
water once it's ready and roughly chop. Use a
kitchen grater to mince each clove of garlic.
Follow with the lemon zest. Squeeze the juice from
both lemons and add the oil. Add the parsley and
give it all a good shake in a jam jar. Set aside.

Slice the pumpkin into wedges using vigour and
vigilance. Scoop out its stringy nest and dice
the flesh into matchbox-sized pieces. If it's
organic, keep the skin on - saves on time and
gives extra nutrition. We've also noticed that
organic pumpkins are 10 times tastier than
conventional ones. Tumble the pumpkin pieces onto
a large baking tray and give it a good lick of
coconut or olive oil. Roast on high for 45-65
minutes, or until it starts browning and caramelising around the edges. The same temperature as
the chicken is fine. Shake the tray once or twice
during roasting to share the juices around the
pan and let your nostrils party.

The pumpkin can start cooking 1 hour before the
chicken finishes cooking so that it all comes out
of the oven at the same time. While the chicken
rests, you can switch off the oven, leave the door
ajar and keep the pumpkin and guests warm.

If you have time, roast a tray of carrots too or
prepare the carrot and mango purée on page 192.
This will help stretch the meal to 8 and bump up
your veggie intake.

10-HOUR SHOULDER OF LAMB WITH CRUSHED CHICKPEAS AND THE BEST SAUCE YOU'RE EVER LIKELY TO TASTE

xxxxxxxxxxxxxxxxxxxxxxxxxxxxxxxxxxxxxxxxxxxxxxxxxxxxxxxxxxxxxxxxxxxxxxxxx

Here's some slow-cooked lamb that effortlessly falls off the bone. Let it cosy up to some messy chickpea smash and a scorching hot Middle Eastern mojo. This recipe was designed to help mend marriages.

For the slow-cooked lamb:
1 shoulder of mutton (an older lamb)
2 tablespoons balsamic vinegar
a few tablespoons sumac (optional)

For the crushed chickpeas:
500g dried chickpeas
1 teaspoon bicarbonate of soda
1 strip of kombu seaweed (optional)
1/2 cup cashew nut butter
3 garlic cloves, crushed
3 tablespoons tamari (or generous seasoning)
squeeze of lemon juice

For the hot anchovy mojo:
1 x 50g tin anchovies (8-10 anchovies)
3-5 mixed medium chillies, deseeded
3 garlic cloves, crushed
1 red pepper, finely chopped
1 yellow pepper, finely chopped
2 large bunches of fresh coriander
1 tablespoon ground cumin
1 tablespoon dried oregano
juice of 1 lemon
dash of sherry vinegar (to taste)
great big glug of extra virgin olive oil

Serves 5

Start tonight by soaking the chickpeas in cold water. Tomorrow, drain and discard the soaking water. Tip the chickpeas into your largest heavy-based pan with the bicarb and ramp up the heat. Stir for 30 seconds without burning the bum off the pan. Pour in 2-3 litres of water and the strip of kombu seaweed (if using). Bring to a rolling boil and cook for 1 hour. While you want the chickpeas to be soft and cooked, try not to let them go mushy. Taste a chickpea every so often and decide how soft you like them to be. A good test is to press one between your middle finger and thumb - the chickpea should just about submit to pressure.

Remove from the heat, drain and set three-quarters of the chickpeas aside. Blitz the other one-quarter in a food processor with the cashew nut butter and garlic. Add a good few splashes of ice-cold water from the fridge, just to loosen it up. Finish whizzing to a smooth cream.

Roll the cream into the drained chickpeas and gently crush some of the chickpeas to let in the flavours of the smooth sauce. Douse with enough tamari and lemon juice to suit your fancy. You can leave this big pot of crushed chickpeas covered in a warm oven until required.

To make the hot anchovy mojo, give all the ingredients a jolly good whizz in your food processor, but not with a hand-held blender. Food processors give chunkier textures, whereas hand blenders are basically creamers. As spicy, captivating and sparkling as that first kiss, this sauce is high octane.

To cook the lamb, preheat the oven to 220°C/200°C fan/425°F.

Rub the lamb with the balsamic vinegar and sumac (if using) and place on a roasting tin with high edges. Bring to room temperature before blasting at high heat in the oven for 20 minutes. Turn down the heat to 140°C/120°C fan/275°F and cook for 8 hours.

Pull some meat away from the bone after 6-8 hours to check how it's doing. If you are doubling up to feed 10, then make sure to give the lamb a few extra hours. Increasing the quantity of food in the oven often dilutes the heat and can result in undercooking, especially at this temperature. Similarly, if the lamb is a small spring shoulder, it probably only needs 6 hours and will feed fewer people. The meat is done as soon as it falls from the bone and practically dissolves in your mouth.

We find the best way to serve this is by piling everything on the table. A simple crisp salad dressed in lemon juice and black pepper can help stretch out the number of mouths to feed.

CHOCOLATE CHILLI CON CARNE WITH COCONUT YOGHURT AND JAZZY ONIONS

xxxxxxxxxxxxxxxxxxxxxxxxxxxxxxxxxxxxxxxxxxxxxxxxxxxxxxxxxxxxxxxxxxxxxxxxxxxxxxxxxxxxxxxxxxx

*If you are a feral carnivore, like my husband, here's a good way of intro-
ducing more beans and veg to your diet without feeling oppressed. The
overtones are there (what man won't wolf down a Chilli Con Beast?), but so
is the nutritional purchase. It doesn't actually taste of chocolate, but
rather, utilises cacao powder as another spice in the mix.*

*By downloading some good podcasts at RadioLab.org, you'll prep this before
you even realise it. Put your feet up, and enjoy the dance your nostrils
will do over the next 2 hours. Serve with great big dollops of cultured
coconut yoghurt, macerated red onions and exceptional company.*

1 1/2 cups dried kidney beans, soaked overnight
2 onions
2 red peppers
1 large carrot
4 garlic cloves
extra virgin olive or coconut oil, for sautéing
2 tablespoons tomato purée (optional)
1 tablespoon dried oregano
1 tablespoon raw cacao powder
1 tablespoon sweet or hot paprika (optional)
1 cinnamon stick
good pinch of dried chilli flakes
pinch of coconut sugar (optional)
500g minced beef
2 x 400g tins chopped tomatoes
just over 300ml vegetable or beef stock
salt and pepper
1 tablespoon ground cumin
2-4 squares dark or raw chocolate (optional)

To serve:
1 small red onion
1 really juicy lime
1 tablespoon nam pla (optional)
fistful of fresh coriander (optional)
natural coconut yoghurt, like CoYo

Serves 10-12

First off, soak the dried kidney beans overnight.
The next day, prep the veggies. I find the easiest
way to dice the onions is to cut each onion
in half, from root to toe. Peel and place the

flat part on the chopping board. With a slicing action, make little matchsticks from the onion lengthways, but not quite cutting all the way to the root end so that they are still held together. Now slice across the matchsticks.

Roughly chop the peppers and carrot into bite-sized chunks, discarding the pepper seeds and stalks. Slice your garlic and line up all your dried spices and herbs. Now you're ready to cook.

Heat a little oil in your largest sauté pan or frying pan (I have 2 going at the same time to speed things up). Sweat the onions first, stirring regularly for 10 minutes, until they become glassy. Put them aside, then sauté the peppers and carrot until soft but not browned. Add the garlic towards the end, along with the tomato purée, spices and coconut sugar (if using). Cook for a good 5 minutes and let your nostrils samba. Remove from the heat and pile on top of the resting onions.

Now whack up the heat and brown the mince all over. Mince needs to be browned or the end result will be disappointingly insipid. You may need to do this in 2 batches.

Tip in the soaked kidney beans (tinned is okay in an emergency), tinned tomatoes and stock. Don't worry if it looks a little icky. The pot will transform in a few hours. Stir in the veg, pop a lid on and let it paddle on a low heat for 2-3 hours. It's done as soon as the beans are soft, but not mushy.

Taste, tickle with salt and pepper and add the cumin and dark chocolate to liven it up. If you feel it needs more pungency, add some yeast extract, blackstrap molasses or chopped anchovies. Sometimes we do, sometimes we don't.

To serve, cut the red onion in half and finely slice into semi-circles. Squeeze the lime over the onions, and allow them to party with the nam pla. Top each bowl of chilli con carne with a little macerated red onion, fresh coriander (if using) and a great big dollop of cultured coconut yoghurt in place of sour cream. It's the holy trinity to a good con carne.

Extra Virgin Treats

I'm through with guilt.

Looking back, I could never get enough sugar hits. I was an addict. Everything I did related to or led to my next sugar fix. I even convinced myself that college projects required kilos of coffee and Curly Wurlies to charge my brain cells. I couldn't possibly perform without them.

Sound familiar?

Having to give up junk food was like a bad break-up with the love of my life. Sudden. Undesired. Unexpected. Grief smothered my senses like a diaphanous veil over my entire body. I struggled deeply to wave goodbye to the things I loved in life: my chocolate bars, ice cream, cupcakes, panna cotta. Clearly, they did not love me back. Like all cases of unrequited love, I had to get over myself, move on, or drown in a pool of self-pity.

Here were my choices - ignore the medical advice I was given and dig my way to the grave with my teeth? Or nosedive into an apron and role-play with Heston Blumenthal?

I chose the latter.

Today, my body is in balance. There are no sugar binges or episodes of overeating. That's because my cravings are satisfied with real food that nourishes my neurotransmitters in a way that white sugar and flour never could.

It's *sooo* good to leave the wheat-sugar-dairy circus, to let your body samba to something less generic and more wholesome. Do it! If you feed your body, your body will feed you. So here are loads of treats to help turn your naughty cravings into a nutritional hit. A word of caution - your wings will go wild and your toes may take off. *Sláinte!*

Raw Cacao Nib Toffee --------------

----------- Goji Berry Smudge

GOJI BERRY SMUDGE

>>>>>>>>>>>>>>>>>>>>>>>>

This is like a smoochy fudge. It's quite possibly my favourite recipe.

We know that good bone health is intimately linked to what we eat. Dr Marilyn Glenville, specialist in women's health, is dubious about dairy's monopoly on calcium in our diet. Why, Glenville asks, is our rate of osteoporosis much higher than Japan's, where they don't even eat dairy? A good question. Glenville is not alone. New York Times best-selling author Dr Joel Fuhrman doesn't rate dairy at all. Fuhrman's medical research and experience as a GP have entirely reversed his thinking about dairy. Worthy of further head-scratching.

So let's explore alternative sources to dairy without having to mourn our cheese board. These include tinned salmon and sarnies, barley grass, chickpeas, broccoli, figs, sesame seeds, tahini, almonds, hazelnuts and green leafy veg. This Goji Berry Smudge is a great place to start.

Melt the coconut oil on a very gentle heat. Stir in the maple syrup, vanilla and salt. The grooviest salt to use in desserts is a vanilla-infused organic salt from Halen Môn in Wales. Find it online or in Fallon & Byrne, Dublin 2.

With a fork, beat through the tahini, goji berries and hemp seeds (if you don't have hemp seeds, no worries). Keep some gojies to tickle the top. Scrape half the mixture into a small rectangular container lined with cling film. Dribble runny honey over it and scrape the remaining mixture on top of the honey. Prod it with a fork and give it a swirl to move the honey about without incorporating it into the tahini. Think caramel swirls.

Freeze for 4 hours. Just like ice cream, it must be stored in the freezer or else it will melt into a holy mess. Slice big wedges from it and marvel at its virtuous decadence.

3 tablespoons extra virgin coconut oil

up to 1/2 cup maple or brown rice syrup

1 teaspoon vanilla extract or powder

1 teaspoon Maldon sea salt flakes

1 x 340g jar light tahini

4 tablespoons goji berries

2 tablespoons hemp seeds (optional nutritional boost)

2-3 tablespoons runny raw honey

Makes 30 servings

RAW CACAO NIB TOFFEE

>>>>>>>>>>>>>>>>>>>>>>>>>>>>>>

Apparently, women think about chocolate more then men. Some scientists think this is because eating cacao helps release a cavalry of dopamine in the female brain, the same substance released during orgasm. It's even been suggested that when women eat raw chocolate, it affects activity in the cerebral hemisphere responsible for regulating sexual desire. Only one way to find out…

1/2 cup date syrup
3 tablespoons extra virgin
   coconut oil
1 mug light tahini (or 1 x
   340g jar)
3 tablespoons raw cacao nibs
2 tablespoons carob powder
2 teaspoons vanilla extract
pinch of sea salt flakes

Makes 25-30 servings

Melt the date syrup and coconut oil together over a low heat. Add the remaining ingredients, mushing with a fork. Ensure the oil is well mixed. Taste, and adjust with vanilla or sweetener. Work quickly, as the oil will begin to separate from the other ingredients as soon as it starts cooling. It needs a warm environment.

Line a small rectangular container (a little lunchbox perhaps?) with cling film so that it comes out over the sides. Transfer your gorgeous gooey gloss into the lined container and tickle with more cacao nibs (if you have any left).

Transfer to the freezer for 4 hours before indulging. Store it there too, as it melts quite quickly at room temperature.

FANCY PANTS LÚCUMA FUDGE

>>>>>>>>>>>>>>>>>>>>>>>>>>>>>>>>>>>>>

I'm a firm believer in the idea that healthy eating should never tax your taste buds. This recipe has an authentic fudgy feel, but with none of the wicked additives or cosmetic gunk. It practically levitates with goodness.

Ever look 20 years older on a Sunday morning? Or sport a dirty big hangover? This recipe will help. Lúcuma is a fancy pants fruit from South America, good enough for the gods and maybe even for Satan. Its creamy flesh falls between an avocado and an egg yolk - a killer combo. Its perfume will even drive your senses wild. Sadly, lúcuma is just too perishable to find fresh in Ireland. Instead, its flesh is freeze-dried before exporting. For helpful online sources of where to find it, see page 253.

Line a very small container with cling film. Gently melt the coconut oil over a low heat and stir in the remaining ingredients with a fork. If you intend using the vanilla pod, split it along the side lengthways, carefully peel the pod open and using the blade of a knife, scoop out its fabulous black seeds. Add to the fudge mix, which should look like wet sand by now. Taste, and adjust the sweetness or saltiness to your preferences.

Spoon into your lined container and let it set in the fridge before cutting into chunks of fudge. It should be ready to devour in 1 hour.

4 tablespoons extra virgin coconut oil
8 tablespoons ground almonds
3 tablespoons lúcuma powder
2 tablespoons maple syrup or raw honey
1 vanilla pod (optional) or 1 teaspoon vanilla powder
sprinkle of decent unrefined salt, like Himalayan pink rock salt

Makes 12 servings

LEMON WHOOPIE PIES

>>>>>>>>>>>>>>>>>>>>>>>>>

Whoopie pies are teeny custard cream cakes with a personality all of their own. Every time my son confides that these whoopie pies are his 'favourite burgers in the world', my chest swells. I think he's an aspiring vegetarian. Or con artist. It's so hard to tell at three, but the pride is definitely undisputed and comical in equal measures.

When I'm baking for kiddies' birthday parties, I use organic cream cheese instead for the vanilla custard cream. If any of their buddies are lactose intolerant, the filling below does the trick.

For the whoopie pies:
1/2 cup coconut flour
1/2 cup ground almonds
zest of 1 small lemon
2 tablespoons desiccated
   coconut
2 teaspoons baking powder
1/2 teaspoon ground turmeric
1/2 teaspoon unrefined
   organic salt
4 medium eggs
1/2 cup extra virgin coconut
   oil
1/2 cup runny honey or brown
   rice syrup (not maple)
good squeeze of lemon juice

For the vanilla custard
   cream:
1 cup cashews, soaked in
   water overnight
1/2 cup water
1/4 cup raw agave, barley
   malt extract or brown rice
   syrup (not maple syrup)
2 teaspoons vanilla extract
   (powder is visually
   better)
squeeze of lemon juice
   (optional kick)
1/2 cup extra virgin coconut
   oil, melted

Makes 10 large or 20 small
   pies

Preheat the oven to 170°C/150°C fan/340°F. Line 2 trays with parchment paper.

To make the biscuit base, you'll be using 2 separate bowls. In the first bowl, stir together the dry ingredients. The second bowl wants the wet ingredients (eggs, oil, natural syrup and lemon juice).

Add the dry ingredients to the wet and mix well. Spoon little puddles onto the lined baking trays. You may need to cook the whoopies in batches, especially if they're teeny tiny ones. Bake large whoopies for 15-18 minutes. If you made smaller whoopies, they'll only require 12-15 minutes.

Remove from the oven and allow to set for 15 minutes before transferring them from their tray and sandwiching with the vanilla custard cream.

To make the vanilla custard cream, discard the soaking water from the cashews. Blitz the nuts in a high-speed food processor with the fresh water, natural syrup, vanilla and optional lemon for a good 2 minutes.

Meanwhile, gently melt the solid coconut oil until liquid. While the motor is still running, slowly add the coconut oil to the whizzed cashew (like you would if making mayonnaise). Blitz until smooth rather than grainy. The custard cream tends to thicken once chilled for a few hours, so don't panic if it looks like milk.

Once it's spreadable, use a knife or fancy implement to slather the filling over a whoopie base, then top with another biscuit. The custard cream should be chilled enough to stay firmly in place and hold the whoopie pie together. Take a deep breath, put on some Frank Sinatra and nosedive into the largest one.

DELINQUENT BROWNIES

>>>>>>>>>>>>>>>>>>>>>>>>>>>

These brownies will fool the most ardent of brownie bingers. Not as saccharine as regular cane sugar, coconut blossom sugar offers a burnt toffee kick to everything it caresses. It's not heavily processed either. The sap of the coconut flower is dehydrated to form honeyed crystals. While coconut sugar can be classified as a palm sugar, it is not to be confused with regular palm sugar, which is no friend to the diabetic. Coconut sugar is thought to have a low glycemic value - good news for hyperactive children, diabetics and bored sedentary workers.

I've used goat's butter in response to many requests over the years to include it in my online recipe portal. This won't suit everyone, but it can be a great alternative for those who react to cow's milk, like my mother. Goat's milk and goat's butter appear to be more alkaline than cow's milk, appealing to those on a calcium-retention diet or alkalising menus.

The ingredients for these brownies need to be measured in grams. For more on this, see page 8. Don't panic - it's just a fling.

250g 85% dark chocolate
200g goat's butter
100g ground almonds
2 teaspoons gluten-free
  baking powder
4 medium eggs
250g coconut blossom sugar

Makes 16-20

Preheat the oven to 180°C/160°C fan/350°F. Line a 30cm x 25cm baking tray with parchment paper and set aside.

Slowly melt most of the chocolate (keep back 30-40g) with the goat's butter over a bain marie. All this means is a saucepan of 2cm of water simmering away and a shallow bowl fit snugly on top in place of a lid. This is where you'll melt the butter and choccie. If the bowl gets too hot the chocolate will go lumpy, so take it off the heat as soon as you see the ingredients melding. Sometimes the water can turn from a mannerly simmer to a violent boil when you're not watching.

Chop the remaining chocolate into mini buttons, throw into a separate bowl and stir through the ground almonds and baking powder.

In a very large bowl, beat together the eggs and sugar with an electric whisk until creamy. The mixture will aerate and change colour slightly, so don't be overly alarmed. Fold in the ground almond mix and the melted chocolate. Swiftly transfer to your prepared tin with a spatula, before all the lovely air bubbles pop.

Bake for 30-35 minutes. Use the chocolate bowl
and sticky spatula as currency with your kids
- after all, there's washing up to be done and
tired feet to be massaged.

Once the brownies are cooked, remove and let
them cool overnight in a locked room. Brownies
improve exponentially in the fridge, so try to
resist looting the tray until they've sufficiently
chilled.

DARK PEANUT BUTTER BROWNIES

>>>>>>>>>>>>>>>>>>>>>>>>>>>

Chocolate is a vaccine against bad moods. Something explosive happens in my veins as well as my mouth. According to scientists, this is because of a neurochemical called dopamine. Once stirred, dopamine can initiate an electrical cavalry through the veins and hit every imaginable spot. And I mean every spot. High levels of dopamine are associated with increased motivation, neuro-aerobics and general rí rá agus ruaile buaile - all diplomatic speak for better nookie.

Luckily for us, Mother Nature gave the cacao bean lots of heart-healthy flavanols and magnesium. Both nutrients are loyal friends of the cardio-vascular system, helping blood flow and circulation. In fact, I believe the smell of chocolate can send a feline's pulse into a frenzy. Quite the defibrillator.

This endorsement of chocolate comes with a rather large qualification: it must be raw or dark. Untreated, raw cacao is the nutritional heavy-weight champion of chocolate. Next best is 85% dark chocolate - indecently rich and muscular. Anything else is disqualified, especially the white or milk varieties. Now for some irritating information: caffeine (in coffee or chocolate) prompts the body to release stored sugars in our system. This is bad news for diabetics or candida warriors. Caffeine's physiological effect can be just as pernicious as sugar. Too much, and we're in trouble.

The ingredients for these brownies are best measured in grams. For more on this, see page 8.

4 tablespoons crunchy peanut butter
1-2 tablespoons maple syrup
125g 85% dark chocolate
100g goat's butter (see note on p.212)
2 medium eggs
125g rapadura sugar or coconut blossom sugar
75g ground almonds or hemp protein powder
1 teaspoon gluten-free baking powder

Makes 10-12

Preheat the oven to 180°C/160°C fan/350°F. Line a small square baking tray (20cm x 20cm) with greaseproof paper.

Beat the peanut butter and maple syrup together in a cup using a fork and litter the lined baking tray with baby blobs. Set aside.

Slowly melt the chocolate with the goat's butter over a bain marie. All this means is a saucepan of 2cm of water simmering away and a shallow bowl fit snugly on top in place of a lid. This is where you'll melt the butter and choccie. If the bowl gets too hot the chocolate will go lumpy, so take it off the heat as soon as you see some action.

In a very large bowl, beat together the eggs and sugar with an electric whisk until creamy. Stir through the ground almonds or hemp and the baking powder, then fold in the melted chocolate. Swiftly transfer to your prepared tin with a spatula. Bake for approximately 18 minutes.

Once the brownies are cooked, remove and let them cool overnight in a locked room. Store in the fridge or other chilled hiding place.

ITALIAN AND RICH

>>>>>>>>>>>>>>>>>>>>>>>

Make Paul Daniels proud – turn your cravings into a nutritional hit by using avocado in place of cream, and prunes in place of sugar. If you're leery about using them, don't be. Their flavour is muted by the cacao content. This Gianduja-style torte is so darn scrumptious, it feels illicit.

For the base:
6–8 soft prunes or soaked
  dates
1 cup roasted hazelnuts
1/4 cup cocoa or cacao
  powder
1/4 cup maple or date syrup
handful of walnuts or pecans
2 tablespoons ground
  linseeds

For the ganache topping:
2 Medjool dates, pre-soaked
1 large avocado, stone and
  skin removed
1/2 cup cacao or cocoa
  powder
1/4 cup maple or date syrup
  (not honey)
2 tablespoons hazelnut
  butter
1 tablespoon tamari
1 teaspoon vanilla extract

Serves 14

To make the base, add the listed ingredients to your food processor and pulse until it starts to stick together. You're looking for a clumpy nut texture, not a purée. Make sure your prunes or dates are plump and juicy, otherwise the mixture won't behave. Soak them in a spot of water for 10 minutes before using if you think this will help.

Once pulsed, scrape the base mixture into a pre-lined tin, one that's about half the size of a magazine page. Refrigerate straight away – I find the base easier to manipulate into place later, when it's chilled.

Now get going on your filling. Whizz all the filling ingredients together with a hand-held blender or food processor. Process until lusciously smooth. Taste to see if it reaches your serotonin and dimples. If not, adjust accordingly: more maple to sweeten, more tamari for depth, more cacao for richness. Set aside.

As soon as the base is cold, press firmly down with the back of a spoon or your fingertips. Fold the filling on top and set for 4 hours in the fridge. Provided it remains in the fridge, it should last for up to 6 days. Pending diligence and discipline, of course.

SEA SALT PROBIOTIC CHOCOLATES

>>>

Probiotic means pro-life. Naturally fermented food like yoghurt is brimming with live probiotic bacteria to keep your internal ecosystem in balance. I understand how foul this may sound, but trust me, these guys are on our side. Without healthy strains of live bacteria, our food would not be sufficiently broken down in our guts or absorbed by our bodies. Thrush, bloating and dodgy bowel movements tend to be the most common symptoms of intestinal imbalance.

If you can't have natural yoghurt, look for alternative sources of probiotics in fermented foods such as sauerkraut, kimchi, unpasteurised miso and coconut yoghurt. Or these chocolates. We use them as currency in our house when necessary. Our toddlers will sing Humpty Dumpty in Mandarin for them. So will my husband.

Melt the cacao butter in a bain marie. All this means is placing the broken shards of butter in a shallow bowl set over a pan of barely simmering water. Make sure the bowl is at least 10cm above the simmering water. Remove from the heat and let the cacao butter naturally melt over the hot water for 5 minutes.

Blitz the remaining ingredients (except the raw cacao powder for dusting) in a food processor. Keep the motor running and slowly add the melted cacao butter in a steady stream. The addition of 1/4 teaspoon cayenne pepper is rumoured to make your tongue dance and your pulse quicken. Just saying.

Refrigerate in the same bowl, with the blade intact, for about 3 hours. If the mixture seems too hard or you've forgotten about it in the fridge, blitz it again to loosen it up. (That's why it's useful to leave the blade in.)

Put the raw cacao powder in a bowl or shallow plate. Roll the mixture into little bonbons between your palms, then drop into the raw cacao powder. They can be frozen for up to 3 months. Glory be to the icebox!

1/3 cup cacao butter
1/2 cup raw agave, barley malt extract or brown rice syrup
1/3 cup cacao or cocoa powder
1/4 cup cashew nut butter
2 tablespoons water
2 tablespoons hazelnut butter (or more cashew butter)
1 tablespoon probiotic powder (we use Udo's)
1 teaspoon vanilla extract or powder
1/2 teaspoon good sea salt, like Maldon flakes
3 tablespoons raw cacao powder, to dust

Makes 40-50

BEETROOT CANDY

>>>>>>>>>>>>>>>>>>

Tiny titans of flavour, no one would guess these candies are scrupulously healthy. Underneath their neon pink dusting lies some of Mother N's finest superfoods: beetroot, seaweed and raw almonds.

That bold pigment that gives beetroot its Harry Potter glimmer is where the magic lies. Deep red-coloured foods like beetroot and onions store powerful chemicals called betacyanins. These compounds love your liver and are believed to support the body's detoxification process. This might be why beets have charmed every detox clinic from North America to the West of Ireland.

You don't need to stick to beetroot powder for the recipe to work - try a Peruvian powdered fruit called lúcuma. Apparently lúcuma is the maple syrup of South America. A mere whiff of this ambrosial substance has the ability to drive the feline persuasion wild. Move over, Justin Bieber, there's a new fixation on the block.

15 plump Medjool dates
2 tablespoons almond or
  cashew nut butter
2 tablespoons extra virgin
  coconut oil
1 tablespoon spirulina
1-2 teaspoons tamari
2 tablespoons beetroot
  powder, to dust

Makes 30-35 candies

Destone the dates before dropping them into a food processor. Add the remaining ingredients except the beetroot powder for dusting later. Whizz on a low speed for 1-2 minutes.

Using a teaspoon amount, mould the candy mix into teeny bonbons. Your hands will become slippery, aiding the process. Expect to get around 30-35 candies from the batch, depending on how many times the teaspoon fell into your mouth.

Chill for 24 hours before rolling in the beetroot powder. Any sooner, and the candy will drink up the coating. No harm in looting one or seven in the meantime. Store in the fridge for up to 1 month.

FIG AND PRUNE CRUMBLE WITH GINGER-LACED YOGHURT AND DATE SYRUP

>>>

This crumble will unleash some serious goodness into your system and prompt a fervent tail-wagging session around the kitchen table.

Whether fresh or dried, figs are a surprisingly good source of calcium. This mineral is the Holy Grail for strong bones, so throw a packet of dried figs in your office drawer to ward off sugar cravings and dodgy hips.

It's worth keeping your health antennae out for cold-pressed extra virgin coconut oil. Once refined, coconut oil's immune-boosting properties substantially diminish. I should add that there is quite a price difference. A large jar of copra, the refined coconut oil that you don't want, is available for the same price as a big bar of chocolate. The equivalent size, raw and unrefined, will be four times more costly. But as Michael Pollan so sensibly exhorts, 'It's better to pay the grocer than the doctor.'

For the filling:
6 small or medium eating
  apples
1 tablespoon ground cinnamon
splash of lemon juice
6 fresh or dried figs,
  stems removed and roughly
  chopped
roughly 1 cup prunes, stones
  removed and chopped

For the topping:
2 cups jumbo oat flakes
4–5 tablespoons maple or
  brown rice syrup, honey or
  raw agave
4 tablespoons extra virgin
  coconut oil
1 cup mixed seeds (sunflower,
  linseeds, pumpkin)
sprinkle of sea salt flakes

For the yoghurt:
coconut or organic soya
  yoghurt
3 tablespoons grated frozen
  ginger
date syrup, to serve

Serves 8

Preheat the oven to 170°C/150°C fan/340°F.

To make the topping, briefly blitz the oats with the syrup and coconut oil (which is solid like butter at room temperature) in a food processor until it clumps together – 5 seconds should do the trick. Stir in the seeds and salt and mix well. It's a good idea to soak the linseeds in twice as much water for 60 minutes or overnight, but it's not essential.

To prep the fruit, chop the apples into bite-sized pieces, binning the core. Don't remove the skins, as these soften once cooked and can add terrific texture and nutrition. In a small saucepan filled with 3cm of boiling water, add the apples, cinnamon and lemon juice. Cover and cook on a medium heat until semi-squishy (anything between 8 and 20 minutes, depending on the variety of apple used). Remember not to let it turn into mush, as it will have additional cooking time in the oven later (but if this happens, don't panic – it will still taste damn fine!). Once it's soft, add the figs and prunes. Pour the filling into an oven dish. Top with the oaty crumble and press down.

Bake for 30 minutes, making sure the top does not brown and turn bitter. Agave will brown quickly, so you may need to adjust the temperature if using this particular sweetener. Allow to cool if you can overcome the temptation to dive straight in. The crumble solidifies when cool, but if you don't mind a crumbly crumble, knock yourself out. Serve alongside natural yoghurt laced with frozen ginger, a bottle of date syrup and someone you're trying to impress.

MACADAMIA AND PASSIONFRUIT CUSTARD PIE

>>>

This recipe will help exorcise those overactive sugar cravings. The base is both crunchy and creamy, in a way that only a team of macadamia can achieve. You'll be getting a fair whack of heart-healthy magnesium and cholesterol-lowering oleic too, something junk food could never brag.

The passionfruit filling is sweet and buttery, with a halo hovering over it. Don't be afraid of egg yolks, as they contain a brain-boosting compound called choline to help find those bloody car keys. And while coconut oil is a source of saturated fat, its unique chemical structure allows us to utilise it as energy straight away.

The snazziest pie dish to use is a 20cm loose-bottomed one, but play with whatever you have. This pie will taste sensational regardless of where you put it. Grease the base and sides with coconut oil.

Using a food processor, briefly pulse all the crust ingredients until they start to clump together in a doughy ball. Scrape into your pie dish and press along the sides and bottom with clean fingers to cover the entire dish and form a crust. If you have any mixture left over, roll into bonbons and use as bribes for stubborn toddlers and teenagers. Chill the pie crust in the freezer until later.

To make the custardy filling, first download a podcast or stick on some great tunes since you will be locked to the cooker for 8 minutes. Gently heat all the ingredients on an extra-low setting in a small saucepan. If it's too hot, the yolks will cook in seconds. Continuous whisking is crucial. When all the coconut oil has melted, keep a watch for little bubbles forming on the surface, telling you the mixture is getting hotter and hotter. By then, you should notice the mixture getting thicker, like a custard. Test it by dipping the back of a spoon into it. If the custard coats the spoon, remove it from the heat. If it runs off, keep the custard over the heat until it thickens a little more. Failure to keep whisking will result in lemony scrambled eggs.

Pour over your chilled base and set in the fridge for 2 hours before serving. Deliciously potent stuff, with a nod to the nutritional gods.

For the crust:
1 cup raw macadamia nuts
  (and/or almonds)
1 cup raisins (not currants)
1/2 cup desiccated coconut
1 tablespoon runny honey or
  maple syrup

For the filling:
4 egg yolks
2 passionfruit
juice and rind of 1 large
  lemon
5 tablespoons runny honey or
  raw agave
4 tablespoons extra virgin
  coconut oil

Makes 12-16 portions

LEMON AND PISTACHIO PIE WITH ORANGE BLOSSOM YOGHURT

>>

This recipe is designed to drive your neurotransmitters wild without driving up your blood sugar levels or gunging your arteries.

But aren't nuts fattening? Not so. Nuts contain monounsaturated fat. That's the healthy one associated with lower rates of heart disease and cholesterol. Commercial candy, on the other hand, is a source of nasty fat, responsible for bumping up your bad LDL cholesterol and haunting your arteries. Please don't confuse the two fats - they behave very differently in the body. In fact, the British Medical Journal published research on Polymeal foods that, if consumed daily, would reduce the risk of cardiovascular disease by 75%. Dark chocolate and nuts were two of the seven foods. Glee.

For the biscuit base:
3/4 cup unsalted cashews
1/2 cup shelled pistachios
1/3 cup sultanas
juice and zest of 1 small
  lemon
2 tablespoons raw agave,
  maple or brown rice syrup
1/4 teaspoon unrefined salt

For the filling:
1 1/2 cups raw unsalted
  cashew nuts, soaked
  overnight
1/2 cup raw agave or brown
  rice syrup (maple is not
  good)
up to 1/2 cup melted extra
  virgin coconut oil
juice of 1 1/2 lemons (or 2
  small lemons)
1/2 teaspoon ground turmeric

handful of shelled
  pistachios, to decorate
coconut or soya yoghurt, to
  serve
orange blossom water, to
  serve

Makes 12 slices

Briefly pulse the base ingredients together using a food processor. Stop the motor when the dough starts to clump together. Spread the nutty dough over the bottom of a lightly oiled 18cm springform tin. These are a special type of baking tin usually used to make cheesecakes. Place in the freezer to chill while you get going on the filling.

Drain the cashew nuts and discard the soaking liquid. Cream the softened cashews with the remaining filling ingredients (except the pistachios) until smooth and glossy. This should take 2 minutes in a blender or food processor. Add more turmeric if you want to achieve an even brighter glow. Too much, though, and planes will start landing on your house. Pour over your base and return to the freezer until beckoned.

Allow to thaw for 5 minutes before cutting the pie from frozen. Crush a handful of shelled pistachios with the bottom of a saucepan and tickle the top of the pie with them. Serve with thick cultured coconut or soya yoghurt splashed with orange blossom water or culinary-grade orange oil. And maybe a pitcher of iced green tea on a sweltering summer's day.

MAPLE AND PUMPKIN PANNA COTTA

>>

The Japanese use agar as a weight-loss aid because of its stellar fibre content. This natural setting agent is made from sea algae, which is frozen and shaved. So make friends with agar, because it's good for your body. After all, you're the one who has to live in it!

Start by peeling the ginger and placing it in the freezer to firm up. Fresh ginger would be too fibrous, overpowering and stringy.

While the ginger is freezing, peel and chop your pumpkin into matchbox-sized pieces, toss in a little olive oil, season and roast on a baking tray at 200°C/180°C fan/400°F for 30 minutes, until soft and tasty. Covering the tray with tinfoil prevents any browning from occurring. Broadly speaking, it's worth cooking about 3 mugs of chopped pumpkin and gleefully gobbling any you don't use in the recipe. As soon as the pumpkin is done, mash it while it's hot and measure out 1 1/2 cups of the purée. Grate the frozen ginger over it using the finest part of a grater. Set aside.

Sprinkle the agar flakes into the cold water and bring to a gentle simmer for 4-5 minutes without stirring.

In the meantime, throw the remaining ingredients (except the blueberries or redcurrants) into your food processor along with the pumpkin mash. Blend everything together on high speed, slowly adding the hot agar mix. Purée until sumptuous and smooth.

Pour into handy jam jars ready to bring into school or work tomorrow. If serving tonight, refrigerate in a suitable large bowl or individual ramekin dishes until set. Excite with redcurrants and a glorious drizzle of maple syrup.

1 x 4cm piece of fresh root ginger, grated
1 small organic pumpkin
a little olive oil
1 tablespoon agar flakes
1 cup cold filtered water
4-5 tablespoons maple syrup, plus extra to serve
1-2 tablespoons extra virgin coconut oil
1/4 teaspoon sea salt flakes
pinch of ground cinnamon
splash of vanilla extract
tiny squeeze of lime juice
redcurrants, to decorate

Serves 5-8

HAZELNUT AND RAISIN FREEZER COOKIES

>>>

It takes 4 pounds of grapes to produce a single pound of raisins. This markedly concentrates raisins' nutritional kick. Counted as one of your five a day, a handful of these chewy little candies will give you astral amounts of antioxidants and phytochemicals, equivalent to a bunch of fresh grapes. (No, not equivalent to a bottle of Merlot, but nice try. Nor does wine count as part of your five-a-day programme, except in December, obviously.)

That same handful contains blushing amounts of resveratrol too, the phyto-nutrient that furnishes our body with anti-cancer infantry. Antioxidants and phytochemicals such as resveratrol are needed to deactivate menacing molecules in our bodies, more commonly referred to as free radicals. Imagine an internal Pac-Man and you've got the idea.

Now for the down sides. Research has shown that grapes carry more pesticides and agrichemicals than most other fruit. Agrichemicals don't exactly sound synonymous with good health, but the jury is still debating this one. If you're worried, the European Working Group has a handy guide to pesticide residues, downloadable online or as an app. It's a simple list of the 'cleanest' fruit and veg and the worst-offending ones for you to consult when shopping at your grocer. The president of the EWG is eager to make the case to eat more fruit and veg, whether conventional or organic. He comes across as a smart and practical shopper rather than a loony food fascist.

With their high glycemic load, raisins are not so good for diabetics. In fact, all dried fruit carries greater glycemic indices (GI) than their fresh equivalent. This is something diabetics have to watch. Low-glycemic fruits to splurge on instead include fresh blueberries, raspberries, black-berries, redcurrants, blackcurrants and strawberries.

2 cups ground almonds
1/2 cup extra virgin coconut
  oil, melted
1/3 cup maple syrup
1/4 cup raisins
handful of roasted
  hazelnuts, roughly chopped
zest of 1 small unwaxed
  lemon
1 tablespoon ground ginger
1/2 teaspoon sea salt flakes

Makes 22 small cookies

Using a fork, mix everything together in a cold bowl. Grab an apricot-sized piece of dough and flatten it into a cookie shape. If it's too sticky, wait until the dough has cooled and dampen your hands slightly.

Place on greaseproof baking parchment and freeze - no need to cook. Once frozen, they can be stored in a freezer bag, ready to pillage at will. Other variations to play with include orange zest and cinnamon, a tablespoon of chia seeds for added omega-3 fuel, or carob powder and cacao nibs.

WHITE CACAO TRUFFLES

>>>>>>>>>>>>>>>>>>>>>>>>>>>>>>>>>>

These are the stunning creation of rawvolutionist Katie Sanderson. Check out her Facebook page Living Dinners for inspiration and super-cool photos. If I won the lotto, I'd have a hotline to her kitchen.

Cacao butter may require a little sat navving to find. I get mine online (see page 253), where I can bulk buy an artillery of scrummy stuff without having to leave my lazy armchair.

Melt the cacao butter in a bain marie. All this means is placing the broken shards of butter in a shallow bowl set over a pan of barely simmering water. Make sure the bowl is at least 10cm above the simmering water. Remove from the heat and let the butter naturally melt over the hot water for 5 minutes.

Cream the other ingredients in a mini electric blender or food processor. Keep the motor running and slowly add the melted cacao butter in a steady stream.

Refrigerate for about 3 hours. If the mixture seems too hard or you've forgotten about it in the fridge, blitz it again to loosen it up. You might want to chill it in the food processor's bowl with the blade still in for this reason. Using a teaspoon, take a teeny amount and form a bonbon between your palms. Drop into lúcuma powder and roll again with dry fingertips. Store in the fridge until the munchies hit. Then kick your feet up and high-five Katie.

1/3 cup melted cacao butter
3/4 cup hazelnut butter
1/2 cup raw agave, brown rice syrup or barley malt extract
3 tablespoons lúcuma powder, plus extra to dust
2 tablespoons water
1 teaspoon vanilla extract or powder
pinch of pink Himalayan salt

Makes 40-50 truffles

PECAN PILLOWS WITH CHOCOLATE PUDDLES

>>>

These are quick and easy to whip up, with remarkably few ingredients. But surely something so tasty has to be bad for you? Nope. Pecans are a rich source of zinc, the 'fertility mineral' responsible for healthy hormones, radiant skin and a Herculean immune system. These unassuming little nuts also proffer a nice dose of age-defying vitamin E, beta-sitosterol for dirty arteries and potassium for mouldy hangovers. Jaysus, pecan, you is one talented nut.

The cacao bean happens to be one of nature's top sources of magnesium, the mineral associated with blood flow and good circulation. No yawning! Circulation affects the entire body, irrespective of what age you are. Think blood flow to the brain, depression, varicose veins, constipation, hypertension, erectile dysfunction and gorgeous skin. We love you, Pecan Pillows!

1 cup pecans
5 Medjool or other very
  sticky dates
4-5 tablespoons cocoa or
  cacao powder
2 tablespoons date, maple or
  brown rice syrup
pinch of unrefined, mineral-
  rich salt
50g 85% dark chocolate
1 tablespoon probiotic
  powder (we use Udo's)

Makes 15

Pulse the pecans, dates, cocoa, syrup and a pinch of salt in a blender until it starts resembling sticky sand. Roll into 15 apricot-sized balls between the palms of your hands. Using your thumb, press a dimple into the crown of each ball. Refrigerate.

For the probiotic frosting, gently melt the chocolate over a saucepan of barely simmering water. It's easiest to use a plate that fits snugly on top of your saucepan, with only 3cm of water beneath. As soon as the chocolate has melted, work very quickly. Remove from the heat, stir through the probiotic powder (or 1 table-spoon of yoghurt will work) and immediately fill each pecan pillow with a puddle of frosting.

Try to refrigerate for 2 hours before looting. They're best hidden behind old jars of capers and gherkins at the back of the fridge. Few will find them.

STRAWBERRY SHORTBREAD

>>>>>>>>>>>>>>>>>>>>>>>>>>>>

These chaps take a mere 3 minutes to whip up, 6 minutes to cook and 2 seconds to devour. The cookie dough can even be eaten straight from the freezer. My mother calls them her La Prairie biscuits. In other words, a cracking anti-ageing brew high in vitamin E, calcium, protein and antioxidants.

For adventurous palates, try lúcuma powder. This golden South American fruit is a scrumptious way of naturally sweetening the dough while providing niacin (vitamin B3) to fight cholesterol and depression. A toughie to find in stores, order lúcuma online or from your local health food supplier. Otherwise, stick to cheap and trusty ginger.

Preheat the oven to 170°C/150°C fan/340°F. Grease a baking tray.

Gently melt the coconut oil in a saucepan, then add the honey or maple syrup. Take off the heat and using a fork, combine with the remaining ingredients. Taste the mixture, ponder a little, and add more dried ginger or salt if you like.

When you're satisfied with your tasting session, mix well and form a squidgy ball of dough. Place on a piece of greaseproof paper and press into an oblong pizza base shape about 5mm deep with the base of your palm or your fingers. Cover with another sheet of greaseproof paper, roll over it with a wine bottle to flatten it some more, then freeze for 15 minutes. This makes it easier to shape and cut into shortbread cookies, but it also ensures they don't turn into puddles in the oven.

Remove the dough from your freezer, cut out your desired shapes with a cookie cutter and place on the greased tray. The quantity you get depends on how thin you manage to press the dough. I normally get about 30 shortbread cookies and freeze 20 of them in their raw state. Bake for approximately 5 minutes before they start to brown or colour, or for 10 minutes if cooking from frozen. Allow to set on the baking tray in a cool place, out of temptation's sight. Best stored in the fridge, or in your tummy.

1/3 cup (80ml) extra virgin coconut oil
1/2 cup honey or maple syrup
2 1/2 cups ground almonds
3 tablespoons dried strawberries
2 tablespoons dried ginger or lúcuma powder
good pinch of unrefined salt

Makes about 30 biscuits

PITCH-DARK CACAO TORTE

I'm through with guilt. As a woman, my brain was trained to deliver remorseful code after every bite of chocolate cake. What if you could turn your cravings into a nutritional hit? Find something sinful but saintly? Here's a recipe for you to flirt with. It's a basic dark chocolate torte, waiting for your personalisation. I decorate it with raspberry leaf tea or bee pollen, but you could try mint, ginger, sea salt, Chinese five spice, blueberry powder or adulation.

Local unpasteurised honey is thought to help introduce manageable amounts of pollen to our bodies, allowing us to prepare for the sneezy season several months in advance. Bee pollen is another unlikely remedy for hay fever. Studies have shown how this superfood can help boost immunity and acts as a natural anti-histamine. Considering the queen bee needs to lay up to 2,000 eggs per day and lives 40 times longer than a worker bee, her stamina is probably testament to this luminous superfood. I think bee pollen tastes like fermented dust balls, so I've hidden it in chocolate. But I've seen people eat it straight from a jar, sober, without flinching.

Chop the dates into small pieces. Whizz in a high-speed blender with the remaining base ingredients until thoroughly socialised. You may need the teeniest splash of water to bring it together. Press the mixture firmly into a 18cm springform circular tin. These are the funny sort of circular tins that detach from its sides. You could make a number of individual tarts too if you have a few cookie-cutter rings. Aim for a thin base. Refrigerate. Any leftover mixture? Freeze for another torte-making day or add to your morning's yoghurt with blueberries and jazz.

To make the filling, cream the cashew butter, ripe avocado (if using), water, cacao, sweetener, tamari and vanilla in a powerful blender. You should have a dense, dark, glossy ganache by now. While the motor is running, slowly add a steady stream of melted cacao butter. Taste, and decide whether you'd like more sweetness from honey or perhaps a salty kick from tamari.

Once you're happy, spread the filling over your base, decorate with bee pollen or raspberry leaf and chill in the fridge. This torte is indecently good straight from the freezer, which is where we store ours.

For the base:
1/2 cup sticky dates, like Medjool
up to 1 cup walnuts
zest of 1/2 orange
2 tablespoons carob, cacao or cocoa powder
pinch of good, organic, unrefined salt

For the filling:
1 x 200g jar cashew nut butter
1/2 ripe avocado (optional)
1/4 cup water
5 tablespoons raw cacao or cocoa powder
4-5 tablespoons local raw honey, maple syrup or date syrup
1 tablespoon tamari
1 teaspoon vanilla extract
2-3 tablespoons cacao butter, melted
bee pollen granules, to decorate (optional)
1 teabag of raspberry leaf tea, to decorate (optional)

Serves 16

BLACKBERRY TART WITH ALMOND PASTRY

>>>

Mother Nature is preparing us for the onslaught of winter bugs by supplying us with free stashes of blackberry bushes every autumn. Blackberries are honking with vitamin C and immune-boosting carotenoids. Look up your local PYO (pick your own) farm instead of shooting back Lemsip this autumn.

But that ain't all, my friends. This tart will arm your body with alarming amounts of anti-ageing artillery. This is because almonds are rich in vitamin E, the undisputed beauty vitamin, and raisins are pumped with resveratrol, a free radical assassin. Free radicals cause damage to our skin and to our bodies. Nasty things. Let's remedy that with some pie!

Using your food processor, briefly blend the pastry ingredients together until it starts to clump into a doughy ball. You might need 1 teaspoon of cold water to help it along. Scrape into a pie dish and press along the sides and bottom to cover the entire dish and form a crust. Place in the freezer.

To make the jammy filling, blitz half the blackberries with all of the remaining ingredients (except the coconut yoghurt) until smooth. Gently stir through the rest of the blackberries with a fork and spread over the chilled pastry. Let it set for 4 hours in the fridge and serve beside a good dollop of natural coconut yoghurt, like CoYo (see page 253).

For the raw pastry:
1 1/2 cups almonds
1 cup desiccated coconut
3/4 cup sultanas or raisins
zest of 1 unwaxed lemon
3 tablespoons raw honey or
  maple syrup
1 teaspoon ground allspice
  or ground cinnamon
good pinch of sea salt flakes

For the filling:
3-4 cups blackberries
8 Medjool dates
2 tablespoons raw honey or
  maple syrup (optional)
squeeze of lemon juice
coconut yoghurt, to serve

Serves 12

POTLETS OF GRAPEFRUIT, LIME AND GINGER CUSTARD

>>>

This is a hummer of a recipe when your body feels like a petri dish. Each serving gives you more than 100% of your daily recommended dose of vitamin C. This is the vitamin hailed as the slayer of free radicals, active campaigner against ageing and loyal deterrent of disease. Pretty impressive for a pot of pleasure.

You'll find that freshly juiced ginger adds an extra karate kick to sore throats. Ginger is one of my top three megafoods. If you don't have a juicer at home, use your best Marilyn Monroe voice and ask your local juicing outlet to press the ginger for you. Failing this, freeze a massive 12cm peeled stick of ginger. Grate the flesh into the mixture, straight from frozen.

6 egg yolks
juice of 1 lime
juice of 1 pink grapefruit
5 tablespoons extra virgin
  coconut oil
5 tablespoons raw honey
3 tablespoons juiced ginger
  (see note above)

Serves 6

Start by downloading a good podcast. You'll be locked to the cooker for 8 whole minutes watching the custard thicken.

Using a small saucepan on a low setting, gently heat all the ingredients. Make sure you are continuously whisking with a metal balloon beater. Keep a watch for little bubbles forming on the surface, telling you the mixture is getting hotter and hotter. By then you should notice it getting thicker. Test by dipping the back of a spoon into it. If the mixture coats the spoon, remove from the heat. If it runs off, keep the mixture over the heat until it thickens a little more.

Pour into little pots and refrigerate until it's no longer possible to ignore. Particularly tasty with crushed pistachio nuts or torn mint leaves.

Don't know what to do with leftover egg whites? Whip 3 into soft white peaks and add to the granola ingredients on page 20 before baking. This gives the granola extra-large clusters. Otherwise, green tea macaroons will happily use them up. See www.susanjanewhite.com.

CHILLI CHOCOLATE MISSILE

>>>>>>>>>>>>>>>>>>>>>>>>>>>>>>>>>>>>>

The addition of chilli powder will give your lips a delicious sting and swell the senses. Chillies can also heighten body temperature and help release natural endorphins to keep your blood gurgling with excitement.

But wait! There's more! Folate in avocados is thought to boost histamine production, apparently necessary for optimal orgasms. Whether this is true or not, its sumptuous flesh is enough to dizzy the senses. In fact, Catholics weren't allowed to eat avocados when the Spanish conquistadors brought them back to Europe in the 16th century. They evoked pleasures of the flesh at a time when contraception was not available. And the Aztec people of South America - the same cunning chaps who invented hot chocolate - called the avocado plant the ahuacatl, which translates as testicle tree.

Cream all your ingredients together with a hand-held blender. It's best chilled for 30 minutes before wolfing, but excitement may override your sensibilities. No shame in that.

Serve in petite wine glasses and top with freshly sliced red chilli if you have it. This mousse is unreasonably tasty after a long day at work. You'll quickly feel the chilli pelt through your veins and service those stubborn limbs.

1 ripe avocado
3 tablespoons cocoa or cacao
  powder
2 tablespoons raw agave or
  maple syrup (not honey)
1 tablespoon almond, cashew
  or macadamia butter
2 teaspoons tamari
pinch of cayenne pepper
1 red chilli, finely sliced,
  to decorate (optional)

Serves 2

'I CAN'T BELIEVE IT'S BEETROOT' CAKE

>>

A study in the Journal of the American Medical Association revealed that older women taking supplements might die younger than non-users. Why? Supplements may deliver too much of a good thing, since nutrients can be toxic at high doses or over long, unsupervised periods. Or perhaps pill-poppers delegate accountability for their health to multivitamins rather than addressing their diet?

We can all agree on one thing: a diet rich in fruit, veg, beans and basketball will rarely backfire. I'm not saying you'll live forever (Dragon's Den still has to crack that one), but we've nothing to lose by eating fresh, unadulterated food. A good diet is the best health insurance you can give your family, not a packet of lab-created pills.

I'm obsessed with beetroot right now. It's one of the tastiest veg on my superfood sonar. (My toddler isn't much convinced.) It may seem odd, but beetroot and chocolate are quite the couple. They get on better than Vladimir Putin and Gerard Depardieu. And the toddler is none the wiser.

Preheat the oven to 180°C/160°C fan/350°F. Grease a 20cm round cake tin or springform tin.

Boil the dates in a small saucepan with about 3cm of water for 10-15 minutes. Purée in a high-speed electric blender. This should yield about 1 1/2 cups of date paste. The recipe only needs 1 cup's worth, so freeze the rest, use it in the Apple-sauce and Cinnamon Cookies on page 71 or scoff with natural yoghurt.

Purée the cocoa powder, beetroot and tamari with the date paste until sumptuously smooth. I cheat by using vacuum-packed beetroot with no vinegar.

Blend in the eggs, oil, vanilla and baking powder until thoroughly incorporated. Immediately pour the batter into the greased cake tin.

Once the cake is in the oven, lower the heat to 170°C/150°C fan/340°F – an important step. Bake for 40-55 minutes. You're looking for a moist, rich cake, not a dry, fluffy cake. It's closer to a ganache torte. Allow to cool, making sure you give it enough time to chill before removing from its tin. Serve with plenty of coconut yoghurt and a large spoon.

2 cups pitted dates
125g cacao or cocoa powder
1 cup puréed beetroot (about
 4 cooked baby beets from a
 vacuum packet)
2 tablespoons tamari
4 medium eggs
1/2 cup extra virgin olive
 oil
2 teaspoons vanilla extract
2 teaspoons baking powder
natural coconut yoghurt, to
 serve (obligatory)

Serves 16-20

PRALINE CUPCAKES

>>>>>>>>>>>>>>>>>>>>

I tend to yearn for childhood recipes, but I also love alchemising healthier versions - coconut flour instead of refined wheat, extra virgin oils instead of butter, maple syrup instead of white sugar. Admittedly, Abba plays a big part in it too.

You can order coconut flour from your local health food store, as it's not that common outside of the US. Coconut flour is whoppingly high in fibre and low in carbohydrates, making it an ideal ingredient for coeliacs, diabetics, paleos and anyone worried about glycemic load. However, it's imperative to follow recipe measurements and not to substitute coconut flour for any other flour. It can be quite the diva.

For the cupcakes:
1/2 cup cocoa powder
1/4 cup coconut flour
1 teaspoon baking powder
1/2 cup raw agave or honey
3 tablespoons almond butter
3 eggs, beaten
5 tablespoons melted coconut
  oil
1 tablespoon tamari
2 teaspoons apple cider
  vinegar
1 teaspoon vanilla extract

For the praline frosting:
2/3 cup cashew nut butter
1/2 cup maple syrup
2 teaspoons tamari

Makes 10 cupcakes

To make the cupcakes, preheat the oven to 180°C/160°C fan/350°F. Sift the cocoa powder, coconut flour and baking powder into a large mixing bowl.

In a medium bowl, beat together the agave or honey and the almond butter with a balloon whisk (those whisky-looking things you see your grandmother using to whip cream). Blend through the remaining ingredients.

Add the wet ingredients to the dry and blend thoroughly with your balloon whisk until glossy and smooth.

Prepare your muffin tray with cupcake liners and fill each one with 1/4 cup of the mixture. Expect a very runny consistency. Don't worry - you're on the right track. Bake for 20 minutes. Touch to feel if they are done. Gently remove from the muffin tray and allow to cool completely on a wire rack before icing with praline frosting.

To make the frosting, mix the nut butter, maple syrup and tamari together with a fork. Smother on top of each cupcake and gleefully tiptoe through the kitchen.

Dispatches from the kitchen: You can replace the almond butter with equal amounts of soya yoghurt. It seems rather important to stick to raw dark agave or honey. Maple syrup, barley malt and brown rice syrup misbehave with the coconut flour.

CINNAMON AND PECAN MALT ICE CREAM

>>

My husband never suspected this was dairy free, let alone sugar free and guilt free. Had I told him, perhaps his spoon would never have ventured in. It was loved, revered and annihilated in one blissful binge.

Chilled, full-fat coconut milk is the key. Go for the organic variety; inorganic can be packed with preservatives and chemical stabilisers that turn the ice cream a dodgy tinge of purple. A top idea is to chill your serving bowls in the freezer beforehand. I use tiny glass preserving jars so that everyone has a pot to themselves.

4 frozen bananas
1 x 400g can full-fat
  coconut milk, chilled
3 tablespoons barley malt
  extract or maple syrup
1/2 tablespoon ground
  cinnamon
handful of pecans, crushed,
  to decorate

Serves 3-4

Peel and chop each banana into many chunks. Try using black-skinned bananas, which are ultra ripe and much sweeter. Place the chunks on a bread-board covered with baking parchment, making sure the banana pieces are not touching each other. Freeze for 60 minutes, then transfer to a freezer bag. This is to prevent the banana sticking together and wearing down your food processor and your patience.

When an ice cream craving hits, take the chilled, unopened can of coconut milk from the fridge and blend in a food processor with your frozen bananas, sweetener and cinnamon. Process in bursts at first until the bananas soften, then continuously until they develop a creamy consistency.

Decorate with crushed pecans, and more maple syrup if you fancy.

Devour immediately, and finish every last slurp because it doesn't like the freezer. Oh well.

ICED GREEN TEA AND MANUKA HONEY CUBES

>>>

When my multiple espresso regime got the heave-ho, I became possessed by the search for a worthy replacement. Decaffeinated coffee was somewhat pointless, having undergone even more chemical adulterations to remove the caffeine than Shane McGowan's liver. Floral teas were cruel. I wanted a hit, not a mug of liquid lawn.

Then I tasted chilled green tea with fresh lemon. Green tea contains one-third the amount of coffee's caffeine and up to 20 times the antioxidant activity as vitamin C. This popular Chinese tea is also bucked up with skin-enhancing polyphenols, something coffee sorely envies.

Choosing to cut down on coffee is a smart decision. Coffee's giant caffeine content releases sugar into your system in the form of glycogen and makes your blood pressure pelt. That's why you love it. But your heart doesn't. Nor does your immune system, which becomes less effective under the influence of raised cortisol levels. Besides, your skin looks parched on coffee, your mouth feels like a badger's bum and you age quicker. Onwards!

Steep the bags in a teapot filled with hot water for around 30 minutes. It doesn't matter if you have a small or large teapot because you can dilute the strength with additional water afterwards. Once cooled, pour into a tall glass jug and top up with filtered water to your preferred strength. I normally use 3 pints of water with 4 teabags as a guideline. Chill in the refrigerator.

To make the ice, *gently* warm the lemon juice and honey together. If using manuka honey, heating too quickly destroys its potency and health-giving properties. Likewise, baking or cooking with manuka honey deletes its effectiveness against bacteria – an expensive lesson to learn. This special honey's efficacy depends on whether or not it is taken on an empty stomach, so it's ideal for this iced green tea in between meals.

Add a little water to the warm lemony mix before pouring into an ice cube tray, then freeze until set. Serve the chilled tea in its jug alongside a tall glass filled with lemony manuka ice cubes for people to help themselves. And perhaps a punnet of raspberries, or a side of last night's gossip.

4 white or green teabags
juice of 2 large lemons
4 tablespoons manuka honey

Serves 8

BANANA TOFFEE ICE CREAM

>>>>>>>>>>>>>>>>>>>>>>>>>>>>>>>>>>>

Eating good food sends my hormones into party mode. It's a sensory pleasure, just like listening to great music or soaking up a swatch of unexpected sunshine. So here's my favourite ice cream recipe to feed your cells as well as your soul.

When you're looking for sweeteners, untreated honey gets my vote. Raw agave is only recommended if you suffer from wonky blood sugar levels. That's because agave has absolutely no nutritional plaudits, though it can serve as a useful alternative to sugar. For more on agave, see page 11.

Roughly mash 2 1/2 bananas with the salt flakes. Stir through the raisins or chopped dates. I use Medjool dates because they are sent from angels. Or demons. Not sure which, but I encourage you to indulge me and try a few licky-sticky yummy ones. Dried dates are fine to use too, but taste crunchy in the ice cream as opposed to squidgy. Raisins are delectably chewy and noticeably cheaper.

In a separate bowl, beat the tahini, sweetener and vanilla with a fork until sumptuously smooth. Fold in the banana mess. Now chop the remaining 1 1/2 bananas into chunks and stir through the entire ice cream mixture. You can swirl a little honey on top if you fancy - it sets like toffee. Pour into a plastic cylindrical tub, seal and freeze overnight. In the morning, you shall rejoice.

4 medium bananas
decent pinch of sea salt
  flakes
handful of plump raisins or
  chopped dates
1 x 340g jar of tahini
1/2 cup raw honey, agave or
  maple syrup
1 teaspoon vanilla extract
  or powder
extra honey, to decorate
  (optional)

Makes 12 servings

COFFEE BEAN ICE CREAM

>>>>>>>>>>>>>>>>>>>>>>>>>>>>>

In Hinduism, the sesame seed stands for immortality. Eyebrows sufficiently raised? Wait until you taste this ice cream. Notions of everlasting life will become much clearer. Theoretically, it might come from the sesame's stash of lignans. These are a group of plant-based compounds associated with fighting cancer. Or perhaps such fancy can be attributed to its bank of B vitamins? This is the vitamin responsible for releasing energy, massaging frayed nerves and mending marriages. Not bad for half a cent per gram, and notably less than a psychotherapist.

Whisk the tahini, date syrup, carob, vanilla and salt crystals with a fork until sumptuously smooth. I find this a little easier if the ingredients are heated ever so gently. As you work, sprinkle in your coffee beans and good humour.

Pour the mixture into a large plastic cylindrical container, just like professional ice cream (we doubled the portions for the photo). You'll need to freeze it for 5 hours before serving.

approx. 1 x 340g jar tahini
1/2 cup date syrup
3 tablespoons carob powder
1-2 teaspoons vanilla
  extract
1 teaspoon sea salt flakes
sprinkle of whole organic
  coffee beans

Serves 6

ICE POPS

>>>>>>>>>>>

Get yourself some fetching ice pop moulds on Amazon. You could also use paper espresso cups from your local café if you ask nicely! Fill three-quarters high with ice pop mixture, cover with tinfoil and gently pop a wooden stick through the centre of the foil. Freeze as usual. Ta-da! Takeaway espresso cups (as opposed to regular paper cups) are lightly lined, making it easier to remove the pop. Nifty, huh?

ISOTONIC POPS

500ml young green coconut water

Pour into moulds and freeze for 8 hours. That's it!

OCTONAUT ICE POPS

My little buddies love The Octonauts. These cartoon sea creatures eat lots of kelp seaweed. One day, Benjamin asked me for green ice cream, just like Captain Barnacles. I couldn't resist, so here it is.

4 pears, peeled and chopped
1 small avocado
1 tablespoon wheat grass or barley grass powder

Cook the pears in a splash of water for 6-8 minutes. Keep the lid on to retain the juices. Purée with the flesh of the avocado and the wheat grass powder. You can try adding slices of kiwi too if you think your little one will eat it.

Pour into ice pop moulds and freeze for 8 hours. Enough to fill 6 regular pops.

EXTRA VIRGIN TREATS

What to Read and Where to Shop

What I'm Reading

Learning about the perils of processed food is a smart move. It's the best insurance policy you can offer your body.

My heroes are authors and campaigners like Marion Nestle, Robyn O'Brien, Joanna Blythman, Bee Wilson, Felicity Lawrence and Michael Pollan. Never heard of them? Nestle, a professor in public health at New York University, has over 100,000 followers on Twitter. Pollan has 200,000. Each of them has a free blog, so it's not necessary to shell out money to access their research and opinions. Here are some great books by these authors. Many of them read like thrillers - scandalous, jaw dropping and haunting.

Not on the Label: What Really Goes into the Food on Your Plate by Felicity Lawrence

Eat Your Heart Out by Felicity Lawrence

Food Rules by Michael Pollan

The Food Our Children Eat by Joanna Blythman

What to Eat by Joanna Blythman

Bad Food Britain by Joanna Blythman

Swindled: From Poison Sweets to Counterfeit Coffee by Bee Wilson

The End of Overeating by David A. Kessler, M.D.

Salt Sugar Fat: How the Food Giants Hooked Us by Michael Moss

Basket Case: What's Happening to Ireland's Food? by Suzanne Campbell and Philip Boucher-Hayes

Gulp: Adventures on the Alimentary Canal by Mary Roach

Diet Delusion by Gary Taubes

Pure, White and Deadly: How Sugar Is Killing Us by Robert Lustig and John Yudkin

Vegan Before Six: Eat Vegan Before 6:00 to Lose Weight and Restore Your Health … for Good by Mark Bittman

Good Food: Can You Trust What You Are Eating? by John McKenna

Food, Inc. (DVD) by Eric Schlosser and Robert Kenner

Farmageddon (DVD) by Linda Faillace and Kristin Canty

Resources: Where I Like to Shop

You'll find me in quirky health stores across Dublin, organic food co-ops and specialist grocers like Fallon & Byrne. Say hi when you see me (unless my toddler is smashing his brother's head through the deli counter again).

Some of the ingredients used throughout this book require a little sat-navving. If you live outside Dublin or Ireland, I recommend exploring your nearest independent health food store, market or savvy deli. Listed below are some useful online sources. Many deliver nationwide and overseas.

**www.irelandsrawkitchen.ie and
www.iswari.net**
Coconut sugar, raw carob, spirulina, barley grass, stevia, dried mulberries, goji berries, raw dark agave, lúcuma, acai and all manner of cacao products.

**www.seaweedproducts.ie and
www.clearspring.co.uk**
Wild harvested Irish sea veg. My favourite is their dulse powder. Clearspring supply hijiki, arame, nori sprinkles, authentic wasabi powder, mirin and tamari.

www.wallandkeogh.ie
My local teahouse. Sells incredible loose-leaf organic tea. International delivery. Favourites include Persian Prince and Barry White. I get my beans for the Coffee Bean Ice Cream recipe on page 249 at Wall & Keogh.

**www.organicsupermarket.ie and
www.waitrose.com**
Home delivery of organic veg, fruit, flours, grains and household sundries.

www.steenbergs.co.uk
Exceptional salts and spices. Also check out the Irish Organic Herb Co. for certified organic herbs.

www.black-blum.com
Bento boxes to transport lunches into work with you.

www.amazon.co.uk
This is where you'll find a Lurch spiraliser, nut milk bags, Tiana coconut flour, matcha green tea powder and oven thermometers.

www.avogel.ie
Three-tier large germinator or sprouter, for your bean zoo on page 126.

www.linwoodshealthfoods.com
If you don't own a coffee grinder to finely mill seeds, Linwoods does a fantastic range of freshly milled flax, sunflower and pumpkin seeds, chia seeds and even goji berries. Essential for recipes such as the Black Bread (page 54), Office Bombs (page 62), Barley Grass Balls (page 66) and Chia Bonbons (page 64).

www.highbankorchards.com
Organic apple syrup, Ireland's answer to maple syrup.

www.coyo.co.uk
Coconut yoghurt made from coconut milk.

www.udoschoice.ie
Udo's Oil is a blend of really healthy oils like linseed, wheat germ, evening primrose, sesame and extra virgin sunflower. We use it for our fresh satay sauce and lots of salads with pomegranate molasses.

www.blackgarlic.com
Fermented and aged black garlic. Keeps for weeks in the fridge.

www.pulsin.co.uk
For the Pea Protein Isolate Powder used in the Protein Grenades on page 69. See also www.sunwarrior.com for really good raw vegan protein powders.

Index